E

Pines and Plantations

Native recipes of Thomasville, Georgia

All profits go to The Vashti Center
for its Christian ministry and
therapeutic treatment to
children and youth in crisis.

Published by

THE VASHTI AUXILIARY

1815 EAST CLAY STREET

THOMASVILLE, GEORGIA 31792

1976

The Vashti Auxiliary
Thomasville, Georgia 31792

First Printing 5,000 books, October, 1976
Second Printing 5,000 books, April, 1977
Third Printing 5,000 books, November, 1977
Fourth Printing 5,000 books, December, 1978
Fifth Printing 5,000 books, December, 1979
Sixth Printing 5,000 books, November, 1980
Seventh Printing 5,000 books, January, 1982
Eighth Printing 5,000 books, June, 1983
Ninth Printing 5,000 books, February, 1985
Tenth Printing 5,000 books, February, 1987
Eleventh Printing 5,000 books, May, 1993
Twelfth Printing 3,000 books, April, 1999
Thirteenth Printing 3,000 books, April, 2002
Fourteenth Printing 3,000 books, March, 2007

ISBN: 978-0-9607860-0-8

WIMMER
COOKBOOKS

A CONSOLIDATED GRAPHICS COMPANY

800.548.2537   wimmerco.com

ORIGINAL PINES AND PLANTATIONS COMMITTEE

CHAIRMEN

Mrs. A.B. Wight, Jr.   Mrs. Joe Beverly

EDITOR
Mrs. Tom Faircloth

RECIPES

Mrs. Fred Cooper   Editor
Mrs. Ken Beverly   Co-Editor
Mrs. Thomas H. Vann, Jr.

ART

Mrs. Elliott McCollum   Editor
Mrs. James Anderson   Plantation Sketches
Reverend Bob Dixon   Plantation Sketches

LONG STANDING COMMITTEE

Mrs. Ames Watkins Kindred   Chairman
Former Vashti Board President
Former Vashti Auxiliary President

Mrs. Harry Tomlinson   Co-Chairman
Local Marketing Chairman

Mr. Russell Fryar   Treasurer
Former Vashti Board Treasurer
Former Vashti Auxiliary Treasurer

Mrs. Louise Hines
Former Vashti Board President
Former Committee Member
Former Auxiliary President

The PINES AND PLANTATIONS committee expresses sincere appreciation to the members of the Vashti Auxiliary and to the many friends who made this book possible.

When the tragic War Between the States ended in 1866, Thomasville, in southwest Georgia, had been left relatively unscathed. Thomas County had sent the flower of its youth off to fight for the Confederacy. The bounty of Thomas County's productive soil had gone off to feed the hungry and tattered soldiers in grey. However, General Sherman and Union invasion armies had not come this far south in their scorched-earth march from Atlanta to the sea. On the contrary, a contingent of captured Yankee soldiers was brought here in the latter days of the war and interned in a temporary prisoner-of-war camp.

The railroad from Savannah to Thomasville was a life-line of the Confederacy until the bitter end. For a while Union troops did occupy the town, but Thomasville was spared the shot and shell and fire that other Georgia towns endured. Consequently, when the war was over, there was not the residue of bitterness here that Sherman's armies left behind in other Georgia towns.

The very railroad that had supplied the Confederate troops during the war was to become the transportation route that in the 1880's and 1890's brought fame and fortune to Thomasville as the first winter resort of the South. A gifted writer, the late Thomas C. Chubb, wrote in 1966 that stories told in the North by a Union soldier who had been for a while a prisoner of war in Thomasville, may have been what started wealthy northerners coming here to escape harsh winter weather.

". . . Word spread in the North," Chubb wrote, "that there was a place to the south of them — and trains ran there — where the air was fragrant with balsam; where the Cherokee roses often bloomed even in December; where an icicle was so rare you almost welcomed it; and where, also, the bobwhite quail whistled from every hedgerow; and where, if you crept out carefully in the early morning, you would hear the put-put-put of the turkey gobbler as he lorded it over his hens."

There was prevalent in the 1880's a belief that the pines had a medicinal quality; so wealthy industrialists and financiers from New York, Philadelphia, Cleveland, and Chicago began coming here to escape winter's snow and ice and to bask in the mild climate of South Georgia. Inhaling the fresh pine-scented air, they relaxed, hunted, fished and enjoyed dining on their wild bounty.

Boarding houses sprang up to accommodate the northern visitors; then came the big, palatial winter hotels like the Piney Woods, the Mitchell House, and the Masury Hotel. When the railroads pushed southward to develop the east coast of Florida, the winter resort era faded here; but many northerners bought plantations around Thomasville and turned them largely into game preserves. Happily, these plantations have been handed down from one generation to the next and their pine forests have been preserved largely intact. Even today the unspoiled natural beauty of these piney woods to the south and west of us remain one of our region's greatest assets.

This cookbook, then, is a collection of unique recipes from the Thomasville area where bountiful tables and gracious entertaining have characterized life-styles for generations. It is with pride that we share our distinctive southern cuisine which reflects our heritage of PINES AND PLANTATIONS.

Albert Riley

TOWN & COUNTRY'S GUIDE TO
Community Cookbooks
A TREASURY OF REGIONAL FOODS

We may live without poetry, music and art
We may live without conscience and live without heart
We may live without friends, we may live without books
But civilized man cannot live without cooks.

Owen Meredith, Earl of Litton, who penned these lines in 1860, might well have added that cooks cannot live without cookbooks. Inevitably, some of the most tempting collections come from the South. The 150-or-so community cookbooks examined in *Town & Country's* survey—necessarily, only a selection—vary enormously in the quality of their recipes and production and, as such, suggest what's really cooking in the melting pots of America—from the bean pot to the *pot de crème*. Our favorites tend to be those that celebrated the riches of their own region, giving unpretentious and traditional recipes and using local ingredients. In the belief that so many worthy local efforts deserve to be better known beyond their own locales, *Town & Country* has poured and picked through piles of cookbooks to bring you this big Christmas stocking stuffed with new ideas. Each of the cookbooks recommended here has its own charm and originality—so much so that even readers who are not—yet—keen cooks will enjoy curling up with them.

PINES AND PLANTATIONS
The book contains favorite recipes of plantation owners and families in the region. Chestnut Stuffing, Strawberry Cream Squares Salad, Hootenholler Whiskey Cake, Squash Fritters and pies: Key Lime or Pumpkin Praline, Williamsburg Pecan and Georgia Peach Cobbler are among the recipes.

TABLE OF CONTENTS

Plantation Menus

DINNER PARTY FOR TWELVE

CHINQUAPIN PLANTATION

Mr. and Mrs. Lewis B. Flynn, Jr.

Vichyssoise*

Quail with White Grapes*

Wild Rice

Artichoke Hearts with Foie Gras*

Spinach Pie with Cherry Tomatoes*

Ice Box Rolls*

Strawberry Kisses*

VICHYSSOISE

¼ cup butter
3 medium onions, chopped
4 cups chicken broth (use
    6 bouillon cubes)
3 large or 4 medium
    potatoes, peeled

2 cups milk
1 teaspoon salt
⅛ teaspoon white pepper
Chives

Saute' the onions in butter slowly until onions are transparent. Add 2 cups of the chicken broth, simmer 15 minutes, and allow to cool. Quarter the potatoes and cook in the other 2 cups of chicken broth until soft. Cool. Put the onions, potatoes and broth into blender and blend twice. Add milk, salt, pepper and blend once more. Chill thoroughly. When time to serve, thin vichyssoise to desired consistency with cold milk. Serve cold topped with chopped chives.

QUAIL WITH WHITE GRAPES

12 quail
4 cups dry white wine
2 cups seedless white grapes
¾ cup blanched almonds, sliced

6 tablespoons butter, melted
4-8 tablespoons flour
Kitchen Bouquet (optional)

Place quail in a roasting pan. Brush them with melted butter and pour wine over them. Bake in 350 degree oven for 30 minutes. Add grapes cut in half lengthwise and almonds. Baste birds with sauce in pan and cook 10 minutes longer or until done. Remove quail from pan. Add flour a little at a time until you reach desired consistency for gravy. Add salt and pepper to taste and a few drops of Kitchen Bouquet, if desired, for color. Serve quail with grape and almond gravy poured over them. Garnish with wild rice cooked according to package directions and sprigs of parsley.

ARTICHOKE HEARTS WITH FOIE GRAS

30 whole artichoke hearts
    (3 large cans)
½ cup butter

30 slices canned pâté
    de foie gras
Béarnaise Sauce

Melt butter in skillet. Carefully place artichoke hearts in skillet; cover and simmer for ten minutes or until hot. Place a round of pâté de foie gras in each heart and place in serving dish. Cover each heart with a spoonful or two of Béarnaise Sauce and place the dish under the broiler for a few seconds to brown the sauce. Garnish with parsley and serve.

BÉARNAISE SAUCE

2 cups butter
8 egg yolks
4 tablespoons lemon juice
½ teaspoon salt
½ teaspoon Tabasco

½ cup white wine
4 tablespoons tarragon vinegar
2 teaspoons dried tarragon
2 tablespoons onion, chopped
½ teaspoon pepper,
freshly ground

In a small saucepan heat butter until very hot but not brown. Into container of an electric blender put egg yolks, lemon juice, salt, and Tabasco. Cover container and turn motor on lowest speed. Immediately remove cover and pour in the hot butter in a steady stream. When all butter is added, turn off motor. In a small saucepan combine white wine, tarragon vinegar, dried tarragon, chopped onion and ground pepper. Bring liquid to a boil and cook rapidly until liquid is reduced to about two tablespoons or less. Pour remaining liquid and seasonings into container and stir to blend. Cover and blend on high speed for ten seconds.

SPINACH PIE AND CHERRY TOMATOES

1 pastry shell
1½ cups frozen spinach
4 tablespoons butter
Salt and pepper
½ pound ricotta cheese

3 eggs, lightly beaten
1 cup Parmesan cheese
½ cup heavy cream
Nutmeg
30 cherry tomatoes

Line a pie pan with pastry, fluting the edges; chill. Prick bottom with a fork and cover bottom with a piece of wax paper. Fill pastry shell with dried beans and bake in a hot oven (450 degrees) for about 15 minutes, just enough to set the crust without browning it. Allow to cool. Cook spinach with butter and salt and pepper to taste. Drain thoroughly and then add ricotta cheese with beaten eggs, ½ cup Parmesan cheese, cream, and nutmeg to taste. Spread mixture in pastry shell and bake the tart in a moderate oven (375 degrees) for 30 minutes, or until the crust is brown and the cheese mixture has set. Slice cherry tomatoes in half, sprinkle with remaining ½ cup Parmesan cheese and place under broiler until cheese is melted. Cut spinach pie into 16 wedges. Arrange slices of pie on round serving tray with broiled tomatoes between pieces.

ICE BOX ROLLS

3 tablespoons lard
1 teaspoon salt
1 egg, beaten
2 cups lukewarm water

1 package yeast
½ cup sugar
7 cups all-purpose flour

Melt lard and cool. Into large mixing bowl crumble yeast and mix with salt and sugar. Pour water in, gradually dissolving yeast thoroughly. Add to mixture the egg, then 3½ cups flour, then lard. Beat thoroughly and then add remaining 3½ cups flour. Set aside to rise until double in bulk. Punch down and place in refrigerator, or make into rolls and put to rise until double in bulk. Be sure to butter top before putting into refrigerator. To make rolls: Roll out dough to ¼ inch thick and cut with large biscuit cutter. Place a small pat of butter on roll and fold over as a turnover. Bake in 400 degree oven for 15 minutes.

STRAWBERRY KISSES

6 egg whites
¼ teaspoon cream of tartar
1½ cups sugar

Vanilla ice cream
Fresh strawberries, cut up

Heat oven to 275 degrees. Cover two baking sheets with heavy brown paper (grocery bags will do). Beat egg whites and cream of tartar until foamy. Beat in the sugar 1 tablespoon at a time. Continue beating until stiff and glossy. Do not underbeat. Drop meringue by ½ cupfuls onto brown paper. Shape mounds into circles building up sides so that they resemble birds' nests. Bake one hour. Turn off oven; leave meringues in oven with door closed 1½ hours. Remove from oven and cool away from draft. Makes approximately 16 shells. When time to serve, fill shells with ice cream and top with fresh strawberries.

TRADITIONAL CHRISTMAS BREAKFAST BUFFET

CHINQUAPIN PLANTATION

Mr. and Mrs. Lewis B. Flynn, Jr.

Quiche Lorraine*

Kentucky Ambrosia*

Champagne or Cold Duck

QUICHE LORRAINE

1 pie crust, uncooked	1 tablespoon flour
1 pound bacon	½ teaspoon salt
1½ cups Swiss cheese,	⅛ teaspoon nutmeg
coarsely grated	2 cups milk
3 eggs	1 tablespoon butter

Line a pie plate with pastry and flute edges. Fry bacon until crisp, drain and crumble into bottom of pie. Grate cheese and put on top of bacon. Pie can be made ahead and put in freezer at this point. Mix the eggs with flour, salt, nutmeg and milk. Pour mixture over the cheese and bacon. Brown the butter and drizzle over the top. Bake 20-30 minutes in 375 degree oven until knife comes out clean.

KENTUCKY AMBROSIA

Place in layers in a large crystal bowl: sliced fresh oranges, grapefruit, bananas, apples and strawberries. Squeeze a little lemon juice over fruit, cover and chill thoroughly. When time to serve, toss fruit lightly and top with freshly grated coconut. Garnish with sprigs of fresh mint.

GAME DINNER

MISTLETOE PLANTATION

Mrs. Jean H. Gallien

Mushroom Consommé

Wild Duck (rare)*

Currant Jelly Sauce*

Wild Rice

Spinach Ring filled with Creamed Onions

Parker House Rolls

Lemon Pudding*

WILD DUCK

Place two strips bacon over duck that is room temperature. Place two celery stalks in cavity and salt and pepper to taste. Cook 20 minutes in 500 degree ·oven.

CURRANT JELLY SAUCE

⅓ currant jelly   ⅓ catsup
⅓ sherry wine

Mix above ingredients in saucepan until hot. Match amount of sauce made to number of ducks served using above proportions.

LEMON PUDDING

Juice and rind of 2 lemons   4 tablespoons self-rising
2 cups milk   flour
6 eggs   4 tablespoons butter
                                  2 cups sugar

Cream butter, flour and sugar. Add well-beaten egg yolks, grated lemon rind and juice. Add milk last. Fold in stiffly beaten egg whites. Place in deep oven-proof dish in pan of hot water. Bake at 350 degrees for about one hour or until delicately brown and pudding begins to leave side of dish. Can be served hot or cold with whipped cream if desired.

TERRACE LUNCHEON

MERRILY PLANTATION

Mr. and Mrs. William H. Flowers

Sherry

Individual Cheese Soufflés*

Salad of Fresh Mushrooms*

Iced Tea

Chilled Apricots

Lacy Oatmeal Cookies*

INDIVIDUAL CHEESE SOUFFLÉS

12 half-cup ramekins
5 level tablespoons all-
purpose flour
1 cup cold milk
3 egg yolks

4 egg whites
½ cup Swiss cheese, grated
Salt, a small pinch
Black pepper, freshly ground
Nutmeg, freshly ground

Heavily butter ramekins and set them in icebox to chill. To make the bouillie: Put flour into a saucepan and gradually add cold milk, stirring, to make a smooth paste. Season and set over medium heat to thicken; continue stirring. Remove from heat and set aside. Add yolks, one at a time, to the bouillie, stirring after each addition. Beat the whites stiff but not dry with a pinch of salt and fold them into the bouillie, gradually sprinkling on the grated cheese at the same time. The bouillie should be lukewarm when folding-in the whites; if necessary, gently reheat the bouillie. Preheat the oven to 375 degrees. Fill the ramekins two-thirds full of the soufflé mixture; set them in a shallow pan and pour simmering water around them to come two-thirds the way up the sides of the molds. Cook 12 to 15 minutes, being careful that the water in the pan does not boil; if it does, adjust oven temperature. Remove soufflés from oven. They will deflate slightly. Serve immediately, or they may be held as much as 24 hours before serving. If held, reheat in a bain-marie, 6-8 minutes, in 350 degree oven. Twenty minutes before serving the soufflés, butter a flat oven-proof dish, unmold the soufflés onto the dish, and prepare the following sauce:

TARRAGON CREAM SAUCE:

1½-2 cups heavy cream
3-4 tablespoons fresh
tarragon (less if dried)

Salt
Pepper, freshly ground

Bring cream to a boil with tarragon and seasonings; simmer slowly for several minutes. Pour this sauce over and around soufflés and return them to oven for 10-12 minutes or until they swell and absorb almost all the cream. You might baste them. Serve immediately. This recipe is for 6. For 8 add an extra egg only.

MUSHROOM SALAD

Toss together fresh sliced mushrooms, almonds, endive, sliced avocado and chopped tomato. Serve with vinaigrette dressing.

LACY OATMEAL COOKIES

½ cup butter
½ cup brown sugar
½ cup white sugar
1 egg
2 tablespoons flour

1 teaspoon baking powder
½ teaspoon salt
1 cup oatmeal
1 teaspoon vanilla
½ teaspoon almond extract

Cream butter, sugar and egg. Mix together and add flour, baking powder, and salt. Combine this with oatmeal, vanilla, and almond extract. Drop by ½ teaspoon on ungreased, open-end cookie sheet sprayed with Pam. Bake at 325 degrees for 10 minutes. Remove quickly from cookie sheet.

FAVORITE RECIPES FROM LABRAH PLANTATION

Mr. and Mrs. R. A. Heinsohn

SHREDDED YAMS

2 pounds sweet potatoes
1 gallon water
1 tablespoon salt
1 cup sugar

1 cup pineapple juice
½ cup white corn syrup
¼ cup butter

Preheat oven to 350 degrees. Peel and shred potatoes in the gallon of water. Add salt. Cook until tender. Drain and place in 11½ x 7½-inch baking dish. Mix sugar, syrup and ½ cup water and cook to a thin syrup. Add butter. Pour pineapple juice over potatoes, then syrup. Bake in preheated oven 35 minutes or until transparent. Serves 12.

CREAMED SPINACH IN PARTY SHELLS

15-20 small party shells,
    baked
2 packages frozen chopped
    spinach, cooked and drained
2 cans cream of chicken soup

A little grated onion
Dash of cinnamon
2 tablespoons flour

To hot, cooked spinach add soup, onion, and cinnamon; carefully blend in flour. When well mixed, pour spinach mixture into warm party shells. Top with hard-boiled eggs which have been pressed through a sieve. Serve around any cold meat or platter of vegetables such as whole cauliflower with cheese, string beans, etc.

BANANA FRITTERS

3 bananas, peeled and mashed
3 tablespoons orange juice
2 tablespoons confectioners'
    sugar

1 cup flour
2 tablespoons baking powder
Dash nutmeg

Combine all ingredients and blend well. Drop batter by tablespoonful into hot fat, constantly turning. Fritters should brown evenly, but not too fast. Sprinkle with confectioners' sugar before serving. Serve piping hot!

DINNER

BOXHALL PLANTATION

Mr. and Mrs. Thomas M. Hines

Fresh Lump Crabmeat

Crab Louis Sauce*   Croutons

Broiled Boned Shad*

Individual Stuffed Eggplant*

English Peas Topped with Toasted Pecans

Sally Lunn Bread*

Danish Apple Cake*

Coffee

CRAB LOUIS SAUCE

1 cup mayonnaise
1 tablespoon lemon juice
¼ cup French dressing
1 teaspoon Worcestershire sauce
Dash cayenne
Salt and pepper to taste
½ teaspoon horseradish
1 tablespoon sweet pickle relish

1 teaspoon McCormick Lemon
    Pepper
1 tablespoon green pepper,
    minced
2 teaspoons onion, grated
½ cup chili sauce
2 tablespoons olives with
    pimento, chopped

Mix above ingredients well and chill until serving time. Serve over cold fresh lump crabmeat.

BROILED BONED SHAD

Sprinkle ready-to-cook boned shad with salt and a little white pepper. Arrange on greased broiler rack and broil about 3 inches from heat for about 20 minutes, turning once. While fish is broiling, brush with mixture of melted butter and lemon juice. Arrange fish on warm serving platter and spread with more melted butter, lemon juice, minced parsley and toasted almonds. Serve with lemon wedges.

INDIVIDUAL STUFFED EGGPLANT

1 medium-size eggplant
    (1¼ inch diameter)
½ cup bread crumbs
1 tablespoon butter
4 tablespoons grated
    Parmesan cheese

2 medium-size fresh tomatoes,
    finely chopped
Chopped onion
¼ teaspoon salt
¼ teaspoon pepper
Butter

Boil whole eggplant in water for 20 minutes. Drain and cut lengthwise. Carefully remove pulp and leave shell ¼ inch thick. Chop the pulp and reserve. Arrange shells in shallow baking dish. Brown bread crumbs in butter. Mix in Parmesan cheese, tomatoes and onion as desired. Add eggplant pulp, salt, and pepper. Cover and cook over low heat for 5 minutes. Pile filling into eggplant and dot each portion with butter. Bake at 400 degrees for 20 minutes. Serve piping hot. Yield: 2 servings, increase quantities as needed.

SALLY LUNN BREAD

1 cup milk, scalded
½ cup butter
2 tablespoons sugar
2 teapoons salt

1 package yeast
½ cup lukewarm water
2 eggs, lightly beaten
6 cups flour

Add butter, sugar and salt to hot milk. Cool until lukewarm. Soften yeast in lukewarm water and add to milk mixture. Beat in 2 cups of flour. Stir in eggs. Add 3 cups flour and beat until batter is smooth and elastic. Knead in about 1 cup flour to make a dough that is soft but not sticky. Cover and let rise in a warm place for 1½ hours, or until dough is doubled in size. Punch down and turn out on lightly floured board. Knead until dough is smooth and elastic. Cut into 2 equal portions. Form each portion into a loaf and put into greased loaf pans, 4½ x 8½ x 2½ inches. Cover and let rise in warm place for about 1 hour or until dough is well-rounded above tops of pans. Bake at 425 degrees for 30 minutes or until lightly browned. Remove from pans to racks and cool. Serve warm. Makes 2 loaves.

DANISH APPLE CAKE

3 pounds cooking apples
¼ cup water
⅔ cup sugar
Grated rind of 1 orange
½ teaspoon vanilla
2 cups fine, dry bread
    crumbs
1 teaspoon cinnamon

¼ cup brown sugar
2 tablespoons butter
Raspberry jam
½ cup butter, melted
⅔ cup red currant jelly
2 tablespoons sherry
Whipped cream

Peel and core apples. Cut into quarters. Simmer, covered in water 25 minutes. Mash and add ⅔ cup sugar, orange rind, and vanilla. Set aside. Mix bread crumbs with cinnamon, and brown sugar. Brown lightly in skillet with 2 tablespoons butter. Butter a round 8-inch baking dish that is 3 inches deep. Alternate layers of crumb mixture, apple purée, and raspberry jam. Finish with a crumb layer on top. Using a large wooden spoon, press layers down firmly. Pour melted butter over cake. Bake at 350 degrees 40 minutes or until cake is firm. In a small saucepan heat currant jelly with sherry until jelly is melted and bubbling and coats wooden spoon lightly. Cool glaze slightly. Cool cake and unmold on serving plate. With a pastry brush, spread currant glaze over top of cake. Decorate with whipped cream.

EASTER DINNER

PEBBLE HILL PLANTATION

Consommé Windsor

Roast Saddle of Lamb or Small Leg of Lamb

White Acre Peas*

Green Vegetable

Apricot Soufflé

Coffee

*A perfect complement to lamb.

CONSOMMÉ WINDSOR

1 quart beef consommé

2 eggs

¼ teaspoon flour

1 tablespoon heavy cream

Slivered, toasted almonds

Place consommé in large saucepan. Bring to a boil over a medium heat. Combine eggs, flour and cream in mixing bowl. Strain through a fine sieve into boiling consommé, stirring constantly. Continue cooking until hot but not boiling. Garnish with almonds. Serves 10 to 12.

ROAST SADDLE OF LAMB

1 6-8 pound lamb saddle

Salt to taste

Pepper to taste

Prepared mustard

Garlic salt

Wash roast. Pat dry and season with salt and pepper. Cover the entire saddle with prepared mustard. Sprinkle with garlic powder or salt. Place on rack in a shallow roasting pan. Place in 400 degree oven. Roast until just done—still a little pink—about 20 minutes per pound, but difficult to be definite. Leg of lamb can be substituted. If using a leg, insert a clove of garlic at each end of the bone before cooking.

APRICOT SOUFFLÉ

3 cups dried apricots

½ cup sugar

1 teaspoon lemon juice

1 teaspoon vanilla

4 egg whites

Pinch salt

Powdered sugar

Slivered, blanched almonds

Lightly whipped cream

Soak apricots overnight. Cover with water and boil until soft. Put in a blender or through a food sieve until you have enough apricot purée to measure 1 cup. Add sugar, lemon juice and vanilla flavoring. Return to heat and cook until sugar dissolves, stirring constantly. Beat egg whites until stiff. Add pinch of salt. Add warm purée to beaten egg whites. Fold in gently. Pour into a buttered 1½ quart casserole. Sprinkle the top with powdered sugar and blanched almonds. Place casserole in pan of hot water and bake at 350 degrees for 30 minutes or until done. Serve immediately. Pour on lightly whipped cream which has been whipped until thickened but will still pour.

SHOOTING PARTY LUNCHEON*

PEBBLE HILL PLANTATION

Hors d'oeuvres Plate

Quail Pie Emma

Cheese Board

Fruits

*To be served as picnic or at home.

HORS D'OEUVRES PLATE

Place lettuce leaves on large chop plate. Arrange on lettuce: cold green beans in groups, separated by quartered tomatoes and deviled eggs - in center, enough sardines for servings desired - pass vinaigrette sauce and mayonnaise.

CHEESE BOARD

Three or four assorted cheeses, with butter pats - serve with stoned wheat or other unsalted crackers.

FRUITS

Bowl of fresh seasonal fruits - as many as possible for time of year.

QUAIL PIE EMMA

6 Quail	1 bay leaf
¾ cup butter, divided	2 tablespoons flour
1 carrot, sliced	Milk
1 stalk celery, sliced	Salt to taste
2 slices onion	Pepper to taste
Sprig of parsley	1 wine glass sherry

Bone birds by cutting down the back of the birds with kitchen shears and pulling out the ribs, saving the bones (neck, back and wings - leave legs on). Dredge birds in seasoned flour and sauté in ½ cup butter until lightly browned. Remove birds and set aside. Place bones and vegetables in pan. Add 1 quart or enough cold water to cover. Add bay leaf. Cook over low heat for 1 hour, adding water if necessary. Drain stock from vegetables. Mix flour with enough milk to pour easily. Add to stock to thicken. Season with salt, pepper, sherry and remaining butter. More butter may be added. Place half the birds and half the sauce in a casserole dish. Cover with strips of pastry made from rich biscuit dough. Bake at 350 degrees for 30 minutes or until pastry is brown. Add remaining birds and sauce. Cover with pastry strips. Continue to bake an additional 30 minutes or until pastry is browned. Serves 4.

BISCUIT PASTRY:

2 cups flour	⅓ cup vegetable oil
3 teaspoons baking powder	⅔ cup milk
1 teaspoon salt	

Combine first 3 ingredients in mixing bowl. Pour milk and oil in measuring cup -do not stir. Add all at once to dry ingredients. Stir until mixture forms a ball. Knead lightly. Roll or pat until ¼ inch thick. Cut into strips.

CHRISTMAS DINNER

SPRINGWOOD PLANTATION

Mrs. Thomas C. Chubb

Oyster Stew*

Roast Wild Turkey with Cornbread Stuffing*

Whole Cranberry Sauce and Cranberry Jelly

Stuffed Sweet Potatoes*

Peas à la Française*

Pecan Tarts with Fresh Whipped Cream*

OYSTER STEW

4 cups light cream	2 tablespoons butter
3 dozen fresh oysters, shucked	Salt, white pepper, and cayenne to taste
½ cup dry white wine	Fresh parsley

Poach oysters in their liquor and wine until their edges curl and they plump up. Place into double boiler; add cream, salt, pepper and cayenne. Cook stew until it is very hot, then add butter and parsley. This can be kept hot this way for several hours without curdling.

ROAST WILD TURKEY WITH CORNBREAD STUFFING

1 10-12 pound turkey	2 cups pecans, chopped
8 strips fat bacon	4 or 5 hard-cooked eggs, chopped
1 package Pepperidge Farm Cornbread Stuffing	1½ cups mushrooms, sliced
2 teaspoons garlic powder	¼ pound butter
1 teaspoon nutmeg	1 shallot, chopped
4 tablespoons parsley	1 cup Madeira wine

Sauté mushrooms in ½ the butter and the shallot in the rest. Combine eggs, stuffing, seasonings and pecans; toss in mushrooms and onion. Add enough of the Madeira to bind the stuffing together. Fill the cavity of turkey with stuffing. Band turkey with bacon strips and roast in a 325 degree oven for 2½ to 3 hours, basting often with remaining Madeira and pan drippings.

STUFFED SWEET POTATOES

8 medium-sized sweet
  potatoes
¾ stick butter
¼ cup heavy cream
¼ cup rum

Salt and white pepper to
  taste
½ teaspoon nutmeg
⅛ teaspoon cinnamon
3 egg yolks, beaten
  until frothy

Bake potatoes for one hour in a 400 degree oven or until fork tender. Slice off a thin piece from the top of each potato and scoop pulp out into a bowl. Beat in the butter, cream, rum and seasonings and continue to beat until the potatoes are smooth. Add beaten yolks, and beat again until potatoes are fluffy. Stuff into potato shells and bake in 400 degree oven for about 20 minutes. These can be made early in the day and heated for 40 minutes until they are very hot.

PEAS À LA FRANÇAISE

5 large lettuce leaves,
  washed but not drained
3 pounds fresh peas, shelled
  or 3 large cans English peas
  drained

Salt and white pepper to taste
3 tablespoons butter
1½ teaspoons sugar, not
  if using canned peas
1½ teaspoons oregano

Line a heavy saucepan with leaves. Add peas, salt, pepper, butter and sugar. Bring to a low, low simmer and cook until lettuce wilts and peas are fork tender. Toss oregano in at the last minute and serve.

PECAN TARTS

1 cup dark corn syrup
½ cup dark brown sugar
3 eggs, beaten
⅓ stick butter
1 cup pecans, chopped

6 halves of pecans
⅛ teaspoon rum
Pinch of salt
6 tart shells, from your
  favorite pastry

Beat eggs, adding sifted sugar, syrup, pecans, butter, rum, and salt. Blend well. Press pecan half into center of each tart. Cook in a 350 degree oven for 40 minutes. Cool on wire rack. Serve with a dollop of freshly whipped cream. Serves 6.

DINNER

MILLPOND PLANTATION

Mr. and Mrs. Dean Perry

Cream of Watercress Soup*

Fillet of Beef Wellington*
with Madeira Sauce*

Broccoli Ring with Hollandaise Sauce*

Boiled New Potatoes with Parsley

Strawberry Ice Cream*

Demitasse

CREAM OF WATERCRESS SOUP
Potage Crème de Cresson

5 to 6 green onion bulbs,
   minced
½ teaspoon salt
3 tablespoons flour
5 cups chicken broth, heated
2 egg yolks
Handful of watercress leaves

3 tablespoons butter
4 packed cups fresh watercress
   leaves and tender stems, washed
   and dried in a towel
   (about ¼ pound)
½ to 1 cup heavy cream

Combine the green onions, butter and ½ cup water in a heavy saucepan. Bring to a boil. Reduce heat and simmer until all the water has boiled away and the onions are tender and translucent. Stir in the watercress and salt. Cover and cook over low heat for about five minutes or until the leaves are tender and wilted. Sprinkle in the flour and stir over moderate heat for three minutes. Stir in the hot broth, then simmer for five minutes. Purée, about half at a time, in an electric blender. Pour back into the saucepan. Taste for seasoning. It may need salt and pepper. Combine the yolks and ½ cup of cream in a bowl. Beat with a whip until mixed. Gradually beat a cupful of the hot soup into the mixture. Then combine with the soup in a thin, steady stream, beating constantly. Place over moderate heat for a couple of minutes. *Do not bring to a boil.* Refrigerate until cold. If too thick, stir in more cream just before serving. Drop the watercress leaves into boiling water for half a minute, refresh in cold water and drain. Use as a garnish.

FILLET OF BEEF WELLINGTON

1 fillet of beef, trimmed of all fat
(Tell the butcher it is for Beef
Wellington and he will shape
it for you so it will wrap
nicely in the pastry.)
3 pounds mushrooms
2 or 3 tablespoons Cognac

1 stick butter
6 strips bacon
¾ pound shallots
1 8-ounce jar or tin of
foie gras
Salt and freshly ground
pepper to taste

Preheat the oven to 450 degrees. Lay the strips of bacon over the fillet, tying them on with string if necessary. Place on a rack in a roasting pan and roast 12 minutes for rare, 20 minutes for medium rare and 25 for medium. Remove from the oven and allow to cool to room temperature before proceeding. Chop the shallots and mushrooms very fine. In a large skillet or two medium ones, heat a couple of tablespoons of butter to bubbling and add the chopped shallots and mushrooms. Cook down over low heat until the mushrooms are quite black, adding more butter if necessary. Add Cognac and cook 5 or 10 minutes more. Mash slightly and cool. (This can be done a day ahead.) Spread the mushroom filling over a pastry rectangle, rolled out to about 18 x 12 inches and preferably, less than ¼ inch thick. Lay the cooled fillet on this and cover the top of the fillet with overlapping slices of foie gras. Wrap up the fillet in the pastry, sealing it well with egg wash, made from 1 egg mixed with 2 tablespoons water. Brush it all over with egg wash and decorate it with little pastry cutouts of various shapes. They will stick to the egg wash. Bake about 30 minutes in preheated 375 degree oven. Mark slices on top, make a few holes to let out steam. Serve with Madeira Sauce.

PASTRY:

3 cups flour
2 sticks butter
1 egg, lightly beaten

1 teaspoon salt
½ cup shortening (Crisco)
½ (about) cup ice water

Blend the butter and shortening into flour and salt with two knives, a pastry blender or the fingers. Add the egg and enough ice water to make a dough that is not wet. Wrap in wax paper and chill.

MADEIRA SAUCE

2 tablespoons butter
1½ cups brown sauce or
    canned beef gravy
2 tablespoons lemon juice

2 tablespoons shallots,
    finely chopped
¼ cup Madeira

Melt the butter in a small pan and sauté the shallots until tender. Add the brown sauce and the lemon juice. When it comes to a boil, add the wine and bring it back to the boil. This can be made ahead of time, it keeps for several days, in the refrigerator.

BROCCOLI RING WITH HOLLANDAISE SAUCE

Cook enough fresh or frozen broccoli and purée to make one cup. In a skillet melt 3 tablespoons butter. Add and sauté for 1 minute 1 tablespoon chopped onion. Stir in until blended 3 tablespoons flour. Combine and stir slowly ½ cup milk or stock and ½ cup cream. When the sauce is boiling add the chopped broccoli. When these ingredients are hot reduce the heat and stir in 3 beaten egg yolks. Cook and stir for 1 minute longer to permit the yolks to thicken. Season with salt, paprika, nutmeg. Add (to improve the looks of the soufflé) a few drops green coloring. Whip until stiff 3 egg whites. Fold them lightly into the broccoli mixture. Grease a 7-inch ring mold. Fill it with the soufflé mixture, set in a pan of hot water and bake it in a moderate oven at 325 degrees until it is firm, for about 30 minutes. Invert the soufflé on a platter and serve with Hollandaise Sauce. (See Sauces)

STRAWBERRY ICE CREAM

To one quart strawberries, add ¾ cup sugar and juice of one lemon. Blend sugar, lemon juice and strawberries in blender. Put in refrigerator. Whip ½ quart whipped cream and ½ quart of light cream until foamy and put in freezer for 3 hours. Mix strawberries and cream together and put in electric churn with a pinch of salt.

DINNER

SINKOLA PLANTATION

Mrs. Warren Bicknell

Cold Borsch with Sour Cream*

Quail with White Wine Sauce*

Corn Soufflé*

String Beans with Celery*

Rolls

Raspberry Ice with Blueberry Sauce*

COLD BORSCH WITH SOUR CREAM

3 cans beets (fresh may
   be used)
1 onion, cut in quarters
3 stalks celery
4 bay leaves
4 cups water

1½ envelopes of gelatin
1 tablespoon vinegar
1 bouillon cube
2 tablespoons sugar

Cook beets, onion, bay leaves and celery with juice until tender; remove onions, celery and bay leaves. Purée a small amount of beets with stock. Mix purée, beets, water, gelatin, vinegar, bouillon and sugar; cook a few minutes. Chill and top with sour cream.

QUAIL WITH WINE SAUCE

Simmer quail with butter in a covered saucepan until tender. Add a small amount of water if necessary.

SAUCE:

1 cup cream
Salt and pepper to taste

1 tablespoon flour
½ cup white wine

Mix and simmer until thick. If mixture is too thick use a little milk to thin. Pour over quail. This is good served on toast or plain.

CORN SOUFFLÉ

2½ cups creamed corn
   (fresh or frozen)
½ cup cream
1 tablespoon flour

3 eggs, separated
1 teaspoon salt
1 tablespoon sugar

Mix corn, cream, flour, egg yolks and salt. Beat egg whites until stiff; add sugar and fold into corn mixture. Bake at 350 degrees in pan of water until brown and well done, about 1 hour and 15 minutes.

STRING BEANS AND CELERY

Combine French beans, salt and water and boil until tender. Thinly slice celery and boil in another saucepan until tender. Drain beans and celery; mix with ½ stick butter or ¼ cup cream.

RASPBERRY ICE WITH BLUEBERRY SAUCE

3 cups raspberries
2 cups sugar

4 cups water
Juice of 2 lemons

SAUCE:

2 cups blueberries
2 cups water

1½ cups sugar

Cook raspberries for 10 minutes and strain. Combine raspberry purée, sugar, water and lemon juice. Mix well and freeze in ice cream churn. Meanwhile, make sauce by mixing blueberries, water and sugar. Cook mixture for 30 minutes or until slightly thickened. Cool and serve over Raspberry Ice.

BARBECUE

SUSINA PLANTATION

Mr. and Mrs. Heywood Mason

Oysters on the Half Shell
Horseradish Sauce

Spare Ribs
Brushed with Barbecue Sauce*

Baked Beans with Sour Cream*

Cole Slaw

Garlic Bread

Hello Dollies*

Coffee

PIT BARBECUE SAUCE

½ pound butter
1 pint catsup
1 pint vinegar
1 tablespoon Tabasco
1 small bottle
    Worcestershire

1 tablespoon brown sugar
1 tablespoon onion juice
2 lemons, cut in half
Dash red and black pepper
1 to 3 tablespoons salt

Mix all ingredients together, squeezing a little juice from lemons. Add more salt if desired. Bring to a boil. Remove lemons. Not necessary to refrigerate. Save unused portion for next time. Makes a little less than 2 quarts. Enough for 17 to 20 pounds of ribs.

BAKED BEANS

Mix baked beans with a dollop or two of sour cream and a good bit of chopped onion. Bake until piping hot.

HELLO DOLLIES

1 stick butter
1 cup graham cracker crumbs
1 6-ounce package chocolate
    chips

1 6-ounce package
    butterscotch chips
1 cup pecans, chopped
1 can sweetened condensed milk

Melt butter in 9 x 13-inch pyrex dish. Sprinkle crumbs, chocolate chips, butterscotch chips and pecans in layers. Last, drizzle milk over all and bake for 25 minutes at 325 degrees. Makes 20 dollies.

DINNER

DIXIE PLANTATION

Miss Geraldine Livingston

Baked Large Mouth Bass with
Cornbread Stuffing*

Spinach Soufflé*

Stewed Tomatoes

Potatoes Anna

Orange Meringue Cups*

Coffee

CORNBREAD STUFFING FOR BASS

Homemade cornbread
1 onion
3 celery stalks

1 bell pepper
4 boiled eggs

Chop onion, celery, pepper and eggs and mix well with crumbled cornbread. Quantities depend on size of fish. Stuff large fish with head on and bake in moderate oven until fish is browned and flakes easily.

SPINACH SOUFFLÉ

1 cup milk
1 cup spinach, cooked
   and chopped
1 onion
½ cup cheese, grated

4 eggs, separated
3 tablespoons butter
3 tablespoons flour
¼ teaspoon salt
⅛ teaspoon pepper

Melt butter; stir in flour and gradually add milk until mixture thickens. Stir in cheese and beaten egg yolks. Fold in onion and spinach. Stir until smooth and slightly cool. Fold stiffly beaten egg whites into mixture. Bake in buttered casserole at 350 degrees until firm on top and soft inside, about 35 minutes.

ORANGE MERINGUE CUPS

Scoop insides out of cold oranges with paring knife after cutting off tops to make cups. Use 1 shell or cup per person. Fill with meringue made with 4 egg whites beaten until stiff with ½ cup sugar and bake in 500 degree oven until lightly brown.

HUNT BREAKFAST
WILLOW OAK PLANTATION
Mr. and Mrs. Edward A. Davis

Eggs Chasseur*

Live Oak Grits*

Beaten Biscuits with Ham*

Tomato Chutney*

Date Nut Squares*

Milk Punch

EGGS CHASSEUR

1 pound chicken livers
4 tablespoons butter
1 cup mushrooms, sautéed
   and sliced
1½ cups white sauce, made
   with cream

Salt and pepper to taste
16 eggs, scrambled with
   ⅔ cup cream
Chopped parsley

Cook livers in butter until they are no longer pink. Remove from heat and dice. Add mushrooms, cream sauce, and salt and pepper. Put this mixture in center of warm serving dish and spoon eggs around it. Garnish with parsley. Serves 12.

LIVE OAK GRITS

3 cups hominy grits, cooked
2 large tablespoons butter
6 eggs, beaten
3 cups cream

3 cups corn meal
1 teaspoon garlic salt
Pepper to taste

While grits are hot, add butter and eggs. Gradually add cream and when mixed well, add corn meal, garlic salt, and pepper. Pour into a large greased casserole and bake at 375 degrees for 20 minutes, until set and crusty. Can be refrigerated before baking and then baked for 45 minutes.

BISCUITS WITH HAM

2 dozen of your favorite
   beaten biscuits
1 pound smoked ham, thinly
   sliced

Butter, melted
Dijon mustard

Split the biscuits and brush with melted butter. Warm them and spread with mustard. Place a thin slice of ham folded in half inside biscuits. Wrap in foil and keep warm in 225 degree oven until serving time. Serves 12.

TOMATO CHUTNEY

1 1-pound, 13-ounce can
   tomatoes
1¼ cups wine vinegar
1¼ cups sugar

1 garlic clove, minced
1 teaspoon ground ginger
¼ cup golden raisins

Put ¼ cup vinegar and garlic in blender. Blend until garlic is ground up. Put tomatoes and sugar in saucepan and bring to boil, stirring sugar back down sides of pot. Add vinegar and garlic mixture and rest of vinegar. Return to boil, then reduce heat and simmer about 1 to 1½ hours, until thickened. Stir in raisins and cook 5 minutes more. Then seal in 2 mason jars.

DATE NUT SQUARES

36 soda crackers, crushed
36 dates, chopped
3 cups sugar
1½ cups pecans, chopped

1½ teaspoons baking powder
9 egg whites, stiffly
   beaten
Almond flavoring to taste

Mix cracker crumbs, dates and nuts with sugar and baking powder. When thoroughly mixed, fold in egg whites and almond flavoring. Pour into a greased 13 x 9-inch pan and bake at 325 degrees about 35 minutes or until a toothpick comes out clean. Cut into little squares.

DINNER

FAIR OAKS PLANTATION

Mr. and Mrs. Brigham Britton

Chilled Chicken Bouillon With Curry*

Roast Beef or Leg of Lamb

Spinach Supreme*

Broiled Tomatoes*

Parkerhouse Rolls

Lemon Fluff*

Coffee

CHILLED CHICKEN BOUILLON

4 tablespoons sherry
2 teaspoons gelatin

8 cups bouillon
4 teaspoons curry powder

Heat sherry in bouillon. Dissolve gelatin in 4 tablespoons cold water, and add to hot bouillon; then add curry. Chill 5 to 6 hours. Serves eight.

SPINACH SUPREME

4 pounds fresh spinach
8 tablespoons butter
Salt and pepper
1½ cups sour cream

1 pound fresh mushrooms
    (optional), thinly sliced
¼ cup Madeira

Put the cooked, chopped spinach in saucepan with 4 tablespoons butter and sour cream. Salt and pepper to taste. Beat all this together and keep warm. In a separate pan melt 4 tablespoons butter and sauté mushrooms for about 7 or 8 minutes. Add mushrooms to spinach mixture with Madeira wine. Mix well and simmer for 2 or 3 minutes over medium flame. Serve at once. Serves eight.

BROILED TOMATOES

8 firm tomatoes
2 eggs
1 cup bread crumbs

3 tablespoons butter
3 tablespoons brown sugar
Salt and pepper to taste

Wash tomatoes, cut slices from top and bottom, and cut in half crosswise. Sprinkle both sides with salt and pepper and allow to drain. Dip in beaten egg, and then in bread crumbs. Dot with butter and broil first on one side, then on other. Sprinkle brown sugar over tomatoes, dot again with butter and brown quickly. Serves eight.

LEMON FLUFF

1 package lemon gelatin
½ cup boiling water
½ cup sugar

1 can unsweetened evaporated
milk
Juice of 1 lemon
Grated rind of 1 lemon

Dissolve gelatin in boiling water. Add sugar and grated rind. Let cool and just gel, not harden. Then whip very cold milk and add to first mixture. Add lemon juice. Beat whole mixture and put in refrigerator in buttered bowl dusted with bread crumbs. (A round platter 2-inches deep can be used.) Serves eight.

SAUCE: A package of frozen raspberries melted and strained through a colander.

Appetizers

ROAST FILLET

7-8 pound fillet of beef
   (rib-eye may be used)
Pepper
Onion salt
⅔ cup A.1. Sauce

1 box paprika
Salt, use plenty
Celery salt
2 lemons
¼ cup Worcestershire sauce

Rub salt, pepper, celery salt, and onion salt into entire roast separately. Use a generous amount of each one. Mix juice of 2 lemons, A. 1. Sauce, and Worcestershire together. Rub this into entire roast and save any left over. Put meat into shallow roasting pan and coat top and sides heavily with paprika. Leave at room temperature for 8 hours. Baste with leftover sauce and meat juices. Pour off sauce before cooking. Bake at 550 degrees for 10 minutes; then reduce temperature to 450 degrees and bake, uncovered, for 8-10 minutes per pound. Slice paper thin and serve on well-buttered rye bread with a selection of mustard.
The Editors

ROQUEFORT SHORTBREAD

1 cup butter or margarine
1 cup blue cheese or
   Roquefort, crumbled

2¼ cups flour

Mix butter, cheese and flour together until well blended. Divide and roll in wax paper. Refrigerate until firm, cut in slices, and bake 10-12 minutes in a 375 degree oven.
Mrs. W. Z. Hayman (Vi)

SHRIMP MOUSSE

1 can tomato soup
¼ cup cold water
1 cup mayonnaise
1 can crabmeat
1 can small shrimp
½ cup onion, chopped

½ cup celery, chopped
½ cup green pepper, chopped
1 package unflavored gelatin
1 8-ounce package cream cheese,
   softened at room temperature

Heat soup to boiling. Dissolve gelatin in cold water and add to soup. Mix cream cheese with mayonnaise. Add soup and beat with rotary beater. Add seafood and chopped vegetables. Pour into round mold and chill. Serve on crackers. Serves 20-25.
Mrs. Fred Cooper (Helen)

MEAT BALLS HAWAIIAN STYLE

1 pound ground beef
2 eggs, beaten
½ teaspoon garlic powder
¼ teaspoon pepper

1 small onion, minced
½ cup chow mein noodles,
   crushed
Flour

Mix above ingredients, except flour and roll into 1-inch balls. Roll in flour and brown in well-oiled pan. Serve meat balls in sauce.

SAUCE:

¼ cup soy sauce
¼ teaspoon powdered ginger
½ cup catsup

¼ cup brown sugar
¼ cup pineapple juice

Combine and heat ingredients. Add meat balls and simmer for 15 minutes. Serves 6.
Miss Ophelia Smith

SAUSAGE SWIRLS

4 cups flour
¼ cup corn meal
¼ cup sugar
2 tablespoons baking powder

1 teaspoon salt
⅔ cup cooking oil
⅔ to 1 cup milk
2 pounds hot bulk sausage

Sift together dry ingredients. Blend in oil. Add enough milk to make a soft dough. Roll thinly into 2 10 x 18-inch rectangles. Spread sausage evenly on dough. Roll up lengthwise. Chill well and slice into ¼-inch slices. Bake at 350 degrees for 15-20 minutes.
Mrs. Charles D. Reichert (Eddie)

MOBILE "COON BALLS"

3 cups Bisquick
1 pound ground hot sausage

2 cups sharp Cheddar cheese,
   grated

Mix all ingredients together. Refrigerate overnight. Roll in small balls and bake 30 minutes in 350 degree oven. May be frozen. If so, reheat before serving.
Mrs. W. W. Alexander (Elise)
Similar recipes submitted by *Mrs. E. B. Cooper (Margaret), Mrs. Stephen Eckels (Beth), Mrs. William Oliver (Naomi), and Mrs. Ray Willett (Ruth).*

BACON WRAP-UPS

10 slices bread
15 slices bacon

1 can cream of mushroom soup
Toothpicks

Trim crusts from bread. Cut bread into 3 strips. Generously spread undiluted soup on each strip. Cut bacon in half. Place half piece of bacon under bread strip (not the soup-spread side). Wrap up as tightly as you can and insert toothpick to hold in place. Place all wrapped pieces on cookie sheet that has sides to catch grease. Bake at 300 degrees for 1 hour. Makes 30.
Mrs. Frederick Jefferson (Marilyn)

CAVIAR PIE

6 eggs, hard cooked
1 stick butter, softened
6 small white onions,
    chopped

2 4-ounce jars lumpfish
    caviar
1 cup sour cream

Sieve eggs and mix with butter. Put the paste into a glass soufflé dish or any pretty glass bowl. Refrigerate for 1 hour. Add a layer of onions, a layer of caviar, and top with sour cream. Return to refrigerator. Serve cold with water crackers.
Mrs. Haywood Mason (Edie)

MARINATED MUSHROOMS

1 pound mushrooms
1 tablespoon salt
Pinch crushed red pepper
⅛ teaspoon black pepper
⅛ teaspoon white pepper
⅛ teaspoon crushed oregano
    leaves

1 tablespoon sugar
1 teaspoon onion, minced
Pinch fresh ground garlic
1 cup wine vinegar
1 cup cottonseed oil

Wash fresh mushrooms and place in large jar. Add seasonings, then pour vinegar and oil over all. Jostle to mix; refrigerate in covered container for 24 hours. Serve in salads or as an appetizer.
Mrs. Robert Maxwell (Ruth Ann)

TENNY BLINI

2 cups packaged Swedish
    pancake mix
Caviar
Sour cream

Chopped onions
Chopped hard-boiled egg

Prepare pancake batter according to directions on package. Using 1 table-spoon batter for each, make 2½-inch pancakes. Stack baked and cooled pancakes on a sheet of foil. Wrap and freeze until ready to assemble and serve. Before serving unwrap and thaw pancakes at room temperature. Arrange pancakes on cookie sheet. Cover with foil and heat at 350 degrees for 20 minutes. Transfer pancakes to chafing dish and serve with caviar, sour cream, eggs, and onions as you wish. Makes 5 dozen.
Mrs. Joe Feinberg (Harriet)

SPICED PECANS (OR WALNUTS)

¼ cup butter
2 tablespoons chili powder
½ teaspoon ground cumin
½ teaspoon ground turmeric

½ teaspoon salt
3 cups nuts
Pinch cayenne

Combine butter, chili powder, cumin, turmeric and cayenne in a skillet. Heat over low heat until butter is hot (do not let smoke). Remove from heat. Add nuts to butter and spices; stir until coated. Spread on paper towel-lined baking pan. Bake at 300 degrees for 20 minutes or until crisp. Sprinkle with salt. Cool.
The Editors

STUFFED MUSHROOMS

1 pound large mushrooms, washed
    and drained
¼ cup butter
¼ cup onion, finely minced
¼ cup celery, finely minced

1 teaspoon Worcestershire
    sauce
½ teaspoon salt
Dash of pepper

In large skillet, heat butter, onion, celery, chopped mushroom stems, and seasonings. Brush mushroom caps with butter. Fill with mixture. Arrange caps, stuffed side up, in same skillet. Simmer 5 minutes. Serve as appetizer, garnish, or side dish. Serves 4-6.
Mrs. Joe Brown (Theresa)   *Leonardwood, Missouri*

MUSHROOM TARTS

Pastry for 2-crust pie
3 eggs
3 tablespoons shallots,
  finely chopped
3 tablespoons dry white wine
⅛ teaspoon nutmeg

1 6 or 8-ounce can mushrooms,
  sliced
¾ cup heavy cream
½ teaspoon salt
⅛ teaspoon pepper
⅛ teaspoon nutmeg

Prepare pastry and roll out, half at a time. Cut into 4-inch circles and line tart pans or large muffin cups. Beat eggs in mixing bowl and brush a small amount of the beaten eggs over the inside of the tart shells. Reserve remaining eggs for filling mixture. Combine shallots, wine, and chives in small saucepan. Bring mixture to a boil, reduce heat, and simmer 2 minutes. Cool. Drain liquid from mushrooms into 2-cup measure. Add heavy cream to make 1½ cups. Add cream mixture to beaten eggs with salt, pepper, and nutmeg. Beat until well blended. Stir in shallot mixture. Divide drained mushrooms among tart shells. Add about ¼ cup of egg-cream mixture to each. Place on baking sheet and bake at 400 degrees for 15-20 minutes. Makes about 14 tarts.
Mrs. A. B. Wight, Jr. (Carolyn)

BRANDIED PÂTÉ

1 cup canned liver pâté
¼ cup brandy
1 cup mushrooms, finely chopped
½ cup butter

2 tablespoons parsley,
  chopped
Salt
Black pepper, freshly ground
Chopped chives

Sauté mushrooms in butter over low heat for about 5 minutes. Add mushrooms and butter to pâté and mix well. Pour in brandy; then add parsley, salt and pepper and mix thoroughly. Let stand at room temperature for 4 hours. Serve spinkled with chopped chives.
Mrs. Raymond D. Hill (Virginia)

GREENWICH FAKE LIVER PÂTÉ

2 packages gelatin
½ cup cold sherry
2 10-ounce cans consommé

1 8-ounce package cream
  cheese
2 cans liverwurst

Soften gelatin in sherry. Heat (do not boil) consommé and dissolve gelatin-sherry mixture. Put half of mixture into a mold and refrigerate. Put the other half of the mixture into the blender with cream cheese and liverwurst. When first mixture is firm to touch, pour on the second mixture. Chill; turn out to serve on toast triangles, wheat thins or melba toast.
Mrs. C. Martin Wood, III (Daphne)
Similar recipe submitted by *Emily R. Jerger*

SOUR PICKLE APPETIZERS

4 or 5 large whole Clausen
pickles (found in refrigerator case)
1 8-ounce package cream cheese

1 3-ounce package corned beef or
ham, sliced

Soften cream cheese to room temperature. Drain pickles on paper towel. With hands cover entire pickle with cream cheese. Then take sliced meat and wrap around cream cheese, making sure cheese is entirely covered. Wrap in foil or plastic wrap and refrigerate several hours. Just before serving slice crosswise.

Mrs. Ken Beverly (Mary Jo)

RUMAKI

10 chicken livers
10 slices of bacon
1 flat can of water
chestnuts

½ cup soy sauce
¼ cup honey
½ teaspoon ginger or 1
teaspoon garlic

Mix soy sauce, honey and ginger or garlic. Put in 13 x 9 x 1-inch pan. Clean and separate chicken livers in half for bite-size pieces. Cut bacon strips in half. Slice water chestnuts into 3 or 4 slices per nut. Wrap a liver piece and water chestnut in bacon and fasten with toothpick. Place in marinade for 4 or 5 hours turning occasionally. Charcoal outside 15-20 minutes or bake on rack over shallow pan in 375 degree oven for about 20 minutes. Turn for even cooking.

Mrs. Lee Mayfield (Patricia)   *Covington, Georgia*

EXTRA CRISP KASESTANGEN
Cheese Twists

2 cups flour, sifted
½ tablespoon salt
2 tablespoons vegetable
shortening

½ pound cold firm butter
6 tablespoons ice water
1½ cups Cheddar cheese,
shredded

Combine flour and salt. Cut in shortening; work with fingers to blend well. Cut in 1 stick (¼ pound) butter until mixture is in pieces the size of peas. Add ice water, 1 tablespoon at a time, and blend to form a firm dough. Divide into half, rolling out one half at a time. Dot each half of pastry with remaining butter. Spread the shredded cheese over each half evenly. Fold each into thirds, let stand 10 minutes; then roll out again. Again fold each into thirds and this time chill pastry in refrigerator for 10 minutes. Roll out a third time, this time over wax paper to prevent sticking. The pastry should be about ¼ inch thick (thicker than for pies). Cut into strips ½ x 2 inches. Twist and place on cookie sheets. Chill 15 minutes. Bake in 425 degree oven until crisp and golden, 15 minutes. Makes about 60 twists.

Mrs. Howard Carnes (Henrietta)

CHEESE STRAWS

1 pound cheese, either 1 pound
    sharp Cheddar or ½ Cheddar
    and ½ New York State
2 cups flour
Salt to taste

½ teaspoon red pepper
1 teaspoon baking powder
1 stick butter, softened

Grate cheese; add other ingredients and mix well. Run through cookie press. Preheat oven to 375 degrees; cook until light brown, about 10 minutes.
Mrs. Ralph Neel, Jr. (Katherine)

Variations: Use 2 sticks of butter to ½ pound of cheese.
Mrs. J. A. Stewart (Melba)

Roll dough and cut with biscuit cutter. Top with pecan half.
Mrs. J. T. Higgins (Virginia)

CHEESE CRUMPETS

2 cups Bisquick
1 cup cream
¼ cup butter

¼ cup olive oil
¾ cup Parmesan cheese,
    grated

Mix Bisquick and cream. Stir in cheese and beat lightly. Drop from spoon into melted butter and oil. Preheat oven to 450 degrees. Bake 12 minutes or until lightly browned. Serve hot.
Mrs. Lonnie Ferguson (Georgia)

CHEESE WAFERS

2 cups sharp Cheddar cheese
2 cups all-purpose flour
Cayenne pepper to taste

2 sticks margarine
2 cups Rice Krispies

Cream cheese and margarine. Blend in flour slowly. Stir in Rice Krispies and cayenne. Drop batter on ungreased cookie sheet and flatten with fork dipped in cold water to make round wafers. Bake at 375 degrees in preheated oven for 10 minutes. Yield: 3 dozen.
Mrs. W. J. Vaughn (Virginia)

Similar recipes submitted by *Mrs. Tom Boyle (Iris), Mrs. Curtis F. Culpepper (Bonnie), and Mrs. Frank Eidson (Phyllis).*

CHEESE AND CURRY ROUNDS

1 4½-ounce can black olives,
   chopped
1 cup sharp Cheddar cheese,
   grated
¾ cup green onions, finely
   chopped

¼ teaspoon curry powder
Salt and pepper to taste
Mayonnaise

Mix together with enough mayonnaise to make the mixture spreadable.
Spread on small rounds of bread and bake in 350 degree oven for 10 to 15
minutes. Yields 30.
Mrs. Robert W. Jackson (Beverly)

BROILED CHEESE SANDWICH LOAF

3 cups Cheddar cheese, shredded
⅓ cup Sauterne or other white
   dinner wine
¼ cup mayonnaise
2 teaspoons prepared mustard
2 teaspoons onion powder

1 French loaf (about 12
   inches long)
Butter
1 5½-ounce package
   cocktail frankfurters
Stuffed green olives

Combine cheese, wine, mayonnaise, mustard and onion powder. Mix well.
Cut loaf in half, lengthwise. Place on flat baking pan, crust side up, and
toast lightly under broiler. Remove from broiler, turn cut side up and spread
with butter, then with a thick layer of cheese mixture. Place small frankfurters
on pan alongside of loaf. Return to broiler with top surface of bread about 6
inches from heat for about 5 minutes, until cheese is melted and lightly
browned. Arrange frankfurters and stuffed green olives on top of loaf with
wooden picks. Cut into thick slices to serve. Serves 8-10.
Mrs. John L. Turner, IV (Sandy)

CHEESE BALL

¾ pound sharp cheese,
   softened
1 3-ounce package cream cheese
⅛ teaspoon garlic powder

2 teaspoons Worcestershire
Nuts or chili powder

Blend all ingredients. Shape into ball. Roll in chopped nuts or chili powder.
Mrs. Ken Beverly (Mary Jo)
Similar recipe submitted by *Mrs. Chris CoCroft (Katie)*

HOLIDAY CHEESE BALL

12 ounces cream cheese,
  softened
6 ounces blue cheese, softened
6 ounces Cheddar cheese, grated
2 tablespoons onion, grated

1 teaspoon Worcestershire sauce
⅛ teaspoon Accent
1 cup ground pecans
½ cup parsley, chopped

Combine first six ingredients and mix well. Stir in ½ cup pecans and ¼ cup parsley. Shape into ball. Wrap in plastic wrap; then wrap in foil. Refrigerate overnight. Roll in remaining pecans and parsley before serving.
Mrs. John Mirocha (Mary Lou)

OYSTER DIP

2 cans smoked oysters
1 can smoked clams
⅓ to ½ bottle Tabasco

¾ to 1 pint sour cream
Worcestershire sauce

Open oysters and clams and drain on paper towels. Dash Tabasco over oysters and clams. Mash or chop finely. Add sour cream and season with Worcestershire sauce. Serve with crackers or Fritos.
Mrs. Pratt Secrest (Sarah)

CURRY DIP

1½ cups mayonnaise
3 tablespoons catsup
3 teaspoons curry powder
1 tablespoon Worcestershire sauce

1 tablespoon onion, grated
Salt and pepper to taste
Garlic bud on toothpick

Mix all ingredients except mayonnaise; then add mixture slowly to mayonnaise. Make a day ahead and refrigerate. Remove garlic. Serve at room temperature. Great with raw cauliflower, celery, carrots, squash, broccoli, etc.
Mrs. Langdon S. Flowers (Bobbie)

Variation: Sour cream may be substituted for mayonnaise and 2 hard-boiled eggs, chopped, give additional flavor.
Mrs. Travis Smith (Dorothy)

KAY'S CLAM DIP

3 large cans minced clams, drained
3 8-ounce packages cream cheese,
   softened
1 tablespoon herb seasoning
1 tablespoon Accent
Juice of 2 lemons (¼ cup)

1 tablespoon Worcestershire sauce
8 drops Tabasco
8 or 10 spring onions,
   tops and bottoms, minced
Black pepper

Mix all ingredients together. Serve cold or hot on English muffin halves or crackers.
Mrs. Chris CoCroft (Katie)
Similar recipe submitted by *Mrs. Paul Bryan (Barbara)*.

CHAFING DISH CLAM DIP

1 7½-ounce can minced clams
2 tablespoons onion, minced
2 tablespoons butter
1 tablespoon catsup

1 teaspoon Worcestershire sauce
Hot pepper sauce (few drops)
1 cup sharp cheese, grated
2 tablespoons ripe olives,
   chopped

Drain clams. Reserve 1 tablespoon liquid. Cook onion in butter until tender but not brown. Add clams and rest of ingredients plus liquid. Heat until cheese melts and mixture is hot. Serve in chafing dish with cocktail crackers.
Mrs. William B. King (Anne)
Similar recipe submitted by Mrs. Marrs Cooper (Jeannette).

TAPFER'S PALM SPRINGS DIP

1 6½-ounce can crabmeat
1 6½-ounce can water
   chestnuts

1 cup mayonnaise
2 teaspoons soy sauce
1 teaspoon chives

Mix and let stand 1 hour before serving. Serve with assortment of cocktail crackers.
Mrs. Thomas Williams (Marguerite)

CHILI CON QUESCO

1 large onion
2 garlic cloves
4 tablespoons butter
1 No. 1 can tomatoes, chopped
1 4-ounce can green chilies,
    chopped
2 tablespoons flour

1 cup milk
1 teaspoon salt
1 tablespoon Tabasco (more
    or less to taste)
2 pounds Velveeta cheese
½ pound Cheddar cheese

Sauté onions and garlic in 2 tablespoons of butter until onions are tender. Add tomatoes and cook until thickened. Add chilies and continue to simmer. In a separate pan mix 2 tablespoons butter and flour. Add milk until it begins to thicken. If it gets too thick, add more milk. Add cheese in chunks. Add salt and Tabasco. Add chili mixture and serve hot or cold with Fritos.
Miss Julia Hickson

ANCHOVY DIP

½ cup mayonnaise
1 8-ounce package cream cheese
½ cup parsley, chopped
2 tablespoons onion, chopped

¼ teaspoon garlic powder
1¼ teaspoons anchovy paste
Dash of pepper
1 hard-cooked egg yolk

Place all ingredients in blender except egg yolk. Blend thoroughly and chill. Set out ½ hour before serving. Sprinkle chopped egg yolk on top. Serve with raw vegetables.
Mrs. Ken Beverly (Mary Jo)

HOT BROCCOLI DIP

½ cup onion, chopped
½ cup celery, chopped
½ cup mushrooms, chopped
3 tablespoons butter or
    margarine, melted

1 10-ounce package frozen
    chopped broccoli, cooked and
    well-drained
1 10¾-ounce can cream of
    mushroom soup, undiluted
1 6-ounce package garlic cheese,
    diced

Sauté onion, celery and mushrooms in butter until tender. Combine cooked broccoli, soup, and cheese; cook over low heat until cheese melts, stirring occasionally. Add sautéed vegetables to broccoli mixture, stirring well. Serve hot. Yield: 1 quart.
Mrs. Bill Lawson (Diane)
Mrs. Lewis Hall Singletary (Mildred)

DANA'S DILL DIP

⅔ cup mayonnaise
1 cup sour cream
1 teaspoon onion, grated
1 teaspoon parsley

1 teaspoon dill weed
1½ teaspoons seasoned salt
1 tablespoon lemon juice
Dash of salt

Mix all ingredients together and refrigerate. Serve with celery, carrots, radishes, and garden onions.
Mrs. Fred E. Murphy, Jr. (Vi)

FRESH DIP

2 cups sour cream
4 teaspoons horseradish
1 tablespoon paprika
1 tablespoon minced chives
1 clove garlic, crushed

1 teaspoon salt
1 teaspoon fresh tarragon or
  dill
¼ teaspoon garlic salt
⅛ teaspoon pepper

Mix and chill.
Mrs. Lewis Hall Singletary (Mildred)

FRESH HERBED GREEN GODDESS DIP

3 egg yolks
3 tablespoons white wine
  vinegar
⅔ cup parsley, snipped
¼ cup chives, snipped
1 2-ounce can anchovy fillets,
  undrained

1 tablespoon tarragon leaves,
  snipped, *or*
1 teaspoon dried tarragon
1 cup vegetable oil
¼ cup olive oil
Assorted fresh vegetables,
  chilled

Place egg yolks, vinegar, parsley, chives, anchovies, and tarragon into blender container; cover. Blend on medium speed about one minute. Add oil gradually in slow steady stream with blender on low speed. Refrigerate. Serve as a dip with fresh vegetables.
Mrs. Bolling Jones, III (Connie)

HOT DRIED BEEF DIP

1 8-ounce package cream cheese
2 tablespoons milk
1 2½-ounce jar dried beef,
 finely chopped
2 tablespoons fresh onion,
 minced

¼ teaspoon pepper
2 tablespoons green pepper,
 finely diced
½ cup sour cream

Blend cream cheese and milk. Stir in dried beef, onion, green pepper, and pepper. Mix well. Stir in sour cream. Spoon into shallow baking dish. Bake at 350 degrees for 15 minutes. Serve with wafers as a hot dip.
Mrs. Howard Carnes (Henrietta)

CHEDDAR CHEESE-SHRIMP DIP

1 pound Cheddar cheese
1 cup mayonnaise
1 small onion,
 finely chopped

1 tablespoon Worcestershire sauce
1 teaspoon garlic salt
¼ pound shrimp,
 chilled and chopped

Grate cheese in blender and add mayonnaise until creamy; then add shrimp, onion, Worcestershire sauce, and garlic. Chill and serve on party rye.
Mrs. William Norwood (Deane)

SHRIMP SPREAD

2 pounds fresh shrimp
Juice of one lemon
1 onion, grated
1 teaspoon curry powder (or
 add to taste)

¾ cup mayonnaise
Salt and pepper to taste

Cook and grind the shrimp, using a fine blade. Add remainder of ingredients and mix well. Put in small mold and chill overnight. Serve on crackers.
Mrs. Maurice Tanner (Peggy)

Beverages

MINT LEMONADE

4 cups sugar
5 cups water
Juice of 12 lemons

Juice of 4 oranges
Grated rind of 2 oranges
2 cups mint leaves, crushed

Simmer sugar and water for 5 minutes and cool. Add lemon juice and orange juice. Pour this mixture over mint leaves and orange rind. Strain into jar. Freeze or store in refrigerator. When ready to serve, add equal amounts of water and above syrup mixture. Skewer lemon slice, pineapple chunk, and cherry; float skewered fruit with mint on top of each glass. Serves 20-24.
Mrs. Ken Beverly (Mary Jo)

PUNCHMELON
Beautiful for a summer party!

1 large watermelon
2 cups orange juice
2 cups lemon juice
1 6-ounce bottle grenadine
   syrup

2 quarts bottled lemon-lime
   beverage, chilled
1 orange, sliced
1 lemon, sliced

With melon standing on end, cut a thin slice off side so it will sit level. Remove top third of melon. Using a coffee cup as a guide, trace scallops around top outside edge. With a sharp knife, carve scalloped edge, following tracing. Scoop out fruit, leaving just a trace of red showing in bowl of melon. Use scraped-out melon as desired. Chill melon bowl. Combine orange juice, lemon juice, and grenadine; chill. When ready to serve, place a small block of ice or ice cubes in melon bowl. Pour juices over ice; pour lemon-lime beverage down side of melon bowl into juice mixture. Float orange and lime slices on top of punch. Makes 3½ quarts.
Mrs. A. B. Wight, Jr. (Carolyn)

MOCK PINK CHAMPAGNE

½ cup sugar
1½ cups water
2 cups cranberry juice
1 cup pineapple juice

½ cup orange juice
2 7-ounce bottles lemon-
lime carbonated beverage

Boil sugar and water until sugar dissolves; cool. Stir in cranberry, pineapple, and orange juices. Chill. Just before serving add carbonated beverage. Serves 14.
The Editors

CRANBERRY PUNCH

2 cups cranberry juice
3 tablespoons frozen orange
juice concentrate

1 pint vanilla ice cream,
cut into chunks

Place all ingredients in blender container in order given. Cover and blend on high speed until smooth and frothy. Makes 6 servings.
Mrs. T. R. Sample (Nell)

FRUIT JUICE PUNCH

1 12-ounce can frozen orange
juice diluted with 1½ cans
water
1 large can grapefruit juice
1 large can pineapple juice

1 6-ounce can frozen lemonade,
diluted with 2¼ cans
water
1 6-ounce can frozen limeade,
diluted with 2¼ cans water
4 28-ounce bottles ginger ale

Mix all ingredients except ginger ale and let "age" overnight. Before serving, add ginger ale. If too strong, add more ginger ale. Note: When making this punch for children, the grapefruit juice may be omitted. It adds a tartness that is more suitable to adult tastes. Makes 45 4-ounce cups.
Mrs. Richard Miller (Charlotte)

VEGETABLE JUICE COOLER

1 22-ounce can cocktail
   vegetable juice
2 teaspoons lemon juice,
   freshly squeezed

½ small garlic clove, minced
Generous dash Tabasco
Avocado slices

Combine all ingredients except avocado; chill. Garnish with avocado cut in strips. Serves 6.
The Editors

SUNSHINE PUNCH

1 quart grapefruit juice
1 quart apple juice
6 oranges
6 lemons

1 quart pineapple or
   lime sherbet
1 28-ounce bottle ginger ale
Sugar to taste

Squeeze oranges and lemons. In punch bowl combine juices, sherbet, and ginger ale. Add sugar to taste, if needed. Stir slightly before serving.
Mrs. Roy S. Heitke

GRAPE BIRTHDAY PUNCH

1 quart vanilla ice cream
1 46-ounce can grape-flavored
   drink

1 28-ounce bottle ginger ale

Place ice cream in punch bowl and add grape drink and ginger ale. Serve in party cups with dipper and straws cut in half to fit cups. Yield: approximately 2½ quarts.
Mrs. Gerald Wolsfelt (Vicki)

COFFEE PUNCH

1 cup instant coffee
3 quarts boiling water
½ cup chocolate syrup
1 cup sugar

2 tablespoons rum flavoring
2 quarts milk
1 gallon vanilla ice cream

Pour 2½ quarts water over coffee and stir. Add other pint to syrup and sugar, bring to boil, and cook 2 minutes. Add to hot coffee and cool. If possible, refrigerate at this point so that punch will be served cold. Before serving, add rum and milk. Put broken-up ice cream into punch bowl, and pour mixture over it. Stir and serve in wide-mouth cup.
Mrs. Paul McCollum (Nancy)

ICED TEA NECTAR

2 tablespoons instant tea
4 cups water
½ cup sugar
1 12-ounce can unsweetened
  pineapple juice

1 12-ounce can apricot
  nectar
2 cups orange juice
1 cup lemon juice

Dissolve tea in water in a large pitcher. Stir in sugar until dissolved; then add pineapple juice, apricot nectar, and orange and lemon juices. Pour over ice in tall glasses. Trim edge of each glass with a wedge of orange if you like. Makes 10 one-cup servings.
The Editors

TOMATO JUICE

4 cups tomatoes
1 cup water
Few celery tops
1 onion, sliced

1 teaspoon salt
⅛ teaspoon pepper
5 or 6 drops Tabasco
¼ teaspoon Worcestershire

Boil all ingredients slowly for 20 minutes. Press through sieve and chill until serving.
Mrs. Wallace Hicks (Margaret)   *Jacksonville, Florida*

RUSSIAN TEA

4 quarts water
1 teaspoon whole cloves
1 stick cinnamon
⅓ cup loose tea or 15 tea bags

1¼ cups sugar
1 cup orange juice
¾ cup fresh lemon juice

Add spices to water and bring to full boil. Remove from heat. Add tea at once. Brew 4 minutes. Strain liquid and add sugar, stirring until dissolved. Add fruit juices. To reheat for serving, place over low heat. Do not boil! Serves 25-30.
Mrs. Archie Pittman (Hattie)

Similar recipe submitted by *Mrs. Jasper Davis (Marthalene).*

HOT MULLED PUNCH

1 1½-quart bottle cranberry
   juice
2 1-quart bottles apple juice
½ cup brown sugar

½ teaspoon salt
4 cinnamon sticks
1½ teaspoons whole cloves

Into 30-cup coffee maker pour fruit juices. Place remaining ingredients in basket and place basket assembly into electric coffee maker. Plug into current. Upon completion of perking cycle, remove basket. Serve hot. Yield: 3½-4 quarts.
Mrs. R. Franklin Smith (Alma)
Mrs. Ray Willett (Ruth)

HOT MULLED GRAPE JUICE

1 quart grape juice
1 pint pineapple juice
2 2-inch cinnamon sticks
3 cups water

1 cup orange juice
12 cloves
6 whole allspice
Sugar

Combine spices with water. Place over low heat and bring to a boil. Cover and simmer 5 minutes. Strain; add to juices and sweeten to taste. Serve hot. (Good with cheese straws.)
Mrs. E. C. Oliver (Clancy)

CUSTOM BLEND VERBENA CITRUS TEA

2 cups orange pekoe tea
    leaves
1 cup lemon verbena (herb tea)

¼ cup lemon rind
¼ cup orange rind

Combine above ingredients. Store in airtight container for at least two weeks before using. Use 1 teaspoon of tea leaves for each cup of boiling water in teapot. Steep 2-3 minutes. Serve hot with an orange and lemon slice and 1 teaspoon sugar per cup.
The Editors

INSTANT RUSSIAN TEA

2 cups sugar
2 cups instant orange-flavored
    breakfast drink
1 cup instant tea

1 teaspoon cinnamon
½ teaspoon ground cloves
1 package instant lemonade
    mix

Mix all dry ingredients well and store in tightly covered jars until ready to use. To serve, measure 2 full tablespoons per 1 cup boiling water. Yield: approximately 30 servings.
Mrs. Richard Atwell (Libby)
Similar recipes submitted by *Mrs. Delmar Conner (Mary), Mrs. Al Lookabaugh (Diana), and Mrs. Paul L. Sampson (Katherine).*

INSTANT HOT CHOCOLATE

1 1-pound box Nestle's Quik
Non-fat dry milk (package
    that makes 8 quarts)

1 7-ounce jar powdered non-
    dairy creamer
⅔ cup confectioners' sugar,
    sifted

Mix together and store in large jar. To serve, fill ½ cup with powdered mix and add hot water.
The Editors

Breads

THREE TOM'S INN SPOON BREAD

2 cups white corn meal
2½ cups boiling water
2 tablespoons butter, melted
1½ teaspoons salt

2 eggs, separated
1½ cups buttermilk
1 teaspoon soda

Add corn meal gradually to boiling water and let stand until cool. Add butter, salt, egg yolks slightly beaten, and buttermilk mixed with soda. Beat 2 minutes and add egg whites which have been beaten until stiff. Turn into buttered bean pot or casserole and bake at 425 degrees for 40 minutes.
Mrs. T. R. Sample (Nell)
Similar recipe submitted by *Mrs. Thomas Hines (Louise)*.

CHARLES' CORN BREAD

1 cup self-rising corn meal
(If plain is used, add 3
teaspoons baking powder,
and 1½ teaspoons salt)

½ cup Wesson Oil
1 cup sour cream
1 cup cream-style corn
2 eggs

Combine all ingredients and mix well. Pour in greased baking pan and bake at 400 degrees for 30 minutes.
Mrs. Fred E. Murphy, Jr. (Vi)
Mrs. Robert Braswell (Sandra)
Mrs. Truman Holland, Jr. (Jimmie)

CORN BREAD

¾ cup flour, sifted
1 teaspoon salt
3 teaspoons baking powder
3 tablespoons sugar

1½ cups yellow corn meal
2 eggs, beaten
1½ cups milk
¼ cup shortening, melted

Sift flour, salt, baking powder and sugar. Add corn meal. Combine eggs with milk and shortening and use to moisten dry ingredients. Turn into a shallow, well-greased pan or iron skillet and bake in 400 degree oven about 30 minutes.
Mrs. Oscar Mims (Candy)

Variation: Substitute buttermilk for sweet milk.
Mrs. Martin Wood, III (Daphne)

(Note: If buttermilk is used, reduce baking powder to 1¼ teaspoons and add ½ teaspoon baking soda.)

YELLOW CORN MEAL MUFFINS

1 cup all-purpose flour, sifted
1 cup yellow corn meal
2 tablespoons sugar
4 teaspoons baking powder

1 teaspoon salt
2 eggs, slightly beaten
1 cup milk
¼ cup vegetable oil

Sift flour, corn meal, sugar, salt, and baking powder into a bowl. Combine beaten eggs, milk and oil. Add all at once to dry ingredients. Stir until smooth. Fill greased muffin tins ⅔ full. Bake at 425 degrees for 15 minutes. Makes 12. May also be baked as corn sticks or as corn bread in an 8 x 8-inch pan.
Mrs. John T. King, Jr. (Clarice)

Variation: Substitute white corn meal for yellow.
Mrs. H. Cook Ray (Mary Jane)

HUSH PUPPIES

1 cup corn meal
¼ cup flour
1 teaspoon baking powder

½ cup onion, grated
¾ cup milk

Mix above ingredients well. Drop batter from spoon and fry in hot fat (275 degrees) until brown.
Mrs. Lloyd Eckberg (Maxine)

HIGH HAT POPOVERS

1 cup flour, sifted
¾ teaspoon salt
2 eggs

1 cup milk
1 tablespoon butter, melted

Sift flour and salt together. Beat eggs until thoroughly blended. Add milk and blend well. Add butter and mix. Make a well in flour and pour in liquid. Beat with beater until smooth. Grease generously 6-8 custard cups and fill half full with batter. Bake at 475 degrees for 15 minutes. Reduce heat to 350 and bake 25 to 30 minutes more or until browned and firm. A few minutes before removing from oven, prick each popover with a fork to let steam escape. Serve hot. To freeze and serve later, set half-filled custard cups on tray and freeze. When frozen, dip bottoms of cups in warm water, slip out batter and pack in freezer bags. When ready to bake put frozen popovers into greased custard cups. Place on baking sheet in cold oven. Turn to 400 degrees and bake 1 hour.
Mrs. William Blackburn (Connie)

BLUEBERRY MUFFINS

1¾ cups self-rising flour   ¾ cup milk
¾ cup sugar   ⅓ cup oil
1 egg   ¾ cup blueberries

Combine all ingredients (except blueberries) in mixing bowl and mix well. Then stir in blueberries. Drop from tablespoon to fill greased muffin pan ⅔ full. Bake in hot oven (400 degrees) 25 minutes. Makes 1 dozen muffins.
Mrs. Harry Park (Mary)

CHEESE BISCUITS

1¾ cups flour, sifted   ¾ cup sharp Cheddar cheese,
1 teaspoon salt   finely grated
Dash cayenne pepper   ¼ cup butter
1½ teaspoons baking powder   ¾ cup milk

Sift together the flour, salt, cayenne and baking powder. Add cheese and toss well to mix. Cut in butter with pastry blender until texture is like cornmeal. Make a well in center and add milk. Stir quickly until ball of dough is free of sides of bowl. Knead 2 or 3 times. With a floured rolling pin, roll to ¼-inch thickness. Cut into 2-inch rounds. Place about 1 inch apart, on lightly greased cookie sheets. Brush lightly with extra milk. Bake at 425 degrees about 16 minutes. Makes 2½ to 3 dozen. These biscuits are perfect split, buttered and filled with ham.
The Editors

PARTY BISCUITS

½ cup butter, softened   1 cup self-rising flour
1 3-ounce package cream cheese

Blend together butter and cheese. Mix in flour and knead mixture to make a dough. Roll out on floured board and cut with small biscuit cutter. Bake in a 350 degree oven until light brown and puffy. About 12 minutes. Serve hot.
Miss Eunice Singletary

SOUR CREAM BISCUITS

2 cups self-rising flour   1 8-ounce carton sour cream
2 sticks margarine, melted

Mix ingredients and drop in muffin tins. Bake at 400 degrees for 12 to 15 minutes. Do not grease tins and do not serve butter with these biscuits as they are rich and "short". Yield: 12 muffins.
Mrs. James McCollum (Wyche)

SAVANNAH ROLLS (Alias Beer Rolls)

3½ cups Bisquick   1 12-ounce can beer
3 tablespoons sugar

Mix well and pour into greased muffin tin. Bake at 400 degrees for about 15 minutes. Makes about 18 rolls.
Mrs. Robert Sullivan (Sally)

SIX-WEEK BRAN MUFFINS

6 cups all-bran   1 cup vegetable shortening
3 cups sugar   4 eggs, beaten
5 cups plain flour, unsifted   1 quart buttermilk
5 teaspoons soda   2 cups boiling water
2 teaspoons salt

In a large bowl, mix 4 cups of all-bran, sugar, flour, soda, and salt. Pour into this the rest of the all-bran mixed with the boiling water and shortening. Add the eggs and buttermilk. Stir well. Cover bowl and refrigerate overnight. Bake as many muffins as needed in a 400 degree oven for 15 to 20 minutes. Batter keeps 6 weeks in refrigerator. Makes 5 dozen.
Mrs. Jack Kelly (Janis)

Variation: Raisins, nuts, or dates may be added to batter before baking.
Mrs. Kenneth Miller (Kathryn)

TIPS ON MAKING YEAST BREADS

1. To facilitate bread rising, turn oven to warm for 1 minute, then turn OFF before placing bread, covered with damp cloth, in oven to rise free from drafts.

2. Bread is easier to knead if you place dough on table lower than counter, or step up on something enabling you to lean over dough.

3. Kneading is what gives bread its fine texture. Don't try to save time on this step.

4. Remove bread from pan as soon as it's done and cool on wire rack so it won't be soggy.

5. For a soft, buttery crust, brush loaves with softened or melted margarine after baking.

6. For a crisp, shiny crust, brush loaves with a mixture of 1 egg and 1 tablespoon water just before baking. May be sprinkled with poppy or sesame seed.

7. Always check the yeast for age; it is always dated. Never use it past the date given on the envelope. If in doubt proof the yeast by mixing it with the warm water called for in the recipe and some of the sweetener. Wait a few minutes and, if the yeast is working properly, you will see it start to bubble up from the bottom. Then add mixture to recipe as instructions say.

8. Add more flour as needed in a recipe to make it easy to handle and workable to knead. Be careful not to add too much or your bread will be dry.

9. When recipes call for dissolving yeast in warm water, this means a temperature of about 115 degrees. Much variation from this temperature will prevent yeast from working properly.

10. Darker breads and flours rise a little less than all-white.

11. Unbleached white flour is often preferred for bread baking because of its nutritional value.

PLAIN ROLL DOUGH

1 cup milk, scalded
¼ cup cooking oil
¼ cup sugar
1 teaspoon salt

2 packages granular yeast
¼ cup lukewarm water
1 egg, beaten
4 cups plain flour

Combine milk, shortening, sugar, and salt; cool to lukewarm. Add yeast which has been softened in water; add egg. Gradually stir in flour until flour disappears; beat about 50 strokes. Cover and let rise in warm place until double in bulk, about 2 hours. Turn out and shape into 4 small loaves, placing in small bread pan; or shape into Parkerhouse rolls by rolling out on floured counter to ¼ inch thickness, cutting with biscuit cutter, folding in half, placing on greased biscuit pan, and brushing tops with oil or butter. Cover and let rise again for one hour. Place in preheated oven at 400 degrees: bake until light brown or about 15 minutes. Whole-wheat flour may be substituted for white flour. These freeze and warm nicely.

Mrs. Roy Lilly (Mary Frances)

Similar recipe submitted by Mrs. Robert C. Brown (Frances).

ICE BOX ROLLS

5 cups flour
⅓ cup sugar
½ teaspoon salt
1⅓ cups milk
1 package yeast

¼ cup hot water
2 eggs
2 teaspoons sugar
6 tablespoons shortening
(Crisco is fine)

Sift together flour, sugar, and salt into large bowl. Scald milk and let cool. Dissolve yeast in hot water. Beat eggs with 2 teaspoons sugar and add to dissolved yeast when it has cooled. Cut 6 tablespoons of shortening into the flour. Then stir into the flour the scalded milk which has been cooled, the beaten eggs, and yeast. Mix until a stiff dough is formed. If dough is too stiff to handle, a small amount of water may be added. Put this dough into a smaller, well-greased bowl, cover with plastic wrap and refrigerate overnight. The next day (or even several days later) roll out on floured board and cut with biscuit cutter. Pat each roll with small amount of cooking oil, fold in half, and put in pan or baking sheet. Let rise for about 2 hours and bake in 400 degree oven for about 20 minutes. After the rolls have been cut out and put into a pan, they may be covered well and frozen until you wish to bake them. After freezing, they will take about 3 hours to rise before baking. They may be kept frozen for a week or two before cooking.

Mrs. Forrest Caldwell (Emily)

DILLY BREAD

¼ cup warm water
1 package yeast
1 tablespoon butter, softened
1 cup cottage cheese
1 tablespoon sugar
2 teaspoons dill seed

1 tablespoon dehydrated minced
  onion or onion flakes
¼ teaspoon soda
1 teaspoon salt
1 egg, unbeaten
2¼ cups all-purpose flour

In warmed mixing bowl, pour in ½ cup warm water. Add yeast and stir with a wooden spoon until dissolved. Blend in butter. Warm cheese slightly in top of double boiler. Add to yeast mixture. Beat in sugar, dill seed, onion flakes, soda and salt. Add egg and beat again. Add flour and stir until all flour is moistened. Keeping the sticky dough in the bowl, knead until it appears slightly smooth, adding as little flour as possible. Grease top of dough with a little oil. Cover with cloth and let rise until amost double in bulk, about 1 hour. Punch down; divide into six portions; pat each into well-greased miniature loaf pan for individual loaves or 1 9x5x3-inch loaf pan. Allow to rise about 40 minutes or until dough has risen at least to top of pan. Bake at 350 degrees for 35-40 minutes. When done, brush with melted butter. Makes 6 miniature loaves or 1 large one. Freezes well.
Mrs. Robert W. Jackson (Beverly)
Mrs. Chip Coffin (Sheila)

BRAIDED ONION BREAD

1 package yeast
¼ cup warm water
1 cup sour cream
1 envelope onion soup mix
  (dry)
¼ teaspoon baking soda
2 tablespoons sugar

2 teaspoons salt
2 tablespoons butter, softened
3 eggs
6½-6¾ cups flour, sifted
1 cup warm water
Sesame seeds

Sprinkle yeast into ¼ cup warm water to soften. In large bowl combine sour cream, onion soup mix, baking soda, sugar, salt, butter, 2 beaten eggs, and 1 cup warm water. Stir in softened yeast until smooth. Gradually add enough flour to form a stiff dough. Knead on a floured board until smooth, about 5 minutes; then place dough in greased bowl and cover with towel. Let it rise in a warm place until doubled in bulk. Punch dough down. Divide half of it into thirds. Roll each part into a strip about 15 inches long. Braid the three strips together sealing ends. Place braids on cookie sheet side by side. Let rise in warm place until they have risen and look light. Brush braids with the remaining beaten egg; sprinkle with sesame seeds. Bake 40 to 45 minutes or until golden and firm. Cool on wire racks and serve. To freeze: wrap braids and freeze. To serve: refrigerate fully-wrapped frozen braids at least 5 hours to thaw. Then heat, wrapped in foil in 400 degree oven about 30 minutes. Unwrap, cut into slices and serve. Makes 2 loaves or braids.
Mrs. T. R. Sample (Nell)

LIGHT ROLLS

1 package yeast
1 teaspoon sugar
¼ cup warm water
1 cup milk, scalded
½ cup shortening

¼ cup sugar
1 teaspoon salt
1 egg
4 cups flour

Mix yeast, sugar and water. To the scalded milk add the shortening, sugar and salt. When cool add the egg and yeast mixture. Add 4 cups of flour, one at a time. Beat with an electric mixer for addition of the first two cups; beat last two in with a wooden spoon. Store in refrigerator until next day. Add the 5th cup of flour a little at a time as needed to make a dough that can be kneaded well. Knead well. Make into rolls and let rise until double in size. Bake in 425 degree oven 15 minutes or until brown. These can be baked but not browned and stored in plastic bags in the freezer. Take them out and brown when ready to serve.
Mrs. E. B. Cooper (Margaret)

GARLIC PARMESAN LOAF

1 package dry yeast
¼ cup warm water
2 cups milk
1 cup Parmesan cheese, grated
2 tablespoons sugar
2 tablespoons shortening or
   salad oil

2 teaspoons salt
⅛ teaspoon cayenne pepper
About 5½ cups sifted all-
   purpose flour
Butter or margarine, melted
2 teaspoons garlic salt

Dissolve yeast in water. Heat milk until almost simmering. Measure cheese, sugar, shortening, salt and pepper into a large mixing bowl. Stir in milk until sugar dissolves and shortening melts. Cool to lukewarm. Stir in about 2 cups flour and beat until smooth. Beat in yeast. Stir in enough flour to make a moderately stiff dough. Onto lightly floured board, turn out dough and knead until smooth and satiny, 5-8 minutes. Shape into a ball and place in lightly greased bowl, turning to grease all sides. Cover and let rise in warm place (80-85 degrees) until doubled, about 1½ hours. Punch down. Divide dough in half; shape each half into a ball. Cover and let rest 10 minutes. Meanwhile, grease two regular loaf pans. Roll out one ball of dough to 10 x 16-inch rectangle. Brush with butter. Sprinkle with 1 teaspoon garlic salt. Cut into four 4 x 10-inch rectangles. Stack rectangles together, spread side up. Cut into 5 stacks, 2 inches wide and 4 inches long. Arrange stacks in row in pan, placing one long, cut-side down. Repeat with remaining dough, filling second pan. Let rise in warm place until doubled, about one hour. Meanwhile, preheat oven to 400 degrees. Bake loaves 30-35 minutes or until a deep golden brown. Immediately remove from pans; cool slightly before serving. To serve, pull "slices" of bread from loaf.
The Editors

NATURAL HEALTH LOAF
Delicious!

3 cups whole-wheat flour
2 packages yeast
2½ cups buttermilk
¼ cup molasses
¼ cup honey
1 tablespoon salt

⅓ cup butter
1½ cup regular rolled oats
2 eggs
2½-3 cups unbleached,
    all-purpose flour, unsifted
2 tablespoons butter

Grease 2 1½-quart round, 2½-inch deep casseroles. Combine whole-wheat flour and yeast. Heat buttermilk, molasses, honey, salt and butter until warm (105-115 degrees). Pour into a 3-quart mixer bowl. Add oats, whole-wheat yeast mixture and eggs. Blend at low speed with electric mixer until moistened. Beat 3 minutes at high speed. Stir in enough flour to make a stiff dough. Brush with melted butter. Cover and let rise in warm place until doubled, about 1 hour. Punch down and shape into 2 round loaves. Place in casseroles; cover. Let rise until doubled, about 45 minutes. Bake at 375 degrees for 25-35 minutes or until loaf sounds hollow when tapped.
The Editors

NUT BREAD

1 package yeast
1 cup milk
1 tablespoon sugar
3 cups sifted flour
⅓ cup sugar

2 tablespoons shortening
White of one egg
¾ cup pecans, chopped
½ teaspoon salt

Dissolve yeast and 1 tablespoon of sugar in lukewarm milk. Add 1¼ cups flour and beat thoroughly. Cover and put in warm place to rise until light. Cream ⅓ cup sugar and shortening. Add to dough. Beat the egg white until stiff and fold it in. Add remainder of flour and salt. Beat with electric mixer until well mixed. Place in greased bowl. Cover and let rise in warm place until doubled. Knead ten minutes and knead in the nuts. Mold into a large loaf or 3 small ones and let rise until doubled. Bake large loaf for 45 minutes at 375 degrees or small ones for 25 minutes at 375 degrees.
Mrs. E. B. Cooper (Margaret)

SOURDOUGH STARTER

Sourdough bread is a traditional western creation. It was standard fare for the cowboys on the trail and now is famous and known as that "San Francisco Bread". It has a crusty exterior, chewy texture and wonderful "sour" taste.

½ cup warm water
1 package yeast
½ cup fresh mashed potatoes,
  cooked and unseasoned

Flour
Water

Dissolve yeast in the water and mix into mashed potatoes. Put in a jar with a loosened screw lid and leave out on counter for 3 days. Stir occasionally. After 3 days, add ½ cup flour and ½ cup water. Stir in and let sit for 8 hours. Then add 1 cup flour and 1 cup water. Stir in and let sit for 8 hours. Now you may add 2 cups flour and 2 cups water. Let sit for 8 hours. From now on it may be doubled every 8 hours, but at this point there is enough starter in the jar to be used and still leave at least a half cup starter in the jar. Store in the refrigerator and stir occasionally through the week. Keeps indefinitely and gets better over the years. To keep the starter going, be sure to add back to the starter equal amounts of water and flour for what was used in a recipe. If your recipe calls for 2 cups of starter, add 1 cup water and 1 cup of flour to starter and stir in and leave out for 8 hours or overnight. If starter is not used for over a week, stir in a teaspoon of sugar and stir well. Store in covered crockery or glass container, not metal.
The Editors

SOURDOUGH BREAD

1 cup milk
⅓ cup sugar
⅓ cup shortening
1 teaspoon salt

1 package yeast
2 tablespoons lukewarm water
1½ cups sourdough starter
5 cups all-purpose flour

Scald milk; add sugar, shortening and salt. Stir to melt sugar and shortening; cool to lukewarm. Dissolve yeast in warm water. Beat together cooled milk mixture, yeast, starter, and 2 cups flour. Add remaining flour to make a stiff dough. Turn onto floured surface and knead 5-10 minutes, adding only enough flour to keep from sticking. Place dough in greased bowl, turning to grease surface. Let rise until doubled, about 1½ hours. Punch down; let rise again, about ½ hour. Divide into 2 balls, cover with towel and let rest 10 minutes. Shape into 2 loaves and put each in a greased 9 x 5 x 3-inch loaf pan. Let rise until doubled, about 1 hour. Bake in 400 degree oven for 40 minutes. Turn out and cool.
Mrs. A. B. Wight, Jr. (Carolyn)

BANANA BREAD I

1 cup sugar
½ cup butter or margarine
½ teaspoon salt
3 ripe bananas, mashed

2 eggs
3 tablespoons buttermilk
1 teaspoon baking soda
2 cups flour, sifted

Cream the sugar, butter, and salt. Add remaining ingredients and mix well. Pour into greased loaf pan and bake at 350 degrees for 50-60 minutes. One half cup chopped nuts may be added to batter before baking.
Mrs. Elliott McCollum (Lorna)
Similar recipes submitted by *Mrs. Lonnie Ferguson (Georgia), Mrs. J. C. Payne (Leola), Mrs. Curtis F. Culpepper (Bonnie), Mrs. R. C. Balfour, III (Virginia), Mrs. Donald H. Price (Judy), and Mrs. Robert Maxwell (Ruth Ann).*

BANANA BREAD II

1 stick margarine
2 cups sugar
½ cup Wesson Oil
4 eggs
3 cups plain flour
2 teaspoons soda

1½ teaspoons cinnamon
½ teaspoon salt
1 teaspoon cloves, ground
1 cup pecans, chopped
6 or 7 bananas, mashed

Cream sugar and butter. Add eggs and then dry ingredients to butter mixture. Add bananas and nuts. Bake in tube pan at 275 degrees for 30 minutes; then 300 degrees about 45 minutes. Serves 12.
Mrs. J. Furman Stewart (Cloe)

BRAN-BANANA-NUT BREAD

1 cup bananas, mashed
1 teaspoon vanilla
2 eggs
⅓ cup salad oil
1 cup flour (can use
    whole-wheat)

1 cup bran
2 teaspoons baking powder
½ teaspoon salt
½ teaspoon soda
⅔ cup sugar
½ cup nuts

Combine bananas, vanilla, eggs and oil. Sift dry ingredients and combine with banana mixture. Bake in greased loaf pan at 350 degrees for 1 hour.
Mrs. Harry T. Jones (Celetta)

PEACH BREAD

2 cups flour
⅔ cup sugar
1 teaspoon baking powder
½ teaspoon soda
½ teaspoon salt

⅓ cup shortening
¼ cup sour milk
2 eggs
1 16-ounce can peaches,
    drained and mashed

Combine all ingredients. Blend well at medium speed. Pour into a 9 x 5-inch greased loaf pan. Bake at 350 degrees for 50-60 minutes.
Mrs. Charles D. Reichert (Eddie)

CRANBERRY BREAD

2 cups flour
½ teaspoon salt
1½ teaspoons baking powder
½ teaspoon soda
1 cup sugar
1 egg, beaten
2 tablespoons butter or
    margarine, melted

½ cup orange juice
2 tablespoons hot water
½ cup nuts, chopped
1 cup cranberries, cut up
Grated rind of one orange

Sift dry ingredients together and add egg, shortening, orange juice and hot water. Mix until dry ingredients are moistened. Fold in nuts, cranberries and orange rind. Bake in greased loaf pan at 350 degrees for 1 hour and 10 minutes. Cool, wrap in wax paper and let ripen in refrigerator for 24 hours.
Mrs. J. H. Jenkins (Essie)

VERMONT GRAHAM BREAD

1 cup sifted flour
1½ teaspoons baking soda
1 teaspoon salt
½ cup light brown sugar

2 cups buttermilk or sour
    milk
2 cups graham flour (whole-wheat)

Sift flour once; add soda, salt, sugar and sift again. Add buttermilk and graham flour. Mix thoroughly. Pour into well-greased loaf pan and bake at 350 degrees for 60-70 minutes. This is an easy-to-make, rich-tasting bread that is a real treat toasted with honey. Plan to make two loaves at once if you want to use up the whole quart of buttermilk.
Mrs. Terry Rouse (Bobbie)

BROWN SUGAR STREUSEL COFFEE CAKE

CAKE:

½ cup butter
1¼ cups sugar
3 eggs
2 cups flour
½ teaspoon baking powder

1 teaspoon soda
½ teaspoon salt
1 teaspoon vanilla
½ pint sour cream

Cream butter and sugar. Add eggs and beat well. Sift together flour, baking powder, soda, and salt. Add dry ingredients alternately with sour cream. Stir in vanilla.

STREUSEL:

1 cup brown sugar
1 teaspoon cinnamon
4 tablespoons butter, melted

4 heaping tablespoons flour
1 cup nuts, chopped

Combine ingredients for streusel and pour one-third of mixture into a well greased Bundt pan. Add one half cake batter, then one third streusel, and the other half of the cake batter and top with the remainder of the streusel. Bake at 325 degrees for 45 to 50 minutes.

Mrs. Ames Watkins Kindred

MEXICAN COFFEE CAKE

2½ cups flour
¾ cup granulated sugar
1 cup brown sugar
1 teaspoon nutmeg
1 teaspoon salt
¾ cup oil

1 cup buttermilk
1 teaspoon soda
1 egg, beaten
2 teaspoons cinnamon
¾ cup nuts, chopped

Mix flour, sugars, nutmeg, salt, and oil. Take out one cup of this mixture and set aside. To the rest of the mixture add buttermilk, soda, and egg. Beat about 2 minutes with an electric beater. Pour into a greased and floured 11 x 17-inch pan. To the one cup of mixture, add the cinnamon and nuts. Mix well and sprinkle over the top of the cake. Bake 25-30 minutes at 350 degrees. While warm, frost with powdered sugar frosting.

FROSTING:

1 cup powdered sugar   Very little water

Combine the above to make mixture to drizzle over cake. Cut into squares before cake is completely cool.

Mrs. Hilton S. Read (Kathryn)

STICKY BUNS

DOUGH:

1 package yeast
¼ cup warm water
2 cups milk, scalded
½ cup sugar

½ cup shortening
2 teaspoons salt
7½-8 cups all-purpose flour, sifted
2 eggs

FILLING:

¾ cup sugar
1½ tablespoons cinnamon

½ cup raisins (optional)
Soft butter

STICKY SYRUP:

½ cup white sugar
½ cup brown sugar

½ cup water

For dough, soften yeast in warm water. Pour milk over sugar, shortening, and salt to dissolve. Add half the flour, eggs, and yeast. Beat well. Turn dough onto floured surface and add enough additional flour to make a soft dough. Cover and let rest 10 minutes. Knead 8-10 minutes until smooth and elastic. Place in greased bowl and grease surface. Cover with damp cloth and let rise 1½-2 hours until double in bulk. Punch down and let rise again for 1 hour. Punch bubbles out and divide dough in half. Roll each half into a 15 x 10-inch rectangle about ½-inch thick. Sprinkle with filling (mixed together) and few drops of water. Roll as for jelly roll beginning at longer side. Slice with knife or cut with scissors to 1-inch rolls and place flat in sticky warm syrup. Boil syrup for 2 minutes and pour into 2 well-greased 9 x 13-inch pans. Chopped nuts may be added to syrup. Allow to rise about 45-60 minutes until almost doubled. Brush with butter just before baking. Bake in 350 degree oven for 35-40 minutes until done. Remove from oven and immediately invert on rack to cool. Otherwise syrup will harden and rolls will stick to pan.
Mrs. Robert Maxwell (Ruth Ann)

CREAM CHEESE COFFEE CAKE

1 3-ounce package cream cheese
4 tablespoons butter or
    margarine
2 cups packaged biscuit mix
⅓ cup milk

½ cup fruit preserves
1 cup confectioners' sugar,
    sifted
1-2 tablespoons milk
½ teaspoon vanilla

Cut cream cheese and butter into biscuit mix until crumbly. Blend in the ⅓ cup milk. Turn onto floured surface; knead 8-10 strokes. On waxed paper, roll dough to 12 x 8-inch rectangle. Turn onto greased baking sheet; remove paper. Spread preserves down center of dough. Make 2½-inch cuts at 1-inch intervals on long sides. Fold strips over filling. Bake in 425 degree oven for 12-15 minutes. Combine sugar, remaining milk, and vanilla. Drizzle on top. Very easy!
The Editors

JANET'S FRENCH BREAKFAST PUFFS

⅓ cup soft shortening
½ cup sugar
1 egg
1½ cups flour

½ teaspoon salt
½ cup milk
1½ teaspoons baking powder
¼ teaspoon nutmeg

Mix shortening, sugar, and egg thoroughly. Blend in flour, baking powder, salt, and nutmeg, stirring in alternately with milk. Fill greased muffin cups ⅔ full. Bake 20-25 minutes at 350 degrees.

⅓ cup butter, melted
½ cup sugar

1 teaspoon cinnamon

Dip in melted butter and roll in cinnamon-sugar mixture. Serve hot. Makes 12 muffins.
Mrs. Ken Beverly (Mary Jo)

CREAM CHEESE DIAMONDS

1 package hot roll mix
1 8-ounce package cream cheese,
    softened
¼ cup sugar
3 tablespoons all-purpose
    flour

1 egg yolk
½ teaspoon lemon rind,
    grated
1 tablespoon lemon juice
½ cup jam
Chopped nuts

Prepare hot roll mix according to package directions. Turn out on lightly floured board and knead until smooth. Put in greased bowl, turn to grease top and let rise in warm place free from drafts until doubled in bulk. Soften cream cheese. Add sugar and beat until light and fluffy. Stir in flour, egg yolk, lemon rind and juice. Roll dough in a 15-inch square, cut in twenty-five 3-inch squares and put on greased baking sheets. Put 1 heaping teaspoonful cheese mixture in center of each square. Bring 2 diagonally opposite corners to center of each square, overlap slightly and pinch together. Cover and let rise 30 minutes, or until doubled. Bake in a moderate oven (375 degrees) for 12 minutes, or until done. Heat jam until melted and brush lightly on hot rolls. Top with nuts.
The Editors

NIGHT BEFORE YEAST WAFFLES

2 cups milk
3 tablespoons sugar
1 teaspoon salt
½ cup margarine

¾ cup very warm water
1 package yeast
3 large eggs, separated
4 cups flour, sifted

Scald milk; stir in sugar, salt and margarine and cool to lukewarm. Measure very warm water into a warm large bowl. Sprinkle in yeast and stir until dissolved. Stir in lukewarm milk mixture, unbeaten egg yolks and flour. Beat until smooth. Cover and refrigerate overnight. While waffle iron heats, beat egg whites until stiff. If batter seems too thick add a little milk. Fold in egg whites and bake. Makes 8 large waffles or 16 medium size. They are best the first day but batter will keep a second day.
Mrs. John T. King, Jr. (Clarice)

MRS. J. L. FOSTER'S PANCAKES

3 tablespoons corn meal
1 cup boiling water
½ teaspoon salt
2 teaspoons sugar
3 tablespoons lard, melted

1 cup of flour, divided
1 egg
3 rounded teaspoons of baking
   powder
Sweet milk

Cook corn meal and water until thick as a soft dough. Remove from heat and beat a few minutes. Add salt, sugar and lard. Beat. When cool, slowly add ½ cup of sifted flour alternately with sweet milk. Mix in 1 well-beaten whole egg. With the other ½ cup of flour mix the baking powder and stir into the batter. Use enough milk to make the batter as thin as buttermilk. Fry on a flat iron griddle using very little grease. Cook on one side until bubbles form, then turn.
Mrs. L. C. Sullivan (Jane)

SOURDOUGH PANCAKES

1 cup all-purpose flour,sifted
2 tablespoons sugar
1½ teaspoons baking powder
½ teaspoon salt
½ teaspoon baking soda

1 egg, beaten
1 cup Sourdough Starter
½ cup milk
2 tablespoons cooking oil

Combine flour, sugar, baking powder, salt and soda. Combine egg, Sourdough Starter, milk and oil; stir into flour mixture until combined. Using 2 tablespoons batter for each pancake, bake on hot, lightly greased griddle until golden, turning once. Makes about 12-16 pancakes.
The Editors

DOUGHNUTS

5 cups flour, sifted
5 rounded teaspoons baking
   powder
1 level teaspoon salt
¼ cup butter
1¼ cups sugar

3 eggs
1 cup sweet milk
1 teaspoon nutmeg, grated
2 teaspoons cinnamon
Powdered sugar

Cream butter and sugar. Beat eggs and blend into mixture. Mix flour, baking powder, salt, nutmeg and cinnamon. Add it to butter mixture alternately with milk. Dough will be a little too soft. Work lightly on floured board adding a bit more flour. Dough must be rather soft. Roll ¼ inch thick and cut into shapes. Have smoking hot grease about 3 to 4 inches deep. Watch closely and turn once. When removed from grease, place doughnuts on brown paper to drain. When cool, coat with powdered sugar by shaking in brown paper bag with the sugar.
Mrs. L. C. Sullivan (Jane)

86

HEALTH CEREAL

5 cups oatmeal
1 cup nuts, chopped
1 cup sesame seeds (optional)
1 cup sunflower seeds
   (optional)
1 cup coconut

1 cup soy flour
1 cup powdered milk
1 cup wheat germ
1 cup honey
1 cup vegetable oil

Mix all ingredients except honey and oil. Gradually add honey and oil. Place on 2 cookie sheets. Bake at 300 degrees for 30-45 minutes, stirring 2 or 3 times during cooking period. Be careful not to let it burn. Raisins and/or chopped dates may be added after cooking. Cool and pack in an airtight container. Serve with milk. Yield: about 10-12 cups.
Mrs. Franklin I. Smith (Doris)

EGG BREAD DRESSING

EGG BREAD:

1 cup yellow corn meal
1 cup buttermilk
1 egg
1 teaspoon salt

2 teaspoons baking powder
¼ teaspoon soda
2 tablespoons cooking oil

DRESSING:

Egg bread
1 package herb-seasoned
   stuffing
1 large onion, chopped
Chicken broth (fresh or canned)
Salt
Pepper

Poultry seasoning
4 eggs
1 cup milk
3 teaspoons baking powder

Make egg bread by mixing all ingredients and baking in an 11x7x1½-inch greased pan for 20-25 minutes at 450 degrees. To make dressing, break egg bread into crumbs in a large bowl. Add the herb-seasoned stuffing, the onion and the seasonings to taste. Pour chicken broth over this mixture until it is well soaked. Let stand overnight or for several hours. Just before cooking, beat the 4 eggs. Mix a cup of milk with eggs. Pour into dressing. Then add 3 teaspoons of baking powder and mix well. Pour into a greased 2-quart pyrex baking dish. Bake at 400 degrees for 25-35 minutes or until brown and firm.
Mrs. Fred Cooper (Helen)

CHESTNUT STUFFING

1½ pounds chestnuts
1 cup butter or margarine
1½ cups celery, chopped
1 cup onions, chopped
2 teaspoons salt

1 teaspoon thyme leaves
1 teaspoon marjoram
½ teaspoon seasoned pepper
8 cups soft bread crumbs

With tip of sharp knife, mark an x in each chestnut. In medium saucepan, cover chestnuts with water. Over high heat, heat to boiling; cook 1 minute. Remove from heat. With slotted spoon, remove 3 or 4 chestnuts at a time; remove shells and skins. Coarsely chop nuts; set aside. (This process is time consuming and if canned chestnuts are available, they may be used. Fresh are delicious though.) In large saucepan over medium heat, in hot butter or margarine, cook celery, onions, salt, thyme, marjoram and seasoned pepper about 10 minutes or until vegetables are tender; remove from heat. Stir in chestnuts and bread crumbs; mix well. Makes about 11 cups, enough stuffing for a 14 to 16 pound turkey.
Mrs. A. B. Wight, Jr. (Carolyn)

GREAT CREPE RECIPE

1 cup sifted flour
Dash of salt
3 eggs

1½ cups milk
About ¼ cup vegetable oil
for frying

Combine flour and salt in large bowl of electric mixer and blend well. Add eggs one at a time and beat well after each addition. Beat until mixture is a smooth paste. Gradually add milk and beat until batter is smooth. The batter should be the consistency of heavy cream. Strain the batter through a fine sieve to remove any lumps. Cover batter tightly with plastic wrap and chill in the refrigerator 1 to 2 hours. To cook crepes, lightly brush the bottom of a 6½ to 7-inch crepe pan with oil. Place over moderately high heat. The pan is hot enough when a few drops of water sprinkled on it will bounce about. Lift the pan from the heat and immediately pour about 2 tablespoons of batter into the pan. Tip the pan so the batter covers the entire bottom surface with an even thin layer of batter. The crepe should be as thin as possible. If there are holes in the crepe, ladle a little more batter into the holes. Set the pan back on the heat and cook about 1 minute, or until the top of the crepe is dry and the bottom is lightly browned. Flip crepe over with a spatula and cook on second side for 20 seconds, or until lightly browned. Remove from pan and repeat until all the batter is used. Crepes may be wrapped tightly in foil or plastic wrap and kept for 48 hours (unfilled) in the refrigerator. Crepes may be frozen for 3 weeks. Makes 16 to 20 crepes, depending on how expert you become!
Mrs. Fred Cooper (Helen)

FILLED FRENCH ROLLS

8 French rolls
½ cup margarine, softened
½ cup Parmesan cheese, grated
2 tablespoons salad oil

½ cup fresh parsley, finely
   chopped
1 clove garlic, finely chopped
½ teaspoon sweet basil
Salt to taste

Turn each roll on its side and cut into ½-inch slices, being careful not to cut all the way through the roll. Make the filling by blending the margarine with the remaining ingredients. Spread the filling between each slice. Wrap each roll in aluminum foil. Bake at 375 degrees for 20 minutes. Serve in foil. Wonderful for a barbecue!
Mrs. Heyward Vann (Mildred)

OPEN-FACED CRAB SANDWICH

6 slices bread
Mayonnaise, enough for
   spreading consistency

Juice of 1 lemon
1 can crab
Grated cheese

Spread mayonnaise on bread. Open crab and remove flecks of shell. Season crab with lemon juice; mix in mayonnaise and spread on bread. Over this put grated cheese; place in oven and broil until cheese is golden brown.
Mrs. Roy Lilly (Mary Frances)

SWISSANDWICHES

½ pound butter, room
   temperature
3 tablespoons mustard
1½ teaspoons poppy seed or
   celery seed

1 teaspoon Worcestershire sauce
1 medium onion, minced
16 slices ham
8 slices Swiss cheese
8 buns

Make mixture of butter, mustard, poppy seed, Worcestershire sauce and onion. Spread each side of bun with mixture, using it generously. Then layer with ham and cheese. Wrap in double foil and bake at 400 degrees for 15 minutes. May be frozen and then baked for 30 minutes.
Mrs. Frederick Jefferson (Marilyn)

OVEN DIVAN SANDWICHES

3 hero rolls, split and
   toasted
6 slices cheese
Sliced chicken
1 package broccoli, thawed

¾ cup mayonnaise
¼ cup Parmesan cheese, grated
1 teaspoon dry mustard
2-3 tablespoons milk
¼ cup red onion, chopped

Cover rolls with cheese, chicken and broccoli. Stir together mayonnaise, grated cheese, mustard, and milk until smooth. Pour over rolls and sprinkle onions on top. Bake 20 minutes at 400 degrees. Serves 6.
Mrs. Hull Searcy (Anne)

ANNE'S DELIGHT
Party Sandwich Filling

1 8-ounce package cream
   cheese, softened
¾ cup nuts, chopped
¼ cup green pepper, chopped
¼ cup onion, chopped
3 tablespoons pimento, chopped

1 tablespoon catsup
3 hard-cooked eggs,
   finely chopped
¾ teaspoon salt
Dash of pepper

Combine all ingredients. Makes 2⅓ cups filling.
Mrs. Rudolph Davis (Anne)

CHEESE CHICKEN SANDWICHES

4 slices toast
4 slices baked chicken or
   turkey
¼ cup Cheddar cheese, grated

4 tablespoons Parmesan cheese
8 strips of bacon
1 cup cream of tomato soup

Place toast, chicken, bacon, and tomato soup in casserole dish. Sprinkle with cheeses. Cook in hot oven until cheese is melted. Serve hot.
Mrs. Lewis Hall Singletary (Mildred)

Soups

SOUP STOCK

Stocks are wonderful things to make up with old bones and meats. Then they may be frozen for later use in recipes calling for them and used as the bases for many tasty sauces.

BASIC BEEF STOCK

8 quarts water
1 beef shank
1 stewing chicken
2 pounds beef bones
2 large carrots
1 large onion, stuck with
   3 cloves

1 stalk celery
1 bay leaf
Few parsley stems
Pinch of thyme
5 tablespoons salt

Bring 4 quarts water to a boil and add beef shank, chicken, and bones. Let water return to a boil and boil 5 minutes. Remove from heat and pour water from pot. To the same pot add 4 quarts fresh water and remaining ingredients. Cook slowly 3 hours, uncovered. Strain. Makes a little more than 2 quarts.
The Editors

BASIC CHICKEN STOCK

3 pounds chicken pieces,
   including bones, wings, fat,
   necks and hearts
3 quarts cold water
1 cup celery, coarsely chopped
1 cup carrots, coarsely chopped
2 large onions, stuck with
   cloves

1 cup leeks or green onions,
   chopped
4 sprigs parsley
½ pound mushrooms, cut into
   chunks
Salt and pepper to taste

Put chicken pieces into a pot and add the water. Bring to boil and skim. Lower heat, cover, and simmer for 2 hours. Add vegetables and simmer, covered for another hour. Strain and season to taste. Makes about 6 cups.
The Editors

VEGETABLE SOUP

Soup bone, with meat on it
1 pound stew meat
½ head cabbage, shredded
4 onions, chopped
2 or 3 potatoes, diced
1 large can tomatoes, mashed

1 large can V-8 juice
1 can or package (frozen)
  mixed vegetables
1 tablespoon sugar
Dash of Accent
Salt and pepper to taste

Cook soup bone and stew meat, covered with water, until meat is tender. Add the other ingredients and cook until vegetables are tender.
Mrs. Hugh Hodges (Sally)

CHINESE PORK AND VEGETABLE SOUP

THE STOCK:

A meaty pork roast bone or
  2 or 3 pork steaks

A chicken bouillon cube
Dash or two of soy sauce

Simmer the pork steaks or pork roast bone in about 2 quarts of water until very tender. Add chicken bouillon cube and soy sauce. You want to make a lightly fragrant stock.

THE VEGETABLES:

1 bunch green onions, green
  tops, too (Slice on the diagonal
  in ½-inch lengths. Save some
  of the tops to chop and
  float on top of soup.)
Water chestnuts, sliced
Celery, thinly sliced on the
  diagonal
Several handfuls of the tiny,
  very thin egg noodles

Spinach, fresh or frozen, chopped
  (Be generous with the amount
  you put in.)
Mushrooms, fresh or canned, chopped
  (The mushrooms, like the spinach,
  are a "must"!)
Bean sprouts (If you use canned,
  be sure to rinse them well.
  You will need only about
  a handful of bean sprouts unless
  they are fresh, then be
  generous!)

Add the vegetables and noodles to the stock and simmer just long enough for the fresh vegetables to be "crunchy" tender. Take the meat out and cut into cubes. Place these in the bottom of your soup bowls. Add the stock and vegetables and sprinkle with some of the chopped green onion tops.
Mrs. Thomas H. Vann, Jr. (Janine)

SOUP OF SMALL BIRDS

This is a fine soup when you have game birds but not enough of them to serve roasted.

3 or more pounds squab, guinea
    hen, quail and/or duck
⅓ cup butter and oil
1 tablespoon brown sugar
½ cup onions, chopped
½ cup carrots, chopped
1 teaspoon marjoram
1 teaspoon thyme

1 cup red wine
6 or more cups chicken broth
1 cup heavy cream, scalded
2 egg yolks
1 jigger Cognac
Parsley, chopped
Croutons, fried in butter

Clean and dry the birds. Sauté them in butter and oil until they are golden all over. They may be split in half so the liquid will more easily cover them. Put them in a big soup kettle. Add the onions, carrots, herbs, wine, and hot broth. Cover; bring to a simmer and skim. Cover and cook gently for 1 hour. Remove all the meat from the bones and cut 2 cups of it into cubes; purée the rest with the strained soup. If too thick, add a little more broth. Put the diced meat in the soup. When ready to serve, reheat and whisk in the scalded cream which has been mixed with the egg yolks. Reheat but do not boil again. Add the Cognac. Sprinkle the top of each plate of soup with a little parsley and pass the crisp croutons. Serves 8.

The Editors

MINESTRONE SOUP

2 quarts beef broth
½ cup fatty ham, chopped
1 cup celery (use leaves
    also), chopped

½ cup fresh kidney beans
¾ cup fresh peas

Combine and simmer for 45 minutes the above ingredients.

1 cup spinach, chopped
1 small zucchini squash,
    chopped
¼ cup fresh onion, minced
1 carrot, diced

1 cup cabbage (green or red),
    chopped
1 cup tomatoes, diced
3 tablespoons olive oil

Sauté the above vegetables in the olive oil. Then add the vegetables to the hot stock.

¼ cup dry rice or pasta
1 tablespoon fresh parsley,
    chopped, or 1 teaspoon dried
    parsley

1 tablespoon fresh sage,
    minced, or 1 teaspoon dried
    sage

Add the rice or pasta to the soup and simmer for 30 minutes; then add the parsley and sage and continue to cook for 5 minutes. Correct the seasoning. Sprinkle servings with grated Parmesan cheese.
Mrs. Robert Maxwell (Ruth Ann)

HEARTY SOUP

1 can tomato soup
1 can cream of chicken soup
1 can green pea soup
1 can cream of mushroom soup

1 cup light cream
2 jiggers sherry
1½ cups crabmeat, lobster,
   or shrimp, cleaned

Put all soups in large pot. Add 1 or 2 cans of water and the cream and sherry. Add cooked seafood and heat well. Can be made the day before.
Mrs. L. G. Hardy (Cile)

TUNA CHOWDER

½ pound bacon, diced
1 medium onion, chopped
1 clove garlic, chopped
1 cup celery, chopped
1 can tomato soup
1 1-pound 4-ounce can
   tomatoes
1 quart water

½ teaspoon celery seed
¼ cup catsup
¼ teaspoon curry powder
2 7-ounce cans tuna (drained
   and flaked)
¼ cup cracker crumbs
¼ cup sherry (optional)
Salt and pepper

Cook bacon, onion, garlic, and celery over low heat until bacon is lightly browned. Add the soup, tomatoes, water, celery seed, catsup, and curry powder. Stir together in a large boiler or soup kettle. Cover and cook over low heat for 1 hour, stirring occasionally. Add the tuna and cracker crumbs. Mix well. Cook 10 minutes to thicken. Before serving add the sherry, salt, and pepper. Makes 3 quarts. This freezes well.
Mrs. Fred Scott, Jr. (Mary)

SHRIMP BISQUE

2 pounds fresh shrimp
3 tablespoons butter
Salt and pepper
1 jigger brandy

½ cup tomato purée
1 cup heavy cream, scalded
2 egg yolks

FISH STOCK:

Ground shells of shrimp
Salt and pepper
1 teaspoon thyme
1 cup dry white wine
½ cup onions, finely chopped
¼ cup carrots, diced

2 whole cloves
1 teaspoon marjoram
4 cups water
2 teaspoons chicken soup
   concentrate
1 pint clam juice

Shell the shrimp and grind the shells. Put them in a heavy pot with all the stock ingredients, cover and simmer very slowly for 15 minutes. Let cool, then strain through a sieve. Cook the shrimp in the butter a minute until they become pink. Season lightly, then blaze with brandy. Add the tomato purée. Reserve 8 or 10 shrimp, the number of persons you will serve. Purée the other shrimp with 2 or 3 cups of the stock until smooth. Add the rest of the stock to the soup. When ready to serve, reheat and whisk in the scalded cream which has been mixed with the egg yolks. Put a sliced (lengthwise) shrimp in each plate of soup. Serves 8-10.
The Editors

CRAB BISQUE

1 can tomato soup
1 can green pea soup
1 can bouillon or consommé
1 cup shrimp, cooked
2 cups milk

1 very small onion, grated
1 cup ripe olives
2 6½-ounce cans crabmeat
Salt and pepper to taste

Mix all ingredients together well. Heat, but do not boil. Serves 8-10.
Mrs. Donald Davis (Sara)
Similar recipe submitted by *Mrs. J. T. Higgins (Virginia)*.

NEW ORLEANS SHRIMP GUMBO

2 pounds shrimp
2 fish heads and bones
2 quarts water
2 bay leaves
2 whole cloves
Salt and pepper
1½ pounds okra
¼ cup butter
¼ cup bacon fat
2 cups onions, finely chopped
½ cup celery, thinly sliced
2 tablespoons tomato paste

2 cloves garlic, crushed
1 green pepper, sliced
½ cup flour
1 cup tomato purée
½ teaspoon Tabasco
1 teaspoon Worcestershire sauce
1 pound fresh crabmeat, cooked
1 pint oysters
1 tablespoon gumbo filé
3 tablespoons parsley, chopped
Rice, cooked

Shell the shrimp and set aside. Put the shells in a large kettle with the fish heads and bones the fish market man gives you. Add 2 quarts of water, bay leaves, cloves, salt and pepper. Cover and simmer gently 1 hour. Strain and use the broth for the soup. For added flavor, add teaspoons of chicken soup concentrate, if you wish. Trim the ends of the okra. It may be washed in water with a pinch of soda to brighten it and rinsed well. Dry okra, then sauté it in the butter and bacon fat and toss over low heat 2 minutes. Add all the vegetables; stir for 3 or 4 minutes until the onions begin to soften. Stir in the flour and when smooth, stir in the tomato purée and all seasonings except the filé. Add a little of the shrimp shell broth and then mix the vegetables with the rest of the broth in the kettle. Add a quart of warm water, cover and simmer gently 1 hour. When ready to serve, add the crabmeat, shrimp and oysters. When it begins to bubble, stir in the filé (a sassafras thickener), add the parsley and serve in a large tureen at the table with hot, cooked rice. Serves 10. In New Orleans fresh live crab are used; this is a simpler version.
The Editors

TAMPICO CRAB SOUP

1 medium onion, chopped
1 clove garlic, mashed
2 tablespoons butter or
    margarine
1 tablespoon parsley, chopped
Dash of pepper

½ teaspoon salt
½ teaspoon dried mint, chopped
1 can tomato soup
1 soup can of milk
2 cans white crabmeat

Sauté the onion and garlic in the butter until golden brown. Add the parsley, salt, pepper, mint, tomato soup and milk. Simmer 15 minutes but do not boil; then add the crabmeat. Heat until crab is hot. Serves 4-6.
Mrs. Lonnie Ferguson (Georgia)

FRESH MUSHROOM SOUP

1 pound fresh mushrooms
⅓ cup onions, finely sliced
4 tablespoons butter
Salt and freshly ground pepper
6 cups rich chicken consommé
½ teaspoon Kitchen Bouquet

3 tablespoons cornstarch
¼ teaspoon nutmeg
1 cup heavy cream
3 tablespoons sherry
Parsley, chopped

A few dried mushrooms, blanched with boiling water, rinsed, and soaked an hour in a cup of the consommé give a rich mushroom flavor to the soup. Cook them in the consommé until tender. Clean the fresh mushrooms and remove ¹⁄₁₆ inch from the stems. Chop them with the dried mushrooms. Put the mushrooms through the meat grinder or chop them quite fine in a wooden bowl. They are not to be puréed. Melt the butter in a skillet and cook the onions 3 minutes, then add the mushrooms and bake in a 375 degree oven for 10 minutes. Salt and pepper them. Combine the mushrooms, consommé, meat glaze, nutmeg, and cream blended with the cornstarch and bring to a simmer. This may stand and ripen until time to serve. Reheat, add the wine, sprinkle the top with chopped parsley and serve. Tiny canned mushrooms may be used as a garnish but they add nothing to the flavor. If 7 cups of consommé are used, this will serve 9 or 10.
The Editors

GAZPACHO

6 large, ripe tomatoes
1 medium cucumber, peeled and
    coarsley chopped
1 garlic clove, minced
½ teaspoon paprika
½ teaspoon sugar
1 teaspoon salt
2 scallions or 1 small onion, chopped

½ medium green pepper, chopped
¼ cup olive oil
2 tablespoons wine vinegar
¼ teaspoon Tabasco
¼ teaspoon crushed oregano
1 cup toasted bread crumbs
4 cups clear chicken broth

Dip tomatoes in boiling water for 5 seconds. Slip off skin, quarter, and remove seeds. Chop tomatoes coarsely. Place tomatoes, cucumber, garlic, paprika, sugar, salt, scallions and green pepper in a blender. Combine olive oil, vinegar, Tabasco, oregano, bread crumbs and 2 cups of chicken broth. Add to vegetables. Blend for 1 minute. Pour into container with cover. Stir in 1 more cup chicken broth and mix well. Cover and chill overnight. Chill also the remaining cup of chicken broth. When ready to serve, if soup is too thick, add as much of the remaining cup of chicken broth as needed to obtain a good purée consistency. Serves 8.
Mrs. Fred Cooper (Helen)

Similar recipe submitted by *Mrs. Russell Fryar (Carole).*

BLACK BEAN SOUP
Delicious and elegant for family and guests!

2 cups dried black beans
½ pound salt pork
¾ pound ground beef
¾ quart water
2 onions, diced
2 carrots, diced
2 stalks celery, sliced
2 teaspoons basil

2 whole cloves
1 tablespoon molasses
1 teaspoon mustard
½ teaspoon mace
2 teaspoons salt
Dash of cayenne
½ cup Madeira wine

Garnish:

Lemon slices
Hard-boiled egg, sieved
Onion, chopped

Wash the beans well and soak overnight in 4 cups of water. Drain them and measure the water. Add enough to make 3 quarts. Put the beans, pork, and beef in the water and bring slowly to a boil. Skim and add all the vegetables and seasonings, except salt, peppers, and wine. Cover and simmer gently 3 hours. Add a little boiling water if needed. Purée the soup. It should be the consistency of heavy cream. Season with salt, pepper and cayenne. When ready to serve, reheat the soup and add the wine. Pass the garnishes with the soup. Serves 10.

Mrs. Thomas H. Vann (Janine)

CREAM OF TOMATO SOUP

6 large ripe tomatoes,
    skinned
⅓ cup butter, melted
1½ cups dry croutons
Salt and freshly ground pepper
3 cloves garlic, crushed

6 cups water
1½ cups heavy cream, scalded
2 egg yolks
Fried croutons, for garnish

Skin and slice the tomatoes into the butter. Stir 3 or 4 minutes over low heat. Stir in the ½-inch cubes of dry croutons, salt, pepper, and garlic. Add the hot water, cover, and simmer gently an hour. Sieve the soup and cook gently, covered, another hour. Sieve again. Scald the cream and mix it with the egg yolks then whisk it into the hot soup. Serve with a bowl of crisp croutons fried in butter. Serves 6.

The Editors

CORN CHOWDER

¾ cup celery, chopped
¾ cup onion, chopped
¼ cup margarine
1¾ cups milk
2 cans cream of chicken soup

1 16½-ounce can whole kernel corn
½ teaspoon basil
½ teaspoon salt
Dash of pepper

Sauté celery and onion in margarine until tender. Add remaining ingredients and heat, stirring occasionally. Do not boil. Serves 4-6.
Mrs. Warren Garrard (Dottie)
Similar recipe submitted by *Mrs. Maureen Otis Adams.*

APRICOT SOUP WITH SOUR CREAM
Perfect for first course of a game dinner.

1 pound dried apricots
½ cup dry white wine
Lemon juice to taste

1 cup heavy cream
Sour cream

Soak apricots in warm water to cover for 1 hour. Whirl apricots in the blender with the water in which they soaked until puréed. (May need to add additional water to keep from being "gummy".) Strain and add wine. Add lemon juice to taste and stir in cream. Chill and serve with garnish of sour cream. Serves 6.
Mrs. A. B. Wight, Jr. (Carolyn)

ONION SOUP

1½ cups butter
4 cups white onions, sliced
1¾ cups flour
12 cups beef stock

½ teaspoon cayenne
1½ tablespoons salt
1 egg yolk
2 tablespoons cream

In a six-quart soup kettle melt butter, add onions and cook over low heat until onions are wilted. Do not brown onions. Add flour and cook 5 to 10 minutes more, stirring occasionally. Blend in stock, salt, and pepper and bring to a boil. Simmer on low heat about 15 minutes. Remove from heat. Beat egg yolk and cream together. Add a little of the hot soup and mix quickly, then add to soup kettle. Serve in soup cups with toasted rounds of bread sprinkled with grated Parmesan cheese. Brown under broiler flame and serve. Makes 3 quarts.
The Editors

SPINACH SOUP

4 tablespoons butter	1 bouillon cube (chicken)
2 tablespoons flour	1½ tablespoons sherry
2 cups milk	1 small onion, studded with
1 cup light cream	2 whole cloves
1 cup spinach, cooked and	Salt, pepper, nutmeg to taste
chopped	

Put butter, flour, 1 cup of the milk, cream and spinach (well-drained) in blender for 5 seconds. Place mixture in top of double boiler, heat over flame quickly, and add bouillon cube and most of remaining milk. Stir over hot water until creamy. Add sherry and onion, and simmer for 10 minutes. If it seems too thick, add a little more milk. Season with salt, pepper, and nutmeg. Remove onion and serve. Serves 4.
Mrs. Thomas H. Vann, Jr. (Janine)

CREAM OF POTATO SOUP
Easy, but delicious . . . cold or hot!

4 tablespoons butter	Pepper
1 onion, chopped	1 can cream of chicken soup
6-7 medium potatoes	¾ pound Velveeta Cheese
Garlic salt	1½ to 2 soup cans of milk
Salt	

Sauté onion in melted butter. Peel potatoes and cut into small cubes. Add to onions and barely cover with hot water. Season with garlic salt, salt, and pepper. Cook until mushy. Stir in one can of cream of chicken soup. Cut cheese into thin slices and stir in. Stir until cheese is melted. Stir in 1½ to 2 soup cans of milk, depending on how thick you prefer soup. Correct seasoning. May be made a day or two before serving. Serve hot one night for supper and cold the next day for lunch.
Mrs. Larry Chamber (Cheryl)   *Tulsa, Oklahoma*

CZECHOSLOVAKIAN CABBAGE SOUP
This soup is delicious.

2 pounds beef bones
1 cup onion, chopped
3 carrots, pared and coarsely
    chopped
2 cloves garlic, chopped
1 bay leaf
2 pounds beef short ribs
1 teaspoon dried leaf thyme
½ teaspoon paprika
8 cups water
8 cups cabbage (1 medium
    cabbage), coarsely shredded

2 1-pound cans tomatoes
2 teaspoons salt
½ to ¾ teaspoon Tabasco
¼ cup parsley, chopped
3 tablespoons lemon juice
3 tablespoons sugar
1 package or 1-pound can
    sauerkraut, rinsed and drained
Sour cream

In a roasting pan place beef bones, onions, carrots, garlic and bay leaf. Top with short ribs and sprinkle with thyme and paprika. Roast uncovered in 450 degree oven 20 minutes, until meat is browned. Transfer meat and vegetables to a large kettle. Add water, cabbage, tomatoes, salt and Tabasco. Bring to a boil. Cover and simmer 1½ hours. Skim off fat. Add parsley, lemon juice, sugar, and sauerkraut. Cook, uncovered, 1 hour. Remove bones and short ribs from kettle. Remove meat from bones, cut into cubes and return to kettle. Cook 5 minutes longer. Serve with sour cream. Serves 10-12.
Mrs. Elliott McCollum (Lorna)

Variation: A meaty ham bone may be used instead of the beef; if the sauerkraut is left out, cut the sugar to 2 tablespoons.
Mrs. Fred Cooper (Helen)

CREAM OF AVOCADO SOUP
A pretty and tasty cold, summer soup.

1 large avocado
1 pint chicken stock
1 teaspoon chili powder

¼ teaspoon ground coriander
1 cup heavy cream
Red caviar (optional)

Peel and cut up avocado. Whirl in the blender with chicken stock, chili powder, and coriander. Heat in top of double boiler for 10 minutes. Cool; add cream and chill thoroughly. Float a teaspoon of caviar on each portion (if available). If not using caviar, garnish with a sprig of parsley. Additional salt may be necessary. Serves 6.
Mrs. A. B. Wight, Jr. (Carolyn)

ICED CUCUMBER SOUP

2 cups unpeeled cucumbers, chopped
1 medium onion, chopped
1 teaspoon salt
Dash cayenne pepper
2 cups clear chicken broth
2 tablespoons cornstarch or flour

1 cup coffee cream
1 cup cucumbers, peeled and finely chopped
1 drop green food coloring
Chopped mint or chives

Cook together unpeeled cucumbers, onions, salt, pepper and broth until very tender. Blend cornstarch with a small quantity of cold water and add to boiling cucumber mixture; stir constantly. Boil two minutes longer, then sieve and chill. Add cream, finely chopped cucumbers and green food coloring when ready to serve. Serves 4-6.

Miss Emily R. Jerger

Salads and Salad Dressings

WILLOW OAK SPECIAL SALAD

1 head Bibb lettuce
1 head romaine lettuce
2 avocados, peeled and sliced

2 large mangoes, peeled and
    sliced (or grapefruit sections)
1 pound fresh mushrooms, sliced

Tear lettuce in bowl. Arrange mangoes and avocados around rim of bowl. Put mushrooms in the center. Chill. Toss with the following dressing just before serving.

DRESSING:

1 8-ounce jar mayonnaise
1¼ cups buttermilk
2 dashes Worcestershire
    sauce
2 dashes Tabasco

White pepper
Garlic salt
1 4-ounce package blue cheese

Place all ingredients in blender. Blend until smooth. Refrigerate.
Mrs. Edward Davis (Rozzie)

AVOCADO WITH HOT SHRIMP SAUCE

2 avocados
Bibb lettuce

Bacon crumbles

Peel and halve 2 avocados. Slice each half into four slices and lay on Bibb lettuce. Sprinkle bacon crumbles on top.

SAUCE:

3 tablespoons butter
3 tablespoons catsup
3 tablespoons sugar
3 tablespoons vinegar

3 tablespoons Worcestershire
    sauce
1 4½-ounce can tiny Danish
    shrimp

Combine all ingredients except shrimp in heavy sauce jar. Heat but do not boil. Rinse shrimp well under running water. Add shrimp to sauce and continue to heat. Serve over avocados. Serves 4.
Mrs. James Evans (Margaret)

AVOCADO MOUSSE

1 3-ounce package lime
   gelatin
½ cup boiling water
2 tablespoons lemon juice
½ cup mayonnaise
1 No. 1 can crushed pineapple,
   drained

½ teaspoon salt
¾ cup whipping cream, whipped
1 cup avocado, diced
½ cup pineapple juice

Mix gelatin and water. Stir well. Stir in ½ cup pineapple juice. Cool. When thickened, add pineapple, salt, and lemon juice. Fold in mayonnaise, whipped cream and avocado. Place in refrigerator until firm. Serve on salad greens. Serves 8.
Miss Ophelia Smith

AVOCADO SALAD

2 3-ounce packages cream
   cheese
⅛ teaspoon white pepper
½ teaspoon Worcestershire
1 teaspoon mayonnaise
⅓ cup ripe olives, chopped

Salt to taste
2 ripe avocados
Lemon juice
1 4-ounce can whole pimentos,
   drained on paper towel

Up to four hours before serving: Mix cream cheese, pepper, Worcestershire, mayonnaise, olives, and salt until creamy. Cut avocados in half and remove seeds. With fork roughen up cavity of each and brush with lemon juice. Cut pimento open on one side; with it line cavity of one of avocado halves. Trim pimento edges even; then add these trimmings to cream cheese mixture. Repeat with other 3 avocado halves. Spoon cheese mixture into avocado halves. Wrap each tightly in foil and refrigerate. To serve, remove foil and cut each avocado half in half. Serves 8.
Miss Ophelia Smith

OVERNIGHT SALAD

1 head lettuce
1 cup celery, chopped
1 cup onions, diced
1 package frozen peas
(seasoned to taste)

8 slices bacon, fried and crumbled
1 pint of mayonnaise
Seasoned croutons
Parmesan cheese

Layer lettuce, celery, onions, peas, and bacon in bowl. Spread mayonnaise over vegetables making sure edges of bowl are sealed tightly. Sprinkle seasoned croutons and Parmesan cheese over mayonnaise generously. Refrigerate overnight. Do not cover! Toss before serving. Serves 8-10.
Mrs. Gerald Wolsfelt (Vicki)
Similar recipe submitted by *Mrs. J. T. Higgins (Virginia)*.

Variation: Add carrots and cover vegetables with 1 cup sour cream, 1/3 cup mayonnaise, and 2 tablespoons sugar.
Mrs. Lewis Hall Singletary (Mildred)

SPINACH SALAD

3 parts spinach
1 part lettuce
Eggs, hard boiled

Cucumber
4 slices bacon, fried and
crumbled

Break lettuce and spinach into bite-size pieces. Slice eggs and cucumber and add to spinach mixture. Fry bacon, drain, crumble and set aside. Reserve 1 tablespoon drippings for dressing.

DRESSING:

1 tablespoon bacon drippings
1 egg, beaten
1/3 cup sour cream

¼ cup vinegar
2 tablespoons sugar
Dash salt

Combine all ingredients and cook until mixture thickens. Place salad greens into the pan and toss with dressing. Sprinkle bacon on top.
Mrs. Gerald Muller (Emmy)

CAESAR SALAD

6 slices white bread
½ cup butter
2 eggs
1/3 cup salad oil
2 to 3 tablespoons lemon
   juice

½ cup grated Parmesan cheese
1 tablespoon prepared mustard
Black pepper
1½ cloves garlic, minced
3 quarts crisp dry romaine
   leaves

Spread butter on bread and brown on both sides. Drain on paper towels and cut into cubes. Place eggs in a bowl and beat. Add oil, lemon juice, cheese, mustard, pepper to taste and garlic. Beat together until blended. Toss with lettuce and croutons.
The Editors

CALICO SALAD

1 can green beans
1 can wax beans
1 can red kidney beans
1 small purple onion
Celery
Olives

½ cup green pepper, chopped
⅓ cup Wesson Oil
⅔ cup tarragon vinegar
¾ cup sugar
1 tablespoon black pepper

Mix and boil vinegar, sugar and pepper. Pour over other ingredients. Cover tightly and refrigerate overnight or longer. Onions may be sliced on top of ingredients, instead of chopped and put in salad.
Mrs. Jasper Davis (Marthalene)

CORN SALAD

2 12-ounce cans white shoe
   peg corn
¾ cup cucumber, diced

¼ cup onion, diced
1 or 2 medium tomatoes,
   diced

SAUCE:

½ cup sour cream
4 tablespoons mayonnaise
2 tablespoons vinegar
2 teaspoons salt

½ teaspoon dry mustard
½ teaspoon celery seed
½ teaspoon pepper

Combine all ingredients for sauce. Pour over diced vegetables and mix well. Marinate in refrigerator, overnight. Serves 10-12 people depending on size of serving. NOTE: Vegetables must be cut the size of corn kernels.
Mrs. Bryant Harvard (Kathy)

BROCCOLI SALAD

2 packages chopped broccoli
1 3-ounce package cream cheese
1 can condensed chicken broth

1 envelope unflavored
   gelatin
1 cup mayonnaise

Cook and drain broccoli. Stir cream cheese into hot broccoli until well mixed. Sprinkle gelatin over broth and stir over low heat until dissolved. Mix broth and broccoli with mayonnaise. Add salt and Tabasco sauce to taste. Pour into a 1½-quart rectangular Pyrex dish and chill until firm. Serve with dressing. Serves 10-12.

SOUR CREAM DRESSING:

2 tablespoons green onion,
   minced
1 tablespoon anchovy paste
2 tablespoons lemon juice

2 tablespoons white wine vinegar
⅛ teaspoon tarragon
1 8-ounce carton sour cream
½ cup mayonnaise

Mix ingredients together and chill. Serve over broccoli salad.
Mrs. A. B. Wight, Jr. (Carolyn)

ASPARAGUS SALAD

¾ cup sugar
1 cup water
½ cup white vinegar
½ teaspoon salt
1 cup celery, chopped
½ cup pecans, chopped

1 small jar pimento strips
1 can green asparagus
2 teaspoons onion, grated
2 envelopes unflavored
   gelatin
8 olives, sliced

Mix the first 4 ingredients and bring to a boil. Add gelatin dissolved in ½ cup cold water. Pour into oblong Pyrex dish. Cool slightly, then add other ingredients. Lay asparagus in rows on top. Chill until set. Cut in squares and serve on lettuce. Serves 12-15.
Mrs. Jimmy Watkins (Raines)   *Albany, Georgia*

CANTALOUPE, AVOCADO, AND TOMATO SALAD

Mix equal amounts of cubed cantaloupe, avocado, and tomato. Sprinkle with lemon juice, salt and pepper. Toss. Serve on bed of crisp lettuce.
Mrs. Joe Rawlings (Bettye Day)

MOLDED EGG SALAD

12 eggs, hard cooked
2 tablespoons (2 packages)
  plain gelatin
½ cup cold water
1 cup boiling water
1 cup mayonnaise
1½ teaspoons salt

½ teaspoon pepper
1 tablespoon lemon juice
2 tablespoons green
  pepper, chopped
2 tablespoons pimento,
  chopped

Sprinkle gelatin over cold water; let stand at least 10 minutes. Dissolve moistened gelatin in boiling water. Put eggs through ricer, or chop them very fine with pastry chopper. Add mayonnaise, salt, pepper, lemon juice, green pepper, and pimento. Add melted gelatin last. Rub mold with oil and pour in mixture. Chill thoroughly, preferably overnight. Serve with Lorenzo Dressing.

LORENZO DRESSING:

¼ cup vinegar
2 teaspoons salt
½ teaspoon mustard
2 teaspoons Worcestershire
  sauce
¾ cup oil

Dash of pepper
Dash of Tabasco
½ cup cocktail sauce
½ cup watercress or parsley,
  finely chopped (optional)

Mix above ingredients. Unmold egg salad on dish and garnish with lettuce. Lorenzo Dressing can be served in separate bowl with ladle and poured over each serving of salad.
Mrs. W. R. Milton (Evie)

GAZPACHO SALAD

2 cucumbers
4 tomatoes, peeled and sliced
2 Italian onions (red),
  peeled and sliced

⅔ cup croutons
½ cup French dressing
Lettuce

In salad bowl, place alternate layers of cucumber, tomato, and onion slices. Refrigerate until thoroughly chilled. When ready to serve pour dressing over vegetables. Place on lettuce leaves. Garnish with croutons on top. Serves 8.
Mrs. J. H. Frobert (Julia)

LOUIS PAPPAS' FAMOUS GREEK SALAD
Louis Pappas' Restaurant, Tarpon Springs, Florida

Make a potato salad from these ingredients:

6 boiling potatoes, cooked
4 green onions (green tops
   also)
¼ cup parsley, chopped

3 tablespoons wine vinegar
2 tablespoons salt
1 cup mayonnaise

Salad ingredients:

1 large head lettuce,
   shredded
Potato Salad (above)
2 or 3 tomatoes, cut into
   wedges
1 cucumber, cut lengthwise
   into fingers
1-2 avocados, sliced
6 slices of Feta (Greek cheese)
1 green pepper, cut into rings

6-8 slices canned beets, cooked
Shrimp, peeled and cooked
6-8 anchovy fillets
Black olives (Greek-style
   preferred)
6-8 whole green onions
½ cup white vinegar
¼ cup olive oil and ¼ cup
   salad oil, blended
Oregano

Mound the potato salad on a large platter. Cover the potato salad with the shredded lettuce, then arrange the remaining vegetables in an attractive pattern on the lettuce. Place the anchovies and shrimp on top of the salad. The entire salad is then sprinkled with the vinegar and then the blended oil. Sprinkle liberally with oregano over all and serve at once. Toasted Greek or French bread is served with the salad. Each person serves himself from the beautiful salad platter. Serves 6-8.
Mrs. Thomas H. Vann, Jr. (Janine)

MACARONI SALAD

2 cups uncooked elbow
   macaroni
¾ cup bottled Italian dressing
1 cup celery, thinly sliced
½ cup onion, thinly sliced

¾ cup green pepper, chopped
¾ cup carrot, shredded
1½ cups Cheddar cheese, diced
1 cup sour cream

Cook macaroni according to package directions. Drain and cool. Mix macaroni and bottled dressing and chill in refrigerator for 3 hours or overnight. Add celery, onion, green pepper, carrot, and cheese. Fold in sour cream. Serves 8 to 10.
Mrs. Fred Cooper (Helen)

MACARONI AND CHEESE SALAD

6 ounces shell macaroni
(about 1½ cups)
1 cup celery, sliced
1 cup carrots, shredded or
chopped
¼ cup onion, chopped
1 10-ounce can condensed
Cheddar cheese soup

¼ cup salad oil
2 tablespoons vinegar
1 teaspoon sugar
1 teaspoon mustard
1 teaspoon Worcestershire
sauce
½ teaspoon salt
Dash of pepper

Cook macaroni; drain and cool. Add celery, carrots and onion to macaroni. Combine remaining ingredients and beat until well blended. Stir into macaroni mixture. Chill several hours. Serves 4-6.
Mrs. Freddy Vonier (Mary Lou)

DEVILED POTATO SALAD

8 eggs, hard boiled
2 tablespoons vinegar
1 tablespoon horseradish sauce
2½ tablespoons prepared mustard
1 cup mayonnaise
1 cup sour cream
½ teaspoon celery seed
½ teaspoon seasoning salt

½ teaspoon salt
4½ cups cooked potatoes, diced
1 cup celery, chopped
¼ cup onion, chopped
2 tablespoons green pepper
2 tablespoons pimento
½ teaspoon lemon-pepper
seasoning

Cut eggs in half and remove yolks. Mash and blend yolks with vinegar, horseradish, and mustard. Add mayonnaise, sour cream, celery seed, salts and seasonings. Chop egg whites. Combine with potatoes, celery, onion, green pepper, and pimento. Fold in yolk mixture and chill. Serves about 8.
Mrs. Philip Leabo (Karen)

POTATO SALAD

6 medium Idaho potatoes,
cooked, peeled, and cubed
1½ teaspoons celery seed
2 teaspoons salt
1 cup sour cream

4 large green onions, chopped
5 ribs celery, chopped
1 cup mayonnaise

Toss cubed potatoes with salt and celery seed. Add chopped green onion and celery. Stir in mayonnaise and sour cream and chill well before serving. Serves 8.
Mrs. A. B. Wight, Jr. (Carolyn)

GERMAN SLAW

4 to 5 pounds red cabbage
Salt
½ cup sugar
2 teaspoons sugar

1 teaspoon dry mustard
1 teaspoon celery seed
1 cup white vinegar
½ cup Wesson Oil

Soak cabbage in salted water. Drain. Then grate and mix with ½ cup sugar. Boil three minutes the following ingredients: sugar, dry mustard, celery seed, vinegar, Wesson Oil. Pour over cabbage and let stand in covered container overnight. Serves 8.
Mrs. Furman Stewart (Cloe)

STAY CRISP COLE SLAW

8 cups cabbage, shredded
1 green pepper, cut in thin
　　strips
¾ cup cold water
⅔ cup sugar
2 teaspoons celery seeds
¼ teaspoon black pepper

2 carrots, shredded
½ cup onion, chopped
1 envelope unflavored gelatin
⅔ cup vinegar
1½ teaspoons salt
⅔ cup salad oil

Mix cabbage, carrots, green pepper, and onion; sprinkle with ½ cup cold water. Mix sugar, vinegar, celery seeds, salt and pepper in saucepan; bring to boil. Stir in gelatin which has been softened in ¼ cup cold water. Cool until slightly thickened; beat well. Gradually beat in salad oil. Drain vegetables. Pour dressing over vegetables; mix until vegetables are coated with dressing. May be served immediately or stored in refrigerator. Stir just before serving. Serves 8.
Miss Ophelia Smith

SWEET AND SOUR SLAW

1 large cabbage
2 medium onions
1 cup vinegar
1 cup sugar

¾ cup salad oil
1 tablespoon salt
1 teaspoon dry mustard
1 teaspoon celery seed

Chop cabbage and slice onions. Mix. Pour sugar over vegetables and mix. Bring remaining ingredients to a boil. Pour over cabbage and age 3 days. Drain and serve.
Mrs. Frederick Jefferson (Marilyn)

Similar recipes submitted by *Mrs. William Smitha (Helen) and Mrs. Richard S. Vann (Ann).*

MARINATED SLICED TOMATOES

3 fresh large tomatoes
⅓ cup olive oil
¼ cup red wine vinegar
1 teaspoon salt
¼ teaspoon pepper

½ clove garlic, finely
   chopped or crushed
2 tablespoons parsley, snipped
1½ teaspoons dried basil leaves,
   crushed
1 teaspoon onion, finely chopped

Slice tomatoes ½ inch thick. Place in single layer in large shallow serving dish. In small jar mix olive oil, vinegar, salt, pepper, and garlic. Cover tightly with lid and shake until well mixed. Pour mixture over tomato slices. Sprinkle parsley, basil, and onion over tomato slices and oil mixture. Cover and refrigerate one to three hours before serving. Serves 4-5.
Mrs. Prince Jinright (Marjorie)

TOMATO ASPIC
This is old-fashioned aspic.

1 quart tomato juice
4 stalks celery, finely chopped
1 small bottle stuffed olives,
   finely sliced
3 tablespoons vinegar
1 tablespoon salt
⅛ teaspoon red pepper

3 envelopes plain gelatin
1 small jar pimento, finely
   chopped (optional)
1 small bell pepper, finely
   chopped (optional)
½ cup cold water

Sprinkle gelatin on cold water. In a saucepan heat one cup of the tomato juice; when the gelatin has absorbed the water, add it to the heated tomato juice. Stir until completely dissolved. In large mixing bowl pour the remainder of tomato juice. Add heated juice, vinegar, salt and pepper; stir. Add celery, olives, pimento and bell pepper; stir. Pour into ring mold or container and place in refrigerator until congealed. Takes a while to congeal.
Mrs. Roy Lilly (Mary Frances)

ASPIC SALAD

1 10-ounce can tomato soup
1 8-ounce package cream
   cheese
1 cup mayonnaise
½ cup water

2 tablespoons onion, chopped
2 tablespoons bell pepper,
   chopped
2 envelopes plain gelatin

Dissolve gelatin in cold water. Add to undiluted soup and warm over low heat. Stir in cream cheese and other ingredients. When mixture is smooth, pour into bowl or mold and congeal.
Mrs. Gene Walker (Hilda)

Variation: Add lemon juice.
Mrs. James Pringle (Mae)

CUCUMBERS WITH SOUR CREAM

2 medium cucumbers, sliced   1¼ teaspoons salt

Chill salted cucumbers at least 30 minutes and dry on paper towel.

1 cup sour cream   ½ teaspoon sugar
1 teaspoon Accent   ¼ teaspoon Worcestershire
1 tablespoon onion, minced   sauce
   (May use more)   Dash pepper
2 tablespoons tarragon vinegar

Combine sour cream, Accent, onion, vinegar, sugar, Worcestershire sauce, and pepper. Add cucumbers. Toss gently. Sprinkle with dried dill weed and parsley if desired. Garnish with paprika.
Mrs. William King (Anne)
Mrs. Jack Kelly (Janis)

CUCUMBER-LIME SALAD

1 3-ounce package lime   1 cup mayonnaise or 1
   gelatin   cup sour cream
¾ cup boiling water   1 cup cucumber, unpeeled
¼ cup lemon juice   and chopped
1 teaspoon onion juice   Dash of salt

Dissolve gelatin in hot water. Add lemon juice and onion juice. Chill until thickened. Fold in cucumber and mayonnaise. Pour into individual molds or one large one. Unmold and serve on crisp lettuce. Serves 6.
Mrs. William Smitha (Helen)

APRICOT SALAD

2 3-ounce packages apricot   2 large cans of apricots,
   or peach gelatin   peeled and drained
1 envelope plain gelatin   1 pint sour cream
1 large can crushed   3 cups juice from cans of
   pineapple, drained   pineapple and apricots

Dissolve flavored and unflavored gelatin in 3 cups of hot juice. Cool. Mash apricots, mix with pineapple and sour cream, and add to cooled mixture. Pour in molds or pan and refrigerate until congealed.
Mrs. J. A. Stewart (Melba)

APRICOT CONGEALED SALAD

2 3-ounce packages apricot
   gelatin
2 cups miniature marshmallows
2 cups boiling water
1 cup cold water

1 No. 2 can crushed pineapple,
   drained
2 bananas, chopped
½ cup nuts, chopped

Drain pineapple and reserve juice for topping. Chop bananas and nuts. Combine apricot gelatin, marshmallows, and boiling water. Mix well. Add cold water, fruit, and nuts. Pour into dish or mold and chill until firm. When firm, pour topping over surface.

TOPPING:

½ cup sugar
½ cup pineapple juice
2 tablespoons flour

1 egg
2 tablespoons butter
1 8-ounce package cream cheese

Combine ingredients (except cream cheese) in top of double boiler and cook until thick. Add cream cheese. Remove from heat and mix until smooth. Spread on firm gelatin.
Mrs. Tom Faircloth (Janice)

PEAR CONGEALED SALAD

1 3-ounce package lime
   gelatin
1 cup hot pear juice
1 16-ounce can pears, mashed

2 3-ounce packages cream
   cheese, softened
½ pint whipping cream

Dissolve gelatin in hot pear juice, add pears and cream cheese. Stir until well mixed. Refrigerate. Whip cream and fold into pear mixture. Pour into mold and congeal.

Variation: Pecans may be added.
Mrs. Bill Lawson (Diane)

CONGEALED FRUIT SALAD

1 No. 2½ can sliced
    pineapple, cut in small pieces
1 pound sharp cheese, grated
4 envelopes unflavored
    gelatin
2 cups sugar

2 cups pecans, chopped
1 pint cream, whipped
1 cup cold water
Pinch salt
Pears, peaches and/or grapes

Soften gelatin in 1 cup cold water. Add sugar and salt to pineapple juice with a little extra water and boil. Dissolve gelatin completely and chill until it begins to congeal. Add nuts, cheese and fruit. Fold in whipped cream. Pour in large ring or Bundt mold. Chill until very firm. Serve on lettuce with mayonnaise in center of mold. Serves a large crowd. This salad is originally a recipe of Mrs. Maggie Jones.
Mrs. Floyd Searcy (Anna)

APPLE SURPRISE SALAD

2½ cups applesauce
¼ cup sugar
2 tablespoons red cinnamon
    candies

1 tablespoon gelatin
2 tablespoons cold water
¼ teaspoon nutmeg
1 tablespoon lemon juice

Bring applesauce to a boil. Remove from heat; add sugar, candies and gelatin which has been softened in cold water. Stir until all are dissolved in applesauce. Add nutmeg and lemon juice. Pour into mold. Chill until firm. Can be frozen.
Mrs. Harry L. Hershey (Patti)

APPLE SALAD SUPREME

1 large package lemon
   gelatin
1½ cups boiling water
160 miniature marshmallows (2 cups)
1½ cups cold water

1 No. 2 can crushed pineapple
   and juice
½ cup pecans
2 large apples, finely diced

Dissolve gelatin and marshmallows in hot water. Add cold water, pineapple and juice, pecans, and apples. Mix together and refrigerate until firm.

TOPPING:

¾ cup sugar
Juice of 1 lemon

2 eggs, beaten
1 package Dream Whip

Combine sugar, lemon juice, and eggs. Cook until thick. Cool. Add whipped Dream Whip. Spread on top of congealed salad.
Mrs. Roscoe Stewart (Eva)

FROZEN WALDORF SALAD

2 eggs, slightly beaten
½ cup sugar
½ cup pineapple juice
¼ cup lemon juice
⅛ teaspoon salt
½ cup celery, diced

½ cup crushed pineapple,
   drained
2 medium apples, diced
½ cup nuts, chopped
1 cup cream, whipped

Combine eggs, sugar, lemon and pineapple juices and salt. Cook over low heat until thick, stirring constantly. Let cool. Add celery, pineapple, apples, and nuts. Gently fold in whipped cream. Put into square or oblong pan and freeze until just before ready to serve. Cut in squares. Serves 10-12.
Mrs. Tom Boyle (Iris)

CHERRY COLA SALAD

2 3-ounce packages red
   gelatin
1 16-ounce can cherries
   (Bing, dark red, or sweet)
1 No. 2 can crushed pineapple

2 3-ounce packages cream cheese
2 6-ounce Coca-Colas
2 cups nuts, broken
   (if desired)

Heat juice from cherries and pineapple to dissolve gelatin. When cool, add Coca-Cola. Allow to congeal slightly and then add broken nuts, cream cheese, cherries, and pineapple. Pour into mold and chill until firm.
Mrs. William Norwood (Deane)

FROSTED CRANBERRY SALAD

1 8½-ounce can crushed
   pineapple
1 1-pound can whole cranberry
   sauce
2 3-ounce packages raspberry gelatin
1 8-ounce package cream
   cheese, softened

2 tablespoons salad dressing
1 cup heavy cream, whipped
½ cup walnuts, coarsely chopped
1 tart apple, peeled and chopped

Drain pineapple and cranberry sauce, reserving liquid; add enough water to juices to make 2 cups liquid. Bring to a boil. Dissolve gelatin in hot liquid. Chill until partially set. Beat softened cream cheese and salad dressing together until fluffy. Gradually beat in gelatin; fold this mixture into whipped cream. Set aside 1½ cups of this mixture for topping. Add drained fruits, nuts, and apple to the remaining cheese mixture. Pour into a 12 x 7½ x 2-inch glass dish and refrigerate until surface sets, about 20 minutes. Frost with reserved topping. Refrigerate several hours or freeze. If frozen, remove from freezer 1 hour before serving. Serves 12.
Mrs. Harry T. Jones (Celetta)

FRESH CRANBERRY-ORANGE SALAD

1 1-pound package cranberries
2 cups sugar
2 cups nuts, chopped
2 oranges, unpeeled, cut in
   sections and seeded

3 3-ounce packages lemon
   gelatin
Red food coloring
2 cups boiling water
2 cups cold water

Wash and drain cranberries. Put ½ cup cold water and ½ package cranberries in blender and chop. Pour in bowl and do the same with remaining cranberries. Take oranges and 1 cup cold water and chop oranges in blender. Pour this in bowl with cranberries. Dissolve gelatin in 2 cups boiling water. Add sugar and few drops of red food coloring. Cool. Combine cranberries, oranges and nuts. Pour into mold. Serves 10-12.
Mrs. Franklin I. Smith (Doris)

FRUIT SALAD

1 package lemon gelatin
1 package orange gelatin
⅓ cup lemon juice
⅓ cup orange juice

1 No. 2 can grapefruit sections
1 small can crushed pineapple
1 can Mandarin oranges, cut
1 small bottle red cherries

Drain all fruit and with juices make 3 cups of liquid. Heat to boiling and dissolve gelatin. Cool. Add fruit and pour into container. Add cherries on top. Chill until firm.
Mrs. J. A. Stewart (Melba)

GAME SALAD

4 oranges	1 cup dates, chopped
2 grapefruits	1 cup black walnuts
1 avocado	Watercress

DRESSING:

2 tablespoons olive oil	¼ teaspoon salt
2 tablespoons brandy	Tarragon, chopped
1 teaspoon sugar	

Peel and remove all membranes from oranges and grapefruits. Arrange with avocado alternately on watercress. Combine dates and walnuts and add over fruit. Mix all ingredients for dressing except tarragon. Pour dressing over all and top with tarragon. Delicious with game.
Mrs. Jack Allen, Jr. (Rebecca)

GRAPEFRUIT SALAD

2 tablespoons gelatin	1 cup sugar
¼ cup cold water	3 cups grapefruit, juice and
½ cup boiling water	pulp
3 tablespoons lemon juice	½ cup pecans, chopped

Soak gelatin in cold water; add hot water and sugar, and cool until thick but not stiff. Add lemon juice, grapefruit juice, and pulp. Add nuts. Let thicken slightly and pour into a slightly greased mold. Serves 8.
Mrs. Richard Miller (Charlotte)

LIME-COTTAGE CHEESE CONGEALED SALAD

1 3-ounce package lemon-
flavored gelatin
1 3-ounce package lime-flavored
gelatin
2 cups boiling water
1 No. 2 can crushed pineapple,
drained (Reserve syrup)

1 cup cream-style cottage
cheese
2 tablespoons mayonnaise
1 cup cold water
¾ cup pecans, chopped

Dissolve gelatin in water. Add enough cold water to pineapple syrup to make 1½ cups; add to gelatin mixture. Chill until partially set. Stir cottage cheese, mayonnaise, nuts and pineapple into gelatin. Refrigerate until firm. Garnish with endive or lettuce leaf. Pass mayonnaise or creamy fruit dressing when served.

Mrs. Prince E. Jinright, Jr. (Marjorie)

Similar recipes submitted by *Mrs. Ethelyn Robertson and Mrs. Gene Walker (Hilda)*.

Variations: Substitute fruit cocktail for pineapple.

Mrs. W. A. Taylor (Julia)

Substitute cream cheese for cottage cheese and add miniature marshmallows.

Mrs. Harry Park (Mary)

TOPPING:

½ cup sugar
2 tablespoons flour
1 cup pineapple juice
1 egg, slightly beaten
2 tablespoons butter

1 cup whipping cream, whipped
¼ cup American cheese,
shredded
3 tablespoons Parmesan cheese,
grated

Combine sugar and flour in saucepan. Stir in pineapple juice and egg. Cook over low heat; add butter. Let cool; chill. Fold into whipped cream. Frost gelatin mixture. Sprinkle with cheese.

Mrs. Arthur Taylor (Thelma)

ORANGE-CARROT CONGEALED SALAD

1 6-ounce package orange
   gelatin
2 cups boiling water
2 cups carrots, grated
1 cup pecans, chopped

1 No. 2 can crushed pineapple
   and juice
½ pint sour cream
¼ cup mayonnaise

Dissolve gelatin in hot water. Chill until mixture begins to thicken and add remaining ingredients. Mix well and return to refrigerator until firm.
Mrs. Tom Faircloth (Janice)

MANDARIN ORANGE SALAD

2 packages orange gelatin
1½ cups boiling water
1 pint orange sherbet

1 11-ounce can Mandarin oranges,
   drained
1 No. 2 can crushed pineapple

Dissolve gelatin in boiling water. Add sherbet and stir until melted. Add fruit and pour into mold. Chill. Serves 12-15.
Mrs. Frederick Jefferson (Marilyn)

Similar recipe submitted by *Mrs. Jim Horner (Zee).*

PEACH PICKLE SALAD

1 package lemon gelatin
1 package orange gelatin
2½ cups water, boiling
½ cup pickle juice

1 can or jar of peach pickles
½ cup celery, chopped
½ cup pecans, chopped

Drain pickles, reserving ½ cup juice. Pour boiling water over lemon and orange gelatin. Stir until gelatin is dissolved. Add pickle juice. Cut peaches into bite-size pieces and add to gelatin. Stir in celery and nuts. Pour into mold and congeal. Serves 8-10.
Mrs. Tom Vann, Jr. (Ann)

STRAWBERRY CREAM SQUARES

2 3-ounce packages strawberry
    gelatin
2 cups boiling water
2 10-ounce packages frozen
    strawberries
1 cup sour cream

1½-2 cups crushed pineapple
2-3 large, firm bananas,
    finely diced
1 cups nuts, coarsely
    chopped

Dissolve gelatin in boiling water. Add strawberries, stirring occasionally until thawed. Add pineapple, bananas, and nuts. Pour half of mixture into a 8 x 8 x 2-inch pan; chill until firm. Spoon an even layer of sour cream over firm gelatin. Gently pour remaining half of gelatin over sour cream. Chill until firm. Cut in squares. Serves 6-8.
Mrs. Delmar Conner (Mary)
Similar recipes submitted by *Mrs. J. H. Jenkins (Essie) and Mrs. William A. Smitha (Helen).*
Variation:

DRESSING:

1 cup thick sour cream
1 tablespoon sugar
Serve over firm gelatin.
Mrs. Heeth Varnedoe, Jr. (Jackie)

1½ cups miniature marshmallows
3 tablespoons lemon juice

CHICKEN SALAD

2 cups chicken, cooked and
   diced
1 cup celery, chopped
½ cup mayonnaise
2 tablespoons Durkee's dressing

2 tablespoons capers
1 tablespoon caper vinegar *or*
   1 tablespoon lemon juice
Dash of Tabasco
Salt as desired

Mix all ingredients and allow to stand in refrigerator to season. Mayonnaise may be increased or reduced. Garnish with paprika and parsley. Serve with boiled egg and sections of pickles and relish.
Mrs. James McCollum (Wyche)

HOT BAKED CHICKEN SALAD

4 cups chicken, cooked and
   diced
3 cups celery, diced
1 cup almonds, chopped or
   slivered

1 cup mayonnaise
4 tablespoons onion, grated
4 tablespoons lemon juice
2 cans cream of chicken soup
1 teaspoon salt

Combine all ingredients and place in shallow baking dish. Spread topping over surface before baking.

TOPPING:

1 cup sharp cheese, grated
5 cups potato chips, crushed

Bake 30 minutes at 350 degrees.
Mrs. J. D. Hall (Willene)
Similar recipe submitted by *Mrs. Dilworth Mills (Mary).*

Variations: Add only 1 can soup and 1 jar pimento.
Mrs. Lewis Hall Singletary (Mildred)

Add 4 hard boiled eggs, diced, to chicken mixture.
Miss Julia Hickson

Add water chestnuts to chicken mixture and top with a can of onion rings.
Mrs. E. J. Williamson (Louise)

CURRIED CHICKEN SALAD

4 chicken breasts, cooked in
water until tender
1 cup celery, chopped

1 apple, pared and chopped
¼ cup green pepper, chopped

DRESSING:

½ cup mayonnaise
½ teaspoon curry powder

½ cup sour cream

Cook chicken, cut in pieces and salt and pepper lightly. Squeeze a little lemon juice over it. Refrigerate in a covered bowl overnight or for several hours. Combine chicken with other ingredients.
Mrs. Pratt Secrest (Sarah)

FRUITED CHICKEN SALAD

½ cup mayonnaise
2 tablespoons milk
1 tablespoon cider vinegar
2 teaspoons onion, grated
1 teaspoon salt

2 cups chicken, cooked and
diced
1 large green pear, cubed
1 large red apple, cubed
1 cup celery, thinly sliced

In large bowl mix first five ingredients. Add chicken, pear, apple and celery; toss gently until well mixed.
Mrs. Henry Pepin (Sarah)

CONGEALED CHICKEN SALAD

1 5-pound hen, cooked and
chopped (no skin or giblets)
3 envelopes plain gelatin,
dissolved in ½ cup cold water
4½ cups chicken stock
1 jar India relish
2 tablespoons lemon juice

2 cups celery, finely diced
2 cups mayonnaise
6 hard-boiled eggs, diced
1 cup almonds or pecans, chopped
2 cups white seedless grapes,
halved

Combine gelatin mixture and hot chicken stock. Add all other ingredients except mayonnaise. Fold in mayonnaise when salad is cool. Pour into two 9 x 12-inch casserole dishes. Refrigerate until firm. Cut in squares and serve on bed of lettuce. Serves approximately 20-24.
Mrs. Tom Faircloth (Janice)

HAM-MACARONI SALAD

2 or 3 cups cooked ham, cubed
½ cup pickle relish
¼ cup onion, chopped
3 hard boiled eggs, chopped
½ cup Longhorn cheese, grated
   (more if you like)

½ cup mayonnaise
2 tablespoons mustard
1 teaspoon salt
1 teaspoon black pepper
1 pound macaroni, cooked and
   drained

Mix all ingredients with macaroni in large mixing bowl. Chill or serve immediately. Serves 8-10.
Mrs. Tom Faircloth (Janice)

HAM RING SUPREME

2 cups ham, cooked and ground
4 eggs, hard-boiled(2 eggs sliced
   and 2 eggs cut in wedges)
¼ cup celery, finely minced
½ teaspoon onion salt
2 dashes of hot sauce
1 teaspoon prepared horseradish

1 teaspoon prepared mustard
3 tablespoons catsup
1 cup sour cream
½ cup mayonnaise
2 envelopes plain gelatin
⅓ cup water
A few stuffed olives, sliced

Oil a ring mold and arrange slices of 2 eggs and olives around bottom in a design. Dissolve gelatin in water and heat over boiling water until liquified. Mix remaining ingredients with the gelatin, adding sour cream and mayonnaise last. Pack into the ring mold carefully so as not to disturb the design. Chill in refrigerator until set. Turn out on platter and garnish with parsley and egg wedges.
Mrs. Martin Cooper (Peggy)

CRAB LOUIS

SALAD:

1 head lettuce
2 to 3 cups crabmeat, chilled
2 eggs, hard cooked and cut in
    wedges

2 large tomatoes, cut in
    wedges

Line 4 large plates with lettuce leaves. Shred remaining lettuce and arrange on leaves. Arrange crabmeat on lettuce and circle with tomato and egg wedges. Sprinkle with salt. Pour Louis dressing over each salad. Sprinkle with paprika. Pass remaining dressing.

LOUIS DRESSING:

1 cup mayonnaise
¼ cup sour cream
¼ cup chili sauce

¼ cup onions, chopped
1 teaspoon lemon juice
salt

Combine mayonnaise, sour cream, chili sauce, onion, and lemon juice. Salt to taste. Chill.
Mrs. Howard Arnold (Margaret)

ST. ANTHONY HOTEL DRESSING
San Antonio, Texas

⅛ cup olive oil
1⅜ cup vegetable oil
3 tablespoons tarragon vinegar
2 tablespoons lemon juice
3 teaspoons parsley, chopped
3 teaspoons onion, chopped
1 teaspoon chives, chopped

2 teaspoons sugar
3 teaspoons salt
1 teaspoon mustard
½ teaspoon thyme
1 teaspoon celery seed
1 clove garlic
1 cup whipping cream

Combine all ingredients except cream and shake well; then add 1 cup whipped cream.
Mrs. T. R. Sample (Nell)

BEST EVER GREEN GODDESS DRESSING

1 clove garlic, minced
½ teaspoon powdered mustard
2 tablespoons anchovy paste
3 tablespoons chives, snipped
1 cup mayonnaise
⅛ teaspoon pepper

½ teaspoon salt
1 teaspoon Worcestershire
3 tablespoons tarragon-wine
  vinegar
⅓ cup parsley, snipped
½ cup sour cream

Place all ingredients in blender and mix thoroughly. Makes about 1½ cups.
Miss Ophelia Smith

CELERY SEED DRESSING

⅓ cup sugar
1 teaspoon dry mustard
1 teaspoon salt
1 cup salad oil

1 teaspoon paprika
1 teaspoon onion, grated
1 heaping teaspoon celery seed
3 tablespoons vinegar

Mix sugar, mustard, salt, paprika, onion and celery seed. Add alternately to
this mixture the oil and vinegar. Beat until smooth. Refrigerate. Makes approximately 1 1/3 cups. Good on avocado and grapefruit salad.
Mrs. H. D. Adams (Martha)
Mrs. Anne W. Wight   *Cairo, Georgia*

Variation: Substitute poppy seed for celery seed.
Mrs. Paul McCollum (Nancy)

THOUSAND ISLAND DRESSING

1 cup mayonnaise
2 eggs, hard cooked, chopped
2 tablespoons celery, chopped

4 tablespoons sweet pickles,
  chopped
4 tablespoons chili sauce
1 cup whipped cream

Combine above ingredients. Mix well. Makes about 2½ cups.
The Editors

BLEU CHEESE DRESSING

2 ounces bleu cheese,
  crumbled
1 ounce buttermilk
Pinch of garlic powder

1 drop hot sauce
1 drop Worcestershire sauce
1 cup mayonnaise
1 cup sour cream

Blend together 1 ounce bleu cheese, buttermilk, garlic, hot sauce and Worcestershire. When well-mixed add mayonnaise and sour cream and blend again. Stir in 1 ounce more of crumbled bleu cheese. Serve on tossed salad.
Mrs. Hull Searcy (Anne)

BLUE CHEESE DRESSING

2 tablespoons green onion,
  chopped
1 clove garlic, crushed, or ⅛
  teaspoon garlic powder
1 teaspoon parsley, chopped
¾ cup mayonnaise
¾ cup sour cream

1 tablespoon lemon juice
¼ cup vinegar
1 4-ounce package blue cheese,
  crumbled
Salt to taste
Pepper to taste

Blend well. Keeps for weeks. Makes about 2 cups.
Mrs. Ken Beverly (Mary Jo)

FRENCH DRESSING I

1 cup sugar
1 can tomato soup
1½ cups salad oil
¾ cup vinegar
1 tablespoon prepared hot
  mustard

1 tablespoon salt
1 tablespoon paprika
1 teaspoon pepper
1 tablespoon Worcestershire
  sauce

Combine all ingredients and beat together in blender for 15 minutes. Makes approximately one quart.
Mrs. W. J. Becknell (Gwen)

FRENCH DRESSING II

2 teaspoons salt
1 teaspoon pepper
¼ teaspoon sugar
½ teaspoon dry mustard
½ teaspoon crushed garlic
¼ teaspoon Worcestershire

¾ cup olive oil
3 tablespoons tarragon
   vinegar
Juice of one lemon
2 tablespoons bleu cheese
   (optional)

Place all ingredients in screw-top jar. Shake well. Put on salad. Toss well. May be kept for weeks in refrigerator. Makes about 1 cup.
Mrs. John Cone (Gloria)
Mrs. R. C. Balfour, III (Virginia)

SALAD DRESSING

¼ cup vinegar
½ cup salad oil
¼ cup catsup
¼ cup sugar (less can
   be used)
Large clove garlic

1 teaspoon onion, grated
1 teaspoon prepared mustard
Salt
Curry powder
Celery seed

Mix above ingredients with wire whisk, adding salt, curry powder, and celery seed to taste. Put in jar with clove of garlic. It is better if it can be allowed to sit in refrigerator before serving. Delicious on green or fruit salad. Makes about 1¼ cups.
Mrs. William B. Turner (Sue Marie)   *Columbus, Georgia*

ZERO SALAD DRESSING

½ cup tomato juice
2 tablespoons lemon juice or
   vinegar

1 tablespoon onion, finely
   chopped
Salt and pepper

Combine ingredients in tightly capped jar. Shake well. Chopped parsley or green pepper, horseradish, or mustard may be added if desired.
Mrs. Rocky Ivey (Mickie)

Variation: V-8 juice can be used with a dash of Worcestershire sauce.

COLE SLAW DRESSING

½ cup mayonnaise
2 tablespoons sugar
1 teaspoon salt

1 teaspoon celery seed
2 tablespoons salad vinegar
1 teaspoon prepared mustard

Combine above ingredients and toss with chopped cabbage. Makes about ¾ cup.
Mrs. Langdon S. Flowers (Bobbie)

PIQUANTE DRESSING

½ cup vinegar
2 teaspoons salt
1 teaspoon sugar
½ teaspoon pepper
1 teaspoon paprika

1 teaspoon dry mustard
1½ cups salad oil
2 teaspoons prepared mustard
1 teaspoon Worcestershire
8 drops Tabasco

Combine first six ingredients. Shake well, then add last four. Shake again. Put ¼ of a cut onion in jar with dressing to season. Do not pour onion out on salad. This is particularly good on spinach or lettuce salad.
Mrs. Frederick Jefferson (Marilyn)

SAP-SAGO CHEESE DRESSING

2¾ teaspoons salt
1 teaspoon sugar
1 teaspoon dry mustard
1 teaspoon Accent
2 teaspoons oregano

1½ teaspoons garlic powder
½ teaspoon pepper
2 tablespoons Parmesan cheese
2 tablespoons Sap-Sago cheese,
  grated

Mix all ingredients together. Set aside. Combine romaine, Boston and iceberg lettuce, 2 or 3 tablespoons olive oil, and 2 tablespoons lemon juice. Mix in 1 teaspoon of the above cheese dressing and serve.
Mrs. William Luckie (Patricià J.)

MAYONNAISE

2 egg yolks
Juice of 2 lemons
½ teaspoon prepared mustard

½ teaspoon salt
Dash of red or cayenne pepper
1½ to 2 cups salad oil

Beat egg yolks until thick. Alternately add oil and other ingredients, beginning and ending with oil. Beat on speed number seven of electric mixer. If mixture separates, beat in another egg yolk.
Mrs. J. L. Turner, Jr. (Nell)

BLENDER MAYONNAISE

1 cup salad oil
1 egg
2 tablespoons lemon juice

½ teaspoon salt
½ teaspoon dry mustard

Combine all ingredients except oil in blender. Blend on medium speed 5 seconds. Steadily pour in oil while blending for 45 seconds. Makes 1 cup.
Mrs. William A. Smitha (Helen)
Similar recipes submitted by *Mrs. Rudolph Bell (Sarah) and Mrs. Robert Boissiere (Madeline)*.

SUNSHINE SALAD DRESSING

½ 6-ounce can frozen orange
  juice
¼ cup honey
2 tablespoons vinegar

¼ teaspoon salt
⅔ cup salad oil
1 tablespoon poppy seed

Combine all ingredients. Use on any fruit combinations. Makes about 1⅓ cups.
Mrs. Donald Davis (Sara)

Cheese
and
Eggs

USES OF EGGS IN COOKING

Eggs are used to thicken, as in custards and puddings; to bind, as in meat loaves; to coat, as in breaded meats; to garnish, as in soups and salads; to stabilize emulsions, as in mayonnaise; and to leaven by beating in air, as in cakes.

COOKING WITH EGGS

Whether cooking eggs on top of the range or in the oven, always use low or moderate and even heat. If cooked at too high a temperature, eggs become tough. If adding hot liquids to beaten eggs, add just a little at a time.

LEFTOVER YOLKS OR WHITES

Yolks will keep 2 to 3 days in refrigerator if placed, covered with water, in a jar with lid. Whites will keep up to 10 days in refrigerator if stored in covered jar.

PREVENTING SHELLS FROM CRACKING WHEN HARD-BOILING

Before cooking, puncture eggs with a pin at center of large end penetrating only the shell. This permits air to escape, reducing the pressure on the shell and preventing it from cracking.

NOODLES ROMANOFF

1 8-ounce package broad
  noodles
1 12-ounce carton cottage
  cheese
1 cup sour cream
¼ cup green onion, chopped
1 clove garlic, minced

1 tablespoon Worcestershire
  sauce
¼ teaspoon Tabasco
¾ teaspoon salt
Pepper
¾ cup Cheddar cheese,
  grated

Cook noodles and drain. Add remaining ingredients except grated cheese. Place in a buttered casserole, top with grated cheese. Bake 30 minutes in a preheated 350 degree oven. Serves 8-10.
Mrs. Thomas H. Vann, Jr. (Janine)

CLASSIC CHEESE FONDUE

1 clove garlic
2 tablespoons butter
2 tablespoons dry sherry or
  Kirsch
2½ tablespoons corn starch
Swiss cheese (3½ ounces per
  serving)

Gruyère cheese (3½ ounces per
  serving)
White wine (½ cup per serving)
Salt and pepper to taste
Dash nutmeg
French bread, slightly stale

Rub fondue pot with garlic. Dissolve 2½ tablespoons corn starch in ½ cup white wine. Pour into fondue pot with enough wine to make ½ cup of wine per serving. (Include the ½ cup of wine mixed with corn starch). Heat the wine on the stove, but do not boil. Cut the cheese into thin strips. (Use 7 ounces of cheese per serving, half Swiss and half Gruyère). When wine is warm, add the cheese, a handful at a time. Stir constantly. After cheese is blended and is bubbling gently, stir in seasonings, butter, and sherry or Kirsch. Serve with French bread which has been cut into bite-size pieces (each piece with one crust side). Fondue must be kept warm over a chafing dish or fondue heating unit.

Mrs. Fred Cooper (Helen)

CHEESE MOUSSE

1 tablespoon unflavored gelatin
¼ cup cold water
2 cups sour cream

1½ teaspoons Italian salad
  dressing mix
¼ cup blue cheese, crumbled
1 cup small-curd cottage cheese

Soften gelatin in cold water. Place over boiling water and stir until gelatin dissolves. Stir softened gelatin into sour cream. Add salad dressing mix, blue cheese, and cottage cheese; beat with electric or rotary beater until well-blended. Pour into 3½-cup mold. Chill several hours or until firm. Unmold and garnish with parsley and carrot curls.

Mrs. Ken Beverly (Mary Jo)

CHEESE ENCHILADAS

1 dozen corn tortillas
(frozen are best)
½ cup cooking oil
2 cups Monterey Jack or
mild Cheddar cheese,
shredded
¾ cup onion, chopped

¼ cup butter or margarine
¼ cup flour
2 cups chicken broth
1 cup dairy sour cream
1 4-ounce can jalapeño peppers,
seeded and chopped

In skillet, cook tortillas one at a time in hot oil for a few seconds, just until softened. Do not overcook or they will not roll. Place 2 tablespoons shredded cheese and 1 tablespoon chopped onion on each tortilla; roll up. Place seam side down in 11¾x7½x1¾-inch baking dish. In saucepan, melt butter and blend in flour. Add chicken broth and cook, stirring constantly, until mixture thickens and bubbles. Stir in sour cream and peppers. Cook until heated through, but do not boil. Pour over tortillas in baking dish. Bake in 425 degree oven for 20 minutes. Sprinkle remaining cheese on top. Return to oven for 5 minutes more or until cheese melts. The cheese filling makes this dish inexpensive and tasty as a main course. Serves 4-6.
Mrs. A. B. Wight, Jr. (Carolyn)

MACARONI CASSEROLE

1 8-ounce package elbow
macaroni, cooked
1 can cream of mushroom soup
1 cup mayonnaise
¼ cup onions, chopped

1 green pepper, chopped and
slightly cooked
¼ cup pimento, chopped
½ pound mild cheese, grated

Combine above ingredients and place in buttered casserole. Bake at 300 degrees for 30 minutes.
Mrs. Terrell Singletary (Nan)
Mrs. Max E. Beverly (Clara)
Mrs. Truman Chastain (Hazel)

CHEESE AND MACARONI

1 pound package of macaroni
1 stick of butter
1 pound sharp cheese, grated
1 teaspoon salt

Pepper to taste
4 small eggs, beaten
1 cup milk
½ cup cream

Boil macaroni in water until tender. Wash and drain thoroughly. Butter a casserole and layer the ingredients: macaroni, slices of butter, salt and pepper, and cheese. Make two layers. Pour the eggs combined with milk and cream over the layers. Cook at 350 degrees for 45 minutes to 1 hour or until custard is set. This can be made the day before and cooked just before serving. Serves 10.

Mrs. Thomas Malcolm McComb (Annie Laurie)
Mrs. Richard Atwell (Libby)

Variation: Chopped onion and green pepper may be added for additional flavor.
Mrs. Mervin Wine (Hettie Love)

MACARONI CHEESE DELUXE

1 7-ounce package elbow macaroni
2 cups cream-style cottage cheese
(small curd)
1 cup dairy sour cream
1 egg, slightly beaten

¾ teaspoon salt
Dash of pepper
2 cups (8-ounce package) sharp
process American cheese, shredded
Paprika

Cook macaroni according to package directions. Drain well. Combine cottage cheese, sour cream, egg, salt and pepper. Add shredded cheese, mixing well; stir in cooked macaroni. Turn into a greased 9x9x2-inch baking dish. Sprinkle top with paprika. Bake at 350 degrees for 45 minutes. Serves 6-8.
Mrs. Robert C. Brown (Frances)

SCRAMBLED EGG PIE

1 10-inch pie shell, unbaked
1½ cups Swiss cheese, grated
1 2½-ounce jar mushrooms,
   drained and sliced
12 slices bacon, fried
   and crumbled

3 eggs, beaten
1 cup whipping cream
½ cup milk
⅛ teaspoon pepper
Dash cayenne pepper

Sprinkle bottom of pie shell with cheese. Add mushrooms and then bacon. Combine other ingredients and pour into shell. Bake at 375 degrees for 45 minutes or until lightly browned and set. Serves 6-8.
Mrs. J. Howard Arnold (Margaret)

QUICHE LORRAINE I

1 9-inch pie shell,
   partially baked (about 8
   minutes at 350 degrees)
8 pieces of bacon.
   cooked and crumbled
3 eggs
½ pint heavy cream

1 pound cheese, grated
   (Gruyère or imported Swiss,
   or mixture of both)
2 onions, (or 1 package raw frozen),
   chopped and sautéed in butter
   until soft and golden

Sprinkle bacon in shell. Add onions and cheese. Whip eggs with cream and pour over cheese mixture. Bake at 325 degrees for 1 hour. Serves 6.
Mrs. James Evans (Margaret)

Variation: ¼ to ½ cup chopped ham may be substituted for bacon.
Mrs. Len Powell (Mary)
Mrs. William Young (Ruth)

QUICHE LORRAINE II

9-inch pie shell
6 rashers bacon
¾ cup Gruyère cheese,
   shredded
Pinch nutmeg

5 eggs
1½ cups light cream
Salt to taste
Fresh parsley, chopped

Bake pie shell at 425 degrees for 8-10 minutes with foil and rice in shell to keep it from puffing. Cook bacon, but not to crisp stage. Cut in pieces and arrange in cooked shell. Add cheese and nutmeg. Beat eggs and cream together lightly, season to taste and add parsley. Bake at 375 degrees until set and a knife comes out clean when inserted 1½ inches from center (about 30 minutes). Serve warm, in wedges. Serves 8 from a 9-inch quiche dish.
Mrs. Charles H. Watt, III (Jan)

MODIFIED QUICHE LORRAINE

½ cup mayonnaise
2 tablespoons flour
4 eggs, beaten
½ cup milk
4 ounces sharp Cheddar cheese, grated

4 ounces Swiss cheese, grated
½ pound bacon, cooked and crumbled
9-inch pastry shell, unbaked

Combine the mayonnaise, flour, eggs, and milk. Add the cheeses and bacon. Bake mixture in pie shell, 40-45 minutes at 350 degrees.
Mrs. Tom Lear (Ann)

CHICKEN QUICHE AMANDINE

1 9-inch pie shell, unbaked
¾ cup of chicken, cooked and diced
3 tablespoons almonds, sliced
1½ cups (6 ounces) Swiss cheese, shredded
3 eggs

½ teaspoon salt
1½ cups milk
¼ teaspoon mace
⅛ teaspoon pepper
2 tablespoons Parmesan cheese, grated

Place chicken and almonds in pie shell; then Swiss cheese. Beat eggs slightly in a medium bowl. Blend in milk, salt, mace and pepper. Pour over cheese. Sprinkle on Parmesan cheese. Bake in a preheated 375 degree oven for 30-35 minutes or until a knife inserted near the center comes out clean. Allow to stand 10 minutes before serving. Serves 6.
Mrs. Emily T. Davies   *Shelbyville, Tennessee*

CHEESE SOUFFLÉ

Rush any soufflé to the table the minute it is done, especially if you bake it the French way, crusty outside but very soft and creamy within.

4 tablespoons butter
2 tablespoons flour
1 cup milk, scalded
½ teaspoon salt

Few grains cayenne
½ to 1 cup cheese, grated
4 egg yolks, beaten very lightly
4 egg whites, beaten stiffly

Melt butter and stir in flour. Add milk gradually and stir until thick and smooth. Add salt, cayenne, and cheese. Stir until smooth. Remove from heat. Add yolks. Cool. Cut and fold in whites. Pour into buttered baking dish or ramekins. Set in pan of hot water. For a firm soufflé, bake 30 to 45 minutes at 325 degrees. For a creamy soufflé, bake 20 minutes at 375 degrees. Serves 4.
The Editors

MOCK CHEESE SOUFFLÉ

9 slices white bread,
   crusts removed
1 pound, medium sharp
   Cheddar cheese
1½ teaspoons salt

2 teaspoons mustard
1 teaspoon Worcestershire sauce
¼ teaspoon garlic powder
6 eggs
3¾ cups milk

Butter large casserole. Butter one side of bread and line casserole. Add grated cheese seasoned with salt, mustard and garlic powder to casserole. Beat eggs and milk together and pour over cheese. Let stand at least 8 hours in refrigerator. It is better if done the night before. Take out 1 hour before baking. Bake in a pan of water 1 hour and 15 minutes at 350 degrees. Serves 6.
Mrs. Randy Malone (Mary)
Similar recipes submitted by *Mrs. Sydney Fleming (Mable), Mrs. Harry L. Hershey (Patti), Mrs. Elliot McCollum (Lorna), and Mrs. Hull Searcy (Anne).*

GARLIC GRITS

1 cup grits
½ pound butter or margarine
1 roll garlic cheese

2 eggs
½ cup milk
Cornflake crumbs

Cook grits until thick and a little dry. Melt cheese and butter. Beat eggs and add milk. Add to cheese and butter. Add all to cooked grits. Put in greased casserole and cover with cornflake crumbs. Dot with butter. Bake at 350 degrees for 45 minutes. Good with ham or other meat.
Mrs. H. D. Adams (Martha)
Similiar recipes submitted by *Mrs. Max E. Beverly (Clara), Mrs. Al Lookabough (Diana), and Mrs. Lloyd Edkberg (Maxine).*

BAKED GRITS AND CHEESE CASSEROLE

6 cups boiling water
1½ cups grits
3 eggs
3 teaspoons savory salt
2 teaspoons salt

1 teaspoon paprika
Dash of Tabasco
1 pound sharp cheese, grated
1 stick butter or margarine

Stir grits into boiling water, stirring constantly until completely mixed. Cook until thickened. Add seasonings and mix thoroughly. Beat eggs slightly and add a small amount of hot grits to eggs, stirring constantly to prevent coagulation of eggs. Add remaining grits gradually. Add cheese and butter and mix well. Pour into a buttered casserole; bake at 350 degrees for 45 minutes. Serves 6.
Mrs. Paul Bryan (Barbara)

WELSH RAREBIT

4 tablespoons butter
2 pounds sharp Cheddar cheese
1 cup light beer
2 eggs

1 teaspoon salt
1 teaspoon dry mustard
Dash cayenne
2 teaspoons Worcestershire sauce

In medium saucepan slowly heat butter. Add cheese and beer. Cook over low heat, stirring frequently until cheese melts. Remove from heat. In small bowl, beat eggs with salt, mustard, cayenne and Worcestershire; gradually add to cheese mixture. Stir over low heat until mixture is heated through and is smooth, about 5 minutes. Serve over toast. To keep rarebit warm, turn into top part of double boiler; let stand over hot water until ready to serve.
Mrs. T. R. Sample (Nell)

FLORENTINE OMELET

1 cup medium white sauce,
   seasoned
¼ teaspoon Tabasco
¼ teaspoon salt

½ cup spinach, cooked and chopped
⅓ cup Parmesan cheese
1 fluffy omelet (See Omelets)

Heat the white sauce. Stir in the salt and Tabasco. Add ½ cup well-drained spinach. Add ⅓ cup Parmesan cheese. Continue heating until the sauce is hot. Serve inside the fluffy omelet.
Mrs. Thomas H. Vann, Jr. (Janine)

FLUFFY OMELET

½ teaspoon salt
¼ cup water
4 eggs, separated

⅛ teaspoon pepper
1 tablespoon butter or margarine

Add salt and water to egg whites. Beat until stiff and shiny. Add pepper to yolks and beat until thick and lemon-colored. Fold yolks into egg whites. Meanwhile, heat butter in a large 10-inch skillet until just hot enough to sizzle a drop of water. Pour in omelet mixture. Reduce heat. Level surface gently. Cook slowly until lightly browned on bottom, about 5 minutes. Lift omelet at edge with spatula to judge color. Place in preheated 325 degree oven. Bake until knife inserted into center comes out clean, about 10 to 15 minutes. Fold omelet in half to serve. Serves 2 to 3.
Mrs. Fred Cooper (Helen)

CREAMED EGGS

8 slices bacon
1 dozen eggs, hard boiled
Large can sliced mushrooms
Butter
Salt and pepper to taste

2 tablespoons butter
2 tablespoons flour
1½ cups milk
½ cup sharp American cheese, grated

Fry bacon slices until crisp and crumble. Peel the eggs, cut in half lengthwise and remove the yolks. Sauté the mushrooms in butter. To this add the egg yolks. Be sure to use enough butter to make soft. Season with salt and pepper. Put stuffing in egg whites and put halves together making a whole egg. Arrange the eggs in layers in buttered casserole. Make a cream sauce by melting the 2 tablespoons butter. Add the flour, stirring with wire whisk. Remove from heat and gradually whisk in the milk. Return to heat and stir until sauce begins to thicken. Add ½ cup sharp American cheese. Stir until melted. Pour sauce over eggs and bake in a 350 degree oven until steaming hot. Just before serving put crumbled bacon all over the top. Serves 6.
Mrs. Heywood Mason (Edie)

EGG AND ARTICHOKE CASSEROLE

1 bunch green onions
2 6½-ounce jars marinated
    artichoke hearts
8 ounces medium Cheddar, grated

1 clove garlic
4 eggs, beaten
6 crackers, rolled

Finely mince onions using half of the tops. Cut artichokes in thirds and reserve oil. Sauté onions and garlic in the artichoke oil. Combine all ingredients. Bake in a greased 9 x 9-inch pyrex dish at 350 degree for 40 minutes. Serves 4 as a main dish. May be prepared a day ahead and refrigerated. Bring to room temperature and warm for about 15 to 20 minutes in a 350 degree oven.
The Editors

EGGS STUFFED WITH BACON

12 eggs, hard-boiled
6 slices bacon
3 tablespoons chives, chopped
2 tablespoons butter, softened

1½ tablespoons vinegar
Dollop of sour cream
Salt
Pepper

Cut hard-boiled eggs in half lengthwise. Fry bacon until crisp and chop finely. Mash egg yolks and mix in chives, butter, vinegar, sour cream, salt and pepper. Fill egg whites and chill.
Mrs. Heywood Mason (Edie)

EGGS BENEDICT

1 English muffin, split and
toasted
2 large thin slices ham,
grilled

2 eggs, soft poached
¾ cup Blender Hollandaise
Sauce (See Sauces)

Cover buttered muffin with ham, then eggs, then sauce. Garnish with sprig of parsley. Serve immediately. 1 Serving.
Mrs. Fred Cooper (Helen)

Seafood

SHRIMP DE JONGHE
Great for a ladies luncheon. Men like it too!

2 pounds shrimp, cleaned
and cooked
¾ cup butter or margarine
⅛ teaspoon garlic salt
¼ teaspoon pepper
¼ teaspoon minced parsley or
diced parsley flakes

½ teaspoon onion, minced
¾ cup sherry or consommé
1 cup Pepperidge Farm stuffing or
dry bread cumbs

Place shrimp in 8 individual baking dishes. Heat together the butter, garlic salt, parsley, pepper, onion, and sherry or consommé. Remove ¼ cup of the butter mixture and toss with the stuffing or bread crumbs. Pour remaining butter mixture over shrimp, dividing equally. Top with buttered crumbs. Place baking dishes in large, shallow pan containing ½ inch of water. Bake in 400 degree oven for 15 minutes. May be prepared ahead.
Mrs. Langdon S. Flowers (Bobbie)

SHRIMP ELEGANTE

2 tablespoons onions, minced
2 tablespoons butter
1 pound fresh or frozen
shrimp, cleaned
¼ pound mushrooms, sliced
1 teaspoon salt
⅓ teaspoon pepper

3 tablespoons chili sauce
1 ⅔ cups water
1 ⅓ cups Minute Rice
1 cup sour cream
1 tablespoon flour
1 tablespoon chives or parsley,
chopped

Sauté onion in butter. Add shrimp and mushrooms. Sauté until shrimp are pink. Combine salt, pepper, chili sauce and water. Add to shrimp and bring to a boil. Stir in Minute Rice. Cover and simmer 5 minutes. Combine sour cream and flour. Add to shrimp mixture and heat gently. Sprinkle with chives. Serves 4.
Mrs. Elliott McCollum (Lorna)

SHRIMP CURRY

1 can consommé	½ teaspoon curry powder
1 teaspoon lemon juice	½ cup coffee cream
2 tablespoons flour	Few drops of Tabasco
Dash of garlic salt	Dash of red pepper
Salt to taste	1½ pounds shrimp, cooked

Make sauce of consommé and other ingredients. Add shrimp and serve over rice with following condiments: crisp bacon, chopped olives, chopped peanuts, chutney, and chopped onions.
Mrs. William B. Turner (Sue Marie)   *Columbus, Georgia*

SHRIMP IN SOUR CREAM

1½-2 pounds shrimp, peeled	1 teaspoon salt
½ cup onion, minced	1 8-ounce can tomato sauce
½ cup butter, melted	Freshly ground black pepper
½-1 pound mushrooms, sliced	⅔ cup sour cream
2 tablespoons flour	¼ cup sherry (optional)

Sauté shrimp with onions in butter for 5 minutes or until shrimp are pink. Add mushrooms and cook 5 minutes longer. Blend in flour, salt and pepper. Add tomato sauce and sour cream gradually; cook until thick, stirring constantly. Remove from heat and stir in sherry. Serves 6.
Mrs. Marrs Cooper (Jeanette))

SHRIMP FOR CHAFING DISH

½ cup butter	3 tablespoons cornstarch
½ cup vinegar	3 pounds shrimp
1 cup water	2 tablespoons soy sauce
½ teaspoon pepper	2 bay leaves
½ teaspoon salt	2 whole cloves
2 cups bell pepper, cut	Pineapple juice (from 32-ounce
into 1-inch squares	can of pineapple chunks)

Brown shrimp in butter. Season with salt and pepper. Add vinegar, soy sauce, water, bay leaves and whole cloves. Cover and simmer for 20 minutes. In another container mix cornstarch with pineapple juice. Bring to boil, stirring constantly. Stir into shrimp mixture. Cook until sauce is thick and clear (about 5 minutes). Add more cornstarch, thinned in cold water, if necessary. Add pineapple chunks and two cups bell pepper. Place in chafing dish and eat with toothpicks.
Mrs. Ames Watkins Kindred

SHRIMP TETRAZZINI

3 tablespoons margarine or
    butter
1 small onion, grated
⅓ green sweet pepper
1 pound fresh mushrooms,
    sliced
1 10½-ounce can condensed tomato
    soup diluted with 1 18-ounce can
    tomato juice

1 pound boiled shrimp
1 8-ounce package spaghetti,
    cooked
1 8-ounce package sharp
    cheese spread
Salt and white pepper to taste

Melt butter or margarine; sauté onion, green pepper and mushrooms and cook five minutes. Stir in tomato juice and tomato soup, shrimp, cooked spaghetti, and three-fourths of the cheese spread; season to taste. Pour into a greased 13 x 9 x 2-inch casserole and dot with remaining cheese spread. Bake in a 350 degree oven for 30 to 45 minutes, or until thoroughly heated and light brown. Serves 8.
Mrs. J. H. Frohbert (Julia)

SHRIMP FLORIDAN

2 pounds shrimp, cooked and
    cleaned
8 ounces cream cheese
8 ounces sour cream
4 ounces blue cheese
2 tablespoons garlic, finely
    chopped

4 tablespoons parsley,
    finely chopped
½ cup dry white wine
1 lemon, sliced very thin on
    the round
6 potatoes, baked

Blend together the cheeses and sour cream being careful to get a smooth and even mixture. Add garlic and parsley and mix well. Add wine, adding less or more to keep mixture from being too thin. Place shrimp in baking dish and top with sauce and lemon slices. Cover and bake at 300-325 degrees for 15 minutes or until lemon slices are tender. Do not let mixture boil. Slice hot baked potatoes into fourths. Spoon the shrimp mixture over potatoes; top with slices of lemon. Garnish with parsley and paprika. Serves 6.
Mrs. Julian Neel (Phoebe)

"FINGER-LICKIN' GOOD" SHRIMP

5 pounds raw unshelled
   shrimp, washed
1 stick butter, melted
Generous amount ground black
   pepper (up to 2 ounces)
Juice of 2 lemons

Vegetable oil
Vinegar
Water
2 packages Good Seasons'
   Italian Dressing Mix

Use the oil, vinegar and water to make the dressing according to directions on back of packages. Combine the butter, pepper, lemon juice and dressing. Pour sauce over the shrimp in a large ovenproof casserole. Cover casserole and bake in 350 degree oven for 1 hour. Serve shrimp and plenty of sauce in soup bowls. Hot French bread and a salad are all you need. Everyone shells his own shrimp and dips the French bread into the sauce. You'll need large napkins. It's messy, but oh so good! Serves 8.
Mrs. Thomas H. Vann, Jr. (Janine)

SHRIMP AND ARTICHOKE BAKE

1 pound fresh shrimp,
   cleaned and cooked
2 14-ounce cans artichoke hearts
½ cup butter
½ cup flour

1½ cups milk
½ cup dry wine
6 ounces Gruyère cheese, grated
¼ teaspoon salt
¼ teaspoon pepper

Melt butter; stir in flour. Remove from heat to add milk and wine. Then cook until it comes to a boil. Stir in cheese and salt and pepper; cook until cheese melts. Remove from heat. Arrange drained artichoke hearts around the edge of a 9-inch baking dish. Place shrimp in center and pour sauce over all. Sprinkle with dill or paprika. Bake in 350 degree oven for 25 minutes. Serves 4 or 5.
Mrs. W. W. Alexander (Elise)
Similar recipe submitted by *Mrs. William Norwood (Deane).*

SHRIMP WILD RICE CASSEROLE

½ cup onion, thinly sliced
¼ cup green pepper, thinly
  sliced (optional)
½ pound mushrooms, sliced
1 stick butter
1 tablespoon Worcestershire
  sauce
4 drops Tabasco

4 drops Tabasco
1 package Uncle Ben's Wild Rice
  and Herbs, cooked
1½ pounds shrimp, cooked
2 cups thin cream sauce (made
  with chicken broth instead of
  milk)

Sauté onion, pepper, and mushrooms in butter. Add seasonings. Add shrimp, rice, and sauce. Place in casserole and bake 30-45 minutes at 300 degrees. Serves 6.
Mrs. Ken Beverly (Mary Jo)

SHRIMP CREOLE

2 pounds medium-size shrimp
⅓ cup olive oil
3 cloves garlic, peeled and
  chopped
2 onions, peeled and chopped
3 pounds ripe tomatoes, chopped
2 green peppers, chopped

3 ribs celery, chopped
1 carrot, washed and chopped
1 teaspoon dried thyme
2 or 3 stalks parsley
1 cup dry white wine
½ cup tomato purée
Salt and pepper to taste

Shell and devein the shrimp and set aside. Heat the olive oil in a large, heavy casserole. Add the garlic and onion. Brown lightly, then add all remaining ingredients except the shrimp, tomato purée, and salt and pepper. Bring to a boil. Cover and reduce heat to simmer and cook for one hour. Strain through a sieve lined with several layers of dampened cheesecloth. Pour back into the casserole and stir in the tomato purée. Season to taste with salt and pepper. Bring to a boil over good heat. Add the shrimp and cook for exactly three minutes. Serves 6.
The Editors

PICKLED SHRIMP

2 to 2½ pounds raw shrimp
15 to 20 whole allspice
6 to 8 peppercorns
6 buds garlic, sliced
2 large stalks celery, thinly
 sliced
2 pinches dried thyme
Red pepper to taste
4 medium onions, thinly sliced

⅛ teaspoon black pepper
Juice of ½ lemon and rind
15 to 20 cloves
3 small onions, sliced
2 large bay leaves
Several sprigs parsley
1 tablespoon Worcestershire
Box of bay leaves

Season 2½ quarts water with 3 tablespoons salt; then add all ingredients except shrimp, 4 onions and box of bay leaves. Boil and simmer 20 minutes. Add shrimp, bring to a boil and simmer 12-15 minutes. Cool shrimp. In large pan arrange shrimp in layers with 4 onions. Then bay leaves. Pour sauce over each layer.

SAUCE:

1¼ cups salad oil
¾ cup white vinegar, warmed
1½ teaspoons salt
2½ teaspoons celery seed
1 tablespoon yellow mustard

2½ tablespoons capers and
 juice
Dash hot sauce
¼ cup Worcestershire sauce

Cover pan and store in refrigerator not less than 24 hours.
Mrs. Jasper Davis (Marthalene)
Mrs. Lewis Hall Singletary (Mildred)

QUICHE LOUISIANA

1 9-inch pie shell, unbaked
1 cup shrimp, cleaned and split
1 tablespoon butter, softened
4 eggs
2 cups heavy cream
¾ teaspoon salt

Pinch nutmeg, sugar, and
 cayenne pepper
⅛ teaspoon pepper
¼ pound Swiss cheese, grated
2 tablespoons chili sauce
Dash Tabasco

Rub butter over surface of unbaked shell. Combine eggs, cream, salt, sugar, nutmeg, cayenne, and pepper. Beat just long enough to mix well. Sprinkle pie shell with cheese. Toss the shrimp with the chili sauce and Tabasco. Place over cheese. Pour in cream mixture. Bake at 425 degrees for 15 minutes. Reduce heat to 300 degrees and bake 40 minutes or until knife inserted in center comes out clean.
Mrs. T. R. Sample (Nell)

BROILED SHRIMP

2 pounds of large shrimp,
   peeled but with tail on
1 pound bacon
1 cup butter
¼ cup white wine

¼ cup lemon juice
1 teaspoon Worcestershire sauce
1 clove garlic, minced
1 teaspoon parsley, chopped
½ teaspoon salt

Combine all ingredients except bacon and shrimp. Simmer until well mixed. Wrap ⅓ piece of bacon around each shrimp and secure with a toothpick. Broil 5 minutes per side and brush often with the sauce. Serves 6-8.
Mrs. Scott Rich (Peggy)

CHINESE WOK-FRIED SHRIMP

18-24 large shrimp
Pinch of salt
2 tablespoons sherry
1½ cups instant-blending
   flour

1 tablespoon baking powder
½ teaspoon salt
½ cup peanut oil
1 cup ice water
Pinch salt

Remove shells from shrimp, but leave the tail intact. Devein. Mix sherry and salt and toss with shrimp. Put aside while preparing batter. Mix dry ingredients. Add oil slowly while beating mixture thoroughly. When dough forms a lump, add water, a little at a time, until batter is consistency of light cream. Heat oil for frying in wok. Take shrimp by tail and coat with batter. The tail should not be battered. Drop in hot oil and fry until golden brown and puffy. Serve at once. Serves 4.
Mrs. James Carico (Helen)

HAWAIIAN FRIED SHRIMP

2 pounds of shrimp, cleaned
   and butterflied
5 eggs
3 cups milk
1 cup pineapple juice
1 teaspoon salt

1 tablespoon sugar
1 teaspoon baking powder
½ teaspoon ginger
2 cups flour
Shredded coconut

Beat well the eggs, milk, pineapple juice, salt, sugar, baking powder, and ginger. Gradually add 2 cups flour until well blended. Dip the shrimp into the batter then into the shredded coconut. Fry in deep hot fat (375 degrees) for 3 minutes. Serves 6.
Mrs. Scott Rich (Peggy)

SHRIMP CASSEROLE

2 pounds shrimp, cooked
1 8-ounce can sliced mushrooms
or ½ pound fresh mushrooms,
sliced
4 tablespoons butter or margarine

2½ cups rice, cooked
2½ cups cheese, grated (save
½ cup for topping)

TOPPING:

1 cup coffee cream
½ cup catsup
½ cup sherry

1 teaspoon Worcestershire
Salt and pepper to taste
½ cup almonds, slivered

Sauté mushrooms in butter. Blend in catsup, cream and Worcestershire. Mix rice, cheese, shrimp, almonds, salt and pepper. Combine both mixtures and add sherry. Bake in a 2-quart casserole covered with foil for 30 minutes at 350 degrees. Serves 8. (May be prepared ahead of time.)
Miss Josephine Craig
Similar recipe submitted by *Mrs. Eugene Driver (Carol).*

BAKED SHRIMP SHELLS

1½ pounds shrimp, cooked and
split
2 tablespoons butter
¼ cup green onion, chopped
1 clove garlic, crushed

¼ cup all-purpose flour
½ teaspoon salt
1½ cups half and half cream
½ cup white wine

TOPPING:

¼ cup bread crumbs
2 tablespoons Parmesan cheese
2 tablespoons parsley, chopped

¼ teaspoon paprika
1½ tablespoons butter, melted

Sauté onions and garlic in butter. Add flour and salt. Remove from heat and add cream. Return to heat; bring to a boil and boil 1 minute, stirring constantly. Add shrimp and wine. Fill scallop shells or ramekins. To prepare topping, combine crumbs, cheese, parsley, paprika and melted butter. Sprinkle on filled shells. Bake 15 to 20 minutes at 350 degrees. Serves 6.
Miss Josephine Craig

CRAB-SHRIMP CASSEROLE

4½ cups soft bread crumbs
4 hard-boiled eggs, sliced
½ teaspoon salt
⅛ teaspoon pepper
1 pound shrimp, cooked
1 can crabmeat
1 4-ounce can mushrooms,
    drained

2 tablespoons pimento, diced
1½ teaspoons onion salt
2 teaspoons dried parsley
1 can cream of chicken soup
1 cup half and half cream
½ cup mayonnaise
2 tablespoons butter
Paprika

Combine 4 cups bread crumbs, eggs, salt, pepper, shrimp, crab, mushrooms, pimento, onion salt, and parsley. Mix lightly; pour into large buttered baking dish. Mix soup, cream, and mayonnaise, blending well. Pour over fish mixture. Mix ½ cup bread crumbs and butter; sprinkle over casserole. Sprinkle with paprika. Bake 30 minutes at 325 degrees. Makes 10 servings.
Mrs. E. C. Oliver, Jr. (Jerreann)

SHRIMP AND CRABMEAT SOUFFLÉ

1 pound crabmeat and shrimp
4 eggs
1 cup celery, chopped
1 cup sharp cheese, grated

1½ cups mayonnaise
Salt and pepper to taste
1½ teaspoons Worcestershire
    sauce
3 tablespoons sherry

Beat eggs until frothy. Add crabmeat and other ingredients. Put in casserole. Place buttered bread crumbs on top and bake at 325 degrees until knife comes out clean.
Mrs. Lewis Hall Singletary (Mildred)

DEVILED CRAB I

1 pound crabmeat	1 teaspoon salt
8 hard-boiled eggs	1 teaspoon Worcestershire sauce
1 stick butter, melted	Dash Tabasco sauce
1 teaspoon mustard	Paprika
1 teaspoon lemon juice	Cracker crumbs
1 tablespoon vinegar	Parmesan cheese (optional)

Mash egg yolks. Chop whites to fine consistency. Add seasonings to yolks and blend well. Add ½ butter. Combine yolk mixture with whites and crabmeat. Put mixture into 6-8 buttered shells; do not pack. Sprinkle each shell with cracker crumbs and pour remaining half of butter on top. Dust with paprika. Grated Parmesan cheese may be added if desired. Bake 20 minutes at 400 degrees.
Mrs. Lloyd Megahee (Frances)

DEVILED CRAB II

2 cups crabmeat	Salt and pepper to taste
2 cups tomatoes, cut up	1 bell pepper, chopped
3 eggs, beaten	2 pieces celery, chopped
2 lemons, squeezed	1 medium onion, chopped
1 bay leaf	1 button garlic, chopped
2 tablespoons catsup	3-4 tablespoons butter
1 tablespoon Worcestershire sauce	Cracker crumbs
½ dozen shakes of Tabasco	

Sauté pepper, celery, onion, and garlic in butter until tender, not brown. Mix crab, tomatoes, lemon juice, catsup, Worcestershire sauce, Tabasco, and sautéed mixture. Add beaten eggs and mix well. Add enough cracker crumbs to this mixture to make it the consistency of chicken salad, but not too dry. Put this mixture into a buttered casserole or crab shells, sprinkle with cracker crumbs and dot with butter. Bake at 325 degrees until top is golden brown and mixture bubbles. Grated cheese can be used in mixture. Serves 4-6.
Mrs. Marx Gaines (Claire)

CRAB CAKES I

1 pound crabmeat (or any boned fish available)	1 egg, slightly beaten
2 tablespoons mayonnaise	¼ cup hush puppy mix
½ teaspoon dry mustard	Salt and pepper to taste

Mix above ingredients and form into patties. Brown in oil. Serves 4.
Mrs. Paul Hjort (Frances)

CRAB CAKES II

6 tablespoons butter
1½ cups onions, diced
3 eggs, beaten
2 teaspoons dry mustard
½ teaspoon salt

¼ teaspoon pepper
1½ cups bread crumbs
1½ cups mayonnaise
3 pounds crabmeat

In melted butter sauté onions slightly. Add to other ingredients and mix well. Form 12 patties. Brown in butter in large skillet. Serves 6.
Mrs. Charles B. Hitchcock (Anita)

CRABMEAT AU GRATIN

2 tablespoons butter
6 tablespoons flour
3 tablespoons Italian cheese
    (Parmesan or Romano),
    grated
2 cups coffee cream, heated

½ cup milk
1 pound crabmeat
2 tablespoons sherry
Italian cheese

Melt butter and stir in flour and 3 tablespoons of Italian cheese. Add cream and milk and blend well. Stir until thickened. Add crabmeat and remove from heat. Pour into buttered casserole and pour wine over. Sprinkle generously with Italian cheese. Brown under broiler. Serves 6.
Miss Ophelia Smith

IMPERIAL CRAB

1 pound crabmeat
1 medium onion, chopped
¼ cup green pepper, chopped
¼ cup margarine
3 tablespoons flour

1 cup milk
¼ teaspoon salt
½ teaspoon prepared mustard
1 teaspoon Worcestershire
Dash of pepper and Tabasco

Clean crab and leave in chunks. Cook onion and pepper in margarine until tender. Stir in flour, then gradually add milk and cook until smooth and thick. Add seasonings and crabmeat. Place in a greased baking dish. Bake at 350 degrees for 30 minutes. Serves 6.
Miss Ophelia Smith
Similar recipes submitted by *Mrs. John L. Turner, Sr. (Nell), and Mrs. Delmar Conner (Mary).*

Variation: The addition of 4 ounces of grated sharp Cheddar cheese enriches
    the flavor.
Mrs. Len Powell (Mary)

BAKED FISH

Filet of fish
1 part lemon juice
1 part A.1. Sauce

1 part butter
Paprika

Dredge fish in above melted ingredients. Bake 20 minutes in 350 degree oven. Sprinkle heavily with paprika and return to oven for 5 more minutes.
Mrs. Lewis Hall Singletary (Mildred)

STUFFED FLOUNDER OR SNAPPER

1½-pound flounder or snapper,
  cleaned and boned
1 cup crab
2 shallots, chopped
½ teaspoon parsley, chopped
1 tablespoon green pepper,
  chopped
½ teaspoon Worcestershire sauce

Salt and pepper to taste
1 teaspoon Parmesan cheese,
  grated
1 egg yolk
½ cup cream
⅛ teaspoon each anisette
  and Pernod (optional)

Combine crab, shallots, parsley, pepper, Worcestershire, salt and pepper, and Parmesan cheese. Beat egg yolk with cream and add to mixture. Stir in anisette and Pernod and mix well. Stuff center cavity of flounder with this mixture and bake at 350 degrees about 25 minutes, basting with butter. Serve hot with a wedge of lemon. Serves 1-2.
The Editors

TROUT WITH GRAPEFRUIT SAUCE

4 whole trout
¼ cup butter or margarine
¼ cup slivered almonds

2 tablespoons parsley,
  chopped
1 tablespoon frozen grapefruit
  juice concentrate, thawed and
  undiluted

Sprinkle trout on both sides with salt. Place on baking sheet lined with greased foil. Brush fish with oil or melted butter. Bake in 450 degree oven about 10 minutes until fish flakes easily with a fork. Combine butter, almonds, undiluted grapefruit juice and parsley in saucepan. Heat and pour over fish. Garnish with grapefruit sections and sprigs of parsley. Serves 4.
Mrs. Lewis Hall Singletary (Mildred)

CLAIRE VARNEDOE'S CREOLE OYSTERS

1 pint oysters, washed	½ teaspoon Tabasco sauce
⅓ pound of butter	1 tablespoon Worcestershire
3 tablespoons tender green	sauce
onions, chopped	¼ pound of bacon
3 tablespoons parsley, minced	About 1-2 cups bread crumbs

Wash and drain 1 pint oysters. Make a paste of the butter, onions, parsley, Tabasco sauce, and Worcestershire. Put a layer of oysters in baking dish and coat with paste. Fry the bacon until crisp; crumble and sprinkle on top of paste. Sauté bread crumbs in bacon drippings until toasted. Sprinkle on next layer. Repeat until all oysters are used ending with bread crumbs. Bake 450 degrees for 20 minutes. Use as a casserole or serve on rounds. Serves 6.
Mrs. Breck Conoley (Lee Ila)

OYSTERS NORFOLK

1 pint large oysters	2 teaspoons butter
4 thin slices country-cured ham	Salt and pepper to taste
4 squares of muffin bread	
(2-inch squares)	

In butter in saucepan curl oysters that have been washed and drained. Add salt and pepper. Top muffin bread with 1 slice of ham. Pour oysters and liquid over ham. Serves 4.
Mrs. Jasper Davis (Marthalene)

SCALLOPED OYSTERS

Butter	Worcestershire sauce
Fresh oysters	Whipping cream
Salt	Crackers
Pepper	Sharp cheese

Butter casserole slightly. Cover bottom with medium-size fresh oysters and some of their juice. Season with salt, pepper, Worcestershire and dots of butter. Add whipping cream, being careful not to get mixture too soupy. Add a generous layer of cracker crumbs. Cover all with grated sharp cheese. Heat in 325-350 degree oven until bubbly. Quantities of ingredients depend on how many are to be served.
Mrs. Paul McCollum (Nancy)
Similar recipe submitted by *Mrs. John L. Turner, Jr. (Lucille)*.

TUNA HAWAIIAN

2 tablespoons butter
1 cup onion, thinly sliced
1 large green pepper, diced
1 cup celery, sliced
1 13½-ounce can pineapple
   chunks
2 tablespoons cornstarch

1 13¼-ounce can chicken broth
2 teaspoons soy sauce
½ teaspoon salt
2 7-ounce cans tuna,
   drained
½ cup water chestnuts,
   sliced

Heat butter in large skillet. Cook onion, celery, and pepper until just soft. Drain pineapple and reserve juice. Combine juice with cornstarch, chicken broth, soy sauce and salt. Pour into skillet. Cook over medium heat until thick. Add tuna, chestnuts, and pineapple. Cover, heat until bubbly. Serve over chow mein noodles or rice. Serves 6.
Mrs. Charles Ferguson (Jean)

TUNA-CASHEW CASSEROLE

2 tablespoons butter
2 tablespoons onion,
   finely chopped
2 tablespoons flour
2 cups milk
2½ tablespoons soy sauce
1 5½-ounce can chow mein
   noodles

½ teaspoon garlic powder
Dash of Tabasco
2 7-ounce cans tuna,
   drained and flaked
¼ pound cashews
1 cup celery,
   finely chopped

Melt butter over low heat. Add onion, browning lightly. Add flour, stirring until well blended. Gradually add milk, cooking over low heat and stirring constantly until thickened. Add the remaining ingredients except noodles. Turn into a 2-quart casserole and bake at 375 degrees for 20-25 minutes until bubbling. Top with crisp chow mein noodles and serve. Makes 6 servings.
Mrs. William M. Searcy, Jr. (Emily)
Similar recipe submitted by *Mrs. Harry T. Jones (Celetta)*.

GRILLED SCALLOPS
Unusual dish but really delicious.

About 1 pound scallops
½ cup sour cream
2 tablespoons prepared
   mustard

Dash Worcestershire sauce
Bread crumbs
Wesson Oil

Mix together sour cream, mustard, and Worcestershire sauce. Dip scallops in sour cream mixture, then in bread crumbs, and thread on skewers. (May be cooked with tomatoes, green pepper, mushrooms, etc.) Brush skewers with Wesson Oil and grill on barbecue grill for about 9-11 minutes. Serve with accompanying sauce.

SAUCE:

½ cup sour cream
1 teaspoon dry mustard

Horseradish sauce to
   taste

Mix all together and chill until ready to serve. Serves 4.
Mrs. Lee Mayfield (Patricia)   *Covington, Georgia*

SALMON MOUSSE

2 16-ounce cans salmon
1 cup heavy cream
6 eggs
2 tablespoons green onion,
   chopped

1 tablespoon parsley,
   chopped
½ teaspoon salt
¼ teaspoon pepper

In large bowl, stir salmon, cream, eggs, onion, parsley, and salt and pepper until well mixed. In covered blender container at low speed, blend one half of salmon mixture at a time until smooth. Pour into well-greased, 6-cup ring mold. Set mold in large roasting pan and place on oven rack. Fill pan halfway with boiling water. Bake 1 hour at 400 degrees or until knife inserted in center of mousse comes out clean. Remove from pan of water; let stand on rack 20 minutes. Then carefully loosen edges of mousse with narrow spatula. Invert onto platter. Serve with Hollandaise Sauce (see index). Serves 8.
Mrs. A. B. Wight, Jr. (Carolyn)

SEAFOOD ROCKEFELLER

1 cup shallots, chopped
½ cup parsley, chopped
1½ cups spinach, chopped
½ cup flour
1 cup butter, melted
1 cup water (oyster water
    if available)

2 cloves garlic, minced
½ teaspoon salt
¼ teaspoon cayenne
¼ cup anchovies, minced
4 ounces absinthe (optional)

Make sauce by putting shallots, parsley and spinach through food chopper or blender. Stir flour into melted butter and cook 5 minutes; do not brown. Blend in oyster water, garlic, salt and cayenne. Stir in chopped greens and anchovies. Simmer, covered, 20 minutes. Remove cover, stir in absinthe and cook until thickened. Fill individual dishes or casseroles with oysters, shrimp (cooked) or crab. Cover the seafood with the Rockefeller sauce. Bake in preheated 400 degree oven on bed of rock salt for about 5 minutes. Makes enough sauce for 8-12 servings. Sauce freezes well.
The Editors

SEAFOOD MORNAY

Shrimp, crab or fish, cooked
2 tablespoons butter
2 tablespoons flour
4 tablespoons Gruyère cheese,
    grated
6 tablespoons Parmesan cheese,
    grated

1½ cups milk
½ cup dry white wine
½ teaspoon salt
White pepper to taste

Heat butter in a heavy saucepan until bubbling but do not brown. Stir in flour and cook over low heat, stirring constantly, for about 1 minute. Add milk and wine gradually, stirring with wire whisk. Add cheeses and stir until thickened and smooth. Adjust seasoning, adding Tabasco for seafood and garlic for other meats. Yield: 2 cups sauce.

To serve as a casserole dish, line a shallow, buttered baking dish with any cooked seafood: shrimp, crabmeat or flaked fish. Cooked, sliced chicken, turkey, or ham can also be used. Cover the seafood or meat with sauce. Broil in hot oven until the sauce blisters. Delicious as a hot buffet dish with toast points. To serve as a crepe dish, make crepes and place seafood or meat on the crepe. Top with Mornay Sauce, roll the crepe up and place in shallow baking dish. Pour rest of sauce over crepes; sprinkle with paprika and chopped chives and parsley. Run in hot oven until sauce blisters.
Mrs. Julian Neel (Phoebe)

JAMBALAYA

3 bacon slices, diced
2 large onions, minced
2 cloves garlic, minced
1 cup chicken stock
1 cup celery, diagonally cut
1 tablespoon tomato paste
1 No. 2½ can tomatoes
¼ teaspoon pepper,
   freshly ground

1 teaspoon celery salt
⅛ teaspoon Tabasco
2 pounds raw shrimp, cleaned
1 pint fresh or thawed
   frozen oysters
2 cups raw rice, cooked

Sauté bacon until crisp. Add onions and garlic. Cook until onions are tender. Add chicken stock and next 8 ingredients. Simmer gently 30 minutes. Thicken sauce with flour. Add shrimp and simmer 4 minutes. Add oysters and simmer 1 minute. Serve over rice. Serves 8.
Mrs. Al Lookabaugh (Diana)

NASI GORENG
Indonesian Chicken, Shrimp, Crab and Rice

4 pounds chicken
7 cups water
2 onions
1 bay leaf
2 sprigs parsley
3 teaspoons salt
2 cups rice
⅓ cup peanut butter
4 onions, chopped
2 cloves garlic, minced

1½ cups shrimp, chopped and
   cooked
1 cup crabmeat, cooked or canned
1 cup ham, cubed
2 teaspoons coriander, ground
1 teaspoon cumin seed, ground
½ teaspoon dried chili peppers,
   ground
¼ teaspoon mace
⅓ cup oil or butter

Cook chicken in water with onions, bay leaf, parsley and 2 teaspoons of salt. Bring to a boil and cook over medium heat 1½ hours or until chicken is tender. Strain the stock and reserve. Remove the meat from the bones and cut in strips. Wash the rice several times. Combine the rice, remaining salt and 3½ cups of stock. Cover and cook over low heat 20 minutes. Drain. Heat oil and add onions and garlic. Sauté for 10 minutes; stir. Add rice and cook until it browns, stirring frequently. Add chicken, shrimp, crabmeat, ham, coriander, cumin seed, chili peppers, mace and peanut butter. Serve with chilled cucumbers, diced apples and sliced bananas. Serves 8-10.
Mrs. Cyrus Helm (Fran)

MY CHRISTMAS CASSEROLE

1 package king crab legs in
   shells, frozen
4 or 5 sea shells, well-cleaned
1 pound crabmeat
1 pound fish, cooked and flaked
1 pound shrimp, deveined and
   cooked
4 tablespoons of butter
1 medium onion, chopped

1 large green pepper, chopped
Small jar of pimentos
1 large can evaporated milk
Salt, pepper and Worcestershire
   to taste
Juice of 2 lemons
1-2 cups saltine crackers,
   crumbled
2 eggs

Sauté onion and pepper in butter. Do not brown. Add can of milk and can of water. Add salt, pepper and Worcestershire. Beat the eggs and stir in with crumbled saltine crackers. Blend but don't stir too much. Remove meat from crab legs and save shells. Add chopped crabmeat with shrimp, fish and pimento to mixture. If too thin, add more saltine crackers, then lemon juice. Put in a baking dish. Decorate with sea shells and crab legs mixed in. Cook in 375-degree oven until warm. Can be made ahead and refrigerated. More pimento and green pepper make it very festive.
Mrs. John B. Guy (Betty)

SHRIMP AND OYSTER CURRY

1 pound shrimp, cooked and
   cleaned
1 pint oysters, washed
5 ripe tomatoes, chopped
1 sweet onion, chopped
2 tablespoons butter

3 small apples, chopped
   (not peeled)
1 tablespoon hot curry powder
1 tablespoon sugar
Salt, pepper and garlic powder
   to taste

Sauté onion in 2 tablespoons butter until opaque. Add tomatoes and apples. Cook until mushy over medium heat. One tablespoon tomato paste may be added to thicken if necessary. Add curry powder, garlic, sugar, salt and pepper. More curry may be used if you like it hot. Cook mixture for 20 minutes. Add shrimp and oysters and cook in 350 degree oven until oysters have curled and are plump. Serve over rice with curry relishes such as chutney, coconut, and raisins. This can be made ahead of time and reheated successfully. Serves 6-8.
Mrs. Edward Davis (Rozzi)

Game
and
Poultry

WILLIAMSBURG SOUTHERN GAME PIE

1 wild duck
1 small chicken
2½ pounds venison steak
2 cups Taylor's Tawny Port
1½ quarts Brown Sauce
1 tablespoon Worcestershire
1 clove garlic, minced
½ teaspoon black pepper,
    crushed

1 cup currant jelly
1½ pounds mushrooms, quartered
½ cup butter
1 pound slab bacon, cut into
    ½-inch cubes
1 15½-ounce can pearl onions
Pie crust for 12 ramekins, unbaked
Egg wash (2 eggs beaten with
    ¼ cup milk)

To prepare duck: Salt cavity and bake 30 minutes at 400 degrees. Reduce temperature to 325 degrees and cook until tender. To prepare chicken: Boil in water until very tender. To prepare venison: Cut venison into large cubes. Brown in vegetable oil. Drain. Add port and boil 2-3 minutes. Return venison to pan, add Brown Sauce and simmer 45-60 minutes or until tender. Cut cooked duck and chicken into serving-size pieces and keep warm in pan with venison. To meats in pan, add Worcestershire, garlic, salt, pepper and jelly. Mix all together and put in individual ramekins lined with unbaked pie crust. Garnish with mushrooms sautéed in butter, fried and drained bacon, and heated and drained onions. Cover ramekins with pastry. Brush with egg wash. Cook at 350 degrees for 20-25 minutes. Serves 12.

BROWN SAUCE:

1½ cups meat drippings
1 carrot, diced
1 onion, diced
2 center celery ribs, diced
½ bay leaf, crushed
¼ teaspoon thyme
1 tablespoon raw bacon

1 tablespoon butter
½ cup flour
10 black peppercorns
2 cups tomatoes, skinned
½ cup parsley, chopped
8 cups beef stock

Simmer carrot, onion, celery, bay leaf, bacon and thyme in butter until soft. Add to meat drippings and brown. Add flour and stir until mixture is brown. Add peppercorns, tomatoes (without juice) and parsley. Stir and mix well. Add beef stock and simmer until reduced in half, about 2-3 hours. Skim fat from top. Strain and stir while cooling to prevent top from forming a film.
Mrs. Harry M. Tomlinson, Jr. (Barbara)

VENISON ROAST

Olive oil
Red wine vinegar
½ cup red wine

Salt
Pepper
Onions

Coat roast with olive oil, red wine vinegar, ½ cup red wine, salt, and pepper. Place in container with lid. Cover roast with onions. Close up and leave in refrigerator 2, 3, 4, or 5 days. Take roast out of container. Place in roaster on rack of foil. Toothpick squares of beef fat all over for moisture. Pour marinade over roast. Cook at 325 degrees until well done. Remove fat. Delicious served cold. You may toothpick mushroom slices all over roast and then chill. *Mrs. John Cone (Gloria)*

ROAST LOIN OF VENISON

1 whole loin section of
   venison at room temperature
2 cloves garlic, sliced in
   half

6 to 8 slices of bacon
Salt and freshly ground
   black pepper

Preheat oven to 300 degrees. Wash and trim outer skin off loin. Cut small slits in loin and insert garlic. Sprinkle with salt and pepper. Place bacon slices across loin. Place the meat on a rack in a shallow, dry roasting pan, uncovered; cook it about one hour and a half to two hours or a little longer if you want it well done. Transfer the venison to a warm serving tray and let stand a few minutes before carving. (The tenderloins are on the bottom side of roast, so be sure and carve them also.) Serve with pan gravy made by adding a small amount of hot water to the drippings in the roasting pan plus adding juices from carvings. Garnish serving tray with stuffed mushrooms. Serves 8. *Mrs. Leon Neel (Julie)*

VENISON STEW

Venison shoulder or rump
Garlic
Flour
½ cup bacon drippings
3 teaspoons salt
½ teaspoon pepper

8-10 small whole white onions
8-10 whole carrots
1-2 celery stalks
½ pound fresh mushrooms
1 green pepper, sliced

Rub venison with garlic, 1 teaspoon salt and ¼ teaspoon pepper. Flour and brown both sides in 3-6 tablespoons bacon drippings. Cover in cold water to which rest of bacon drippings, salt and pepper has been added. Bring to a boil and then simmer for 2-3 hours or until tender. Add onions, carrots, celery, mushrooms and pepper the last ½ hour. Correct seasonings and serve. *Mrs. Jack V. Allen, Jr. (Rebecca)*

ROUND STEAK OF VENISON

2 round steaks, ¾ inches
    thick
4 slices white bacon, cut in
    small pieces

Salt and freshly ground
    white pepper

Place small pieces of white bacon in cold frying pan; cook slowly, not too brown. Take bacon from pan; into the hot grease put venison steaks which have been cut into serving pieces and sprinkled with salt and white pepper. Sear on each side turning constantly until no red blood runs when pricked. When steak is done as you like, place on hot platter. Make gravy by adding cream to grease, thicken by adding a little flour mixed with milk. Place small white bacon pieces on top of steak and pour gravy over all. Serve with grits or mashed potatoes. Serves 4.
Mrs. Leon Neel (Julie)

VENISON STEAKS

Trim off all fat. Marinate your steaks in your refrigerator for 24 hours in peanut oil and lemon juice. (Mix the juice of 1 lemon to 1 cup of peanut oil.) Turn frequently in order to get all sides of the steaks well soaked in oil. You may have to add more oil during the marinating as the meat soaks it up. I cook my steaks in a hot iron frying pan on top of the stove, or grill them outdoors. Outdoors is better if you are cooking a lot of steaks or a big one because of the smoke made from broiling. Have your pan or your grill very hot, depending on the thickness of the steaks. If they are thin, have your pan or grill almost red hot, in order to brown them on the outside, while keeping them very rare in the middle. It won't hurt to scorch them a little, but do not overcook them. It should only take a few minutes to broil venison steaks. Salt and pepper them when you have finished cooking them. While cooking, do not stick them with a fork but turn them with a spatula. Sticking them with a fork allows the juice to run out.
Mrs. Rosalie Mason White

VENISON-NOODLE MEDLEY

Do not throw away your leftover cooked venison, as this venison chili is delicious. Grind your leftover cooked venison. For this recipe you should have about 1 pound of ground meat. In a heavy pan, fry about ½ pound of diced salt pork until the fat has completely cooked out of the meat. Add and cook until clear: 2 cups diced onion, ½ cup diced green pepper and 1 cup diced celery. Add the ground venison (about 1 pound) and cook for a minute or so. Then add 1 quart tomatoes (or 2 8-ounce cans), 1 4-ounce can button mushrooms, 2 teaspoons seasoned salt, 1 teaspoon plain salt, 1 tablespoon chili powder, and ¼ teaspoon black pepper. Simmer (do not boil) until tender, the longer the better up to two hours. This is even better the next day, and it can be frozen. Just before serving, about ½ hour, add 2 cups of broad noodles. You may have to replace liquid with tomato juice or water as the noodles soak it up.
Mrs. Rosalie Mason White

QUICK VENISON CHILI

1 pound venison, ground
½ pound sausage
1 large onion, chopped
1 garlic clove, minced
32 ounces tomato sauce
2 or more tablespoons chili
    powder

1 teaspoon oregano
½ teaspoon thyme
1 bay leaf
32 ounces red kidney beans,
    drained

Brown venison and sausage in heavy iron skillet. Remove meat and sauté onions and garlic in grease. Mix all ingredients and simmer 15 minutes to an hour or more. Stir occasionally. Correct seasonings and serve.
Mrs. Jack V. Allen, Jr. (Rebecca)

RABBIT STEW

2-3 rabbits
5 quarts boiling water
1 pound bacon, cut in pieces
1 large onion, chopped
4 cups tomatoes, diced
2 cups butter beans
2 cups corn

8 medium potatoes, cubed
1 tablespoon salt
1 teaspoon black pepper
Pinch of cayenne
4 teaspoons sugar
½ cup butter
4 tablespoons flour

Add rabbits, onion and bacon to boiling water. Simmer covered for 2 hours. Skim surface when necessary. Debone and add vegetables and seasonings. Simmer another hour. Stir often. Shape butter and flour into small balls and drop in. Boil 10 minutes, stirring constantly to prevent lumping. Correct seasonings and serve.
Mrs. Jack V. Allen, Jr. (Rebecca)

ALICE'S WILD DUCK STEW

4 duck breasts
2 apples, cut up
1 stalk celery

2 onions, cut up
1 small bay leaf

Cover above ingredients with water and simmer until tender. Remove meat from bones. Strain stock; reserve.

2 stalks celery, cut up
4 onions, cut up
Dash Worcestershire sauce
Garlic

Accent
Salt
Pepper
Flour

Simmer celery and onions in stock until tender. Add cut-up duck meat, Worcestershire sauce and a little garlic. Season with Accent, salt and pepper; then thicken with flour. Serve with medium-sized noodles.
Mrs. Chris CoCroft (Katie)

DUCK CASSEROLE

3 ducks
1 onion
1 potato
1 bay leaf
1 package herb seasoned
    dressing (stuffing)
1½ cups milk
2 eggs, beaten

1 stick margarine, melted
1½ cups onion, chopped
½ cup celery, chopped
1 cup mayonnaise
1 can cream of mushroom
    soup
1 cup cheese, grated

Boil ducks in water with onion, potato and bay leaf until tender, about 2 hours. Remove duck from bone and chop. Save 1½ cups broth. Combine duck and broth with all other ingredients except soup and cheese. Place in 13 x 9 x 2-inch casserole, cover, and let sit overnight. Before baking pour mushroom soup over top. Bake at 400 degrees for 1 hour. Cover with cheese and return to oven until cheese melts. Serves 12.
Mrs. John Wilson (Nell)

MUSHROOM-COVERED DUCK PIECES

Wild ducks	1 stick margarine
Onion	Salt
Celery	1 large can mushroom pieces

Stuff each duck with onion and celery. Melt the margarine and brown ducks quickly. Add water to cover the ducks. Season with salt and simmer 2½ to 3 hours or until meat falls away from bones. When meat is cool, remove the bones. Layer the meat in a casserole dish. Cover with the mushrooms. Pour ½ cup broth (from cooked ducks) over duck. When ready to serve, cover in foil and warm about 30 minutes in a 350 degree oven.

Mrs. Clifford Campbell (Frances)

BEGINNER'S DUCK
What to Do When the Merganser Was Cleaned With the Mallard!

4 wild ducks	2 medium potatoes, diced
¼ cup butter	1 cup red wine vinegar, or
½ cup celery, chopped	lemon juice
2 medium apples, sliced	2 quarts water
2 medium onions, quartered	

GLAZE:

1 cup apricot preserves	1 tablespoon brandy
½ cup honey	1 tablespoon Cointreau

Butter cavity. Fill loosely with celery, apples, onions and potatoes. Place in cold water to which wine, vinegar or lemon juice have been added. Parblanch for 1½ to 2 hours or until tender. Remove stuffing. Add glaze. Place in preheated 500 degree oven. Reduce heat to 350 degrees and roast for 10 to 15 minutes or until glaze hardens.

Mrs. Jack V. Allen, Jr. (Rebecca)

LOUISE McCOLLUM'S WILD DUCK

Ducks, washed and giblets
   removed
Salt and pepper
½ to 1 rib celery per duck
Bacon drippings

Vinegar
2 oranges
1 tablespoon Worcestershire
   sauce
1 onion

Salt and pepper ducks generously inside and out, and place celery inside each. (Apple or carrot may be substituted.) Rub breasts with bacon drippings and arrange ducks in heavy cooker, breasts up. Squeeze 1 orange over all. Add water to duck level, a shake of vinegar, Worcestershire sauce, and one onion. For oven, cover cooker and bake at 325 degrees for 3½ hours. Check halfway through cooking period to see if water should be added. After 3 hours, squeeze second orange over all. In crock pot, cook 8 hours or more on low or at least 4 hours on high.
Mrs. Paul McCollum (Nancy)

WILD DUCKS WITH ORANGE SAUCE

Allow at least ½ duck per person to be served. Salt ducks. In large pot, combine:

1 gallon water
2 onions, peeled and sliced
2 teaspoons sage
2 teaspoons celery salt

1 teaspoon black pepper
Accent
5 tablespoons butter per duck

Place ducks, sage, onions and celery salt in water and cook gently for 4 to 5 hours. Test often for doneness, since age of ducks will determine cooking time. As ducks become tender remove from water and place in roasting pan. Reserve stock. Put 1 tablespoon butter inside each duck. Sprinkle inside and out with Accent and black pepper. Baste pan of ducks with 2 cups of stock. Add 4 tablespoons of butter per duck. Brown slowly for 20 to 30 minutes in 250 degree oven, basting often. Serve with Orange Sauce.

ORANGE SAUCE:

Combine in top of double boiler:

1 6-ounce can frozen orange juice
1 10-ounce jar red currant jelly
Juice of 2 lemons

2 tablespoons ginger marmalade
   (substitute orange marmalade if
   necessary).

Heat thoroughly. When dissolved and smooth, serve hot over roast duck.
Mrs. Langdon S. Flowers (Bobbie)

QUAIL OR DOVE
Wet Method

Flour, salt, and pepper birds. Fry in hot grease (bacon drippings are good) in a heavy fryer or dutch oven. After birds are brown, remove from grease. Pour off grease and return birds to pan. Add enough liquid (chicken stock is ideal; bouillon cubes may be used to make stock) to cover birds halfway. Add fresh or minced dried onions, celery, carrots and an apple cut into large cubes. Add poultry seasoning and salt and pepper if needed. Turn heat very low and let birds simmer for 2 to 3 hours. When birds are tender, remove carefully and place in warm oven. Remove celery, carrots, etc. (Vegetables may be strained and mashed and returned to liquid). Thicken gravy. The amounts of ingredients differ with the number of birds and the cook's judgement.
Mrs. Oscar Mims (Candy)

Variation: Worcestershire sauce may be added to liquid.
Mrs. Lloyd Megahee (Frances)

QUAIL IN A BAG

1 tablespoon flour
½ cup or less dry white wine
½ teaspoon Kitchen Bouquet
2 stalks celery,
  coarsely chopped

1 2-ounce can mushrooms,
  sliced, and liquid
6 quail
Butter or margarine, melted

Preheat oven to 350 degrees. Shake 1 tablespoon flour into 10 x 16-inch cooking bag and place in shallow roasting pan. Combine wine and Kitchen Bouquet. If less than ½ cup wine is used, compensate with water. Pour this into bag and stir until well mixed with flour. Add celery and mushrooms with liquid. Brush quail with melted butter and sprinkle with salt, and lay atop vegetables within bag. Close bag with twist tie, make 6 ½-inch slits in top, and cook for 1 hour. The gravy makes itself, and should be spooned over the quail when served.
Mrs. Paul McCollum (Nancy) from Joan Cone's Easy Game Cooking.

QUAIL IN SOUR CREAM SAUCE WITH WILD RICE

8-10 quail
Salt
White pepper
1 pint sour cream

Butter
Paprika
¼ cup sherry
White wine

Season quail lightly with salt and pepper. Moisten inside and out with white wine; then wash liberally with sour cream. Chill and keep cool. Next day strain off juices. Brush with butter. Brown in 400 degree oven for 10 minutes. Pour sour cream marinade over quail, reduce temperature to 300 degrees and roast until tender. Baste and season sauce to taste, add paprika for color and sherry. Serve with Wild Rice.

WILD RICE:

2 layers of onions
½ cup butter
1 teaspoon sage
1 tablespoon parsley
½ cup green celery, chopped

1½ cups wild rice,
    washed and drained
4 cups meat stock
1½ teaspoons salt
Pepper to taste

Sauté onions in medium skillet in butter. Add sage, parsley, and celery; cook 3 minutes. Add wild rice and moisten with meat stock. Season with salt and pepper. Simmer 35 to 40 minutes.
Mrs. John Cone (Gloria)

DOVE BREASTS STROGANOFF

12 to 18 dove breasts
1 medium onion, chopped
2 tablespoons butter,
    melted
1 10½-ounce can cream of
    celery soup, undiluted
1 4-ounce can mushrooms
½ cup Sauterne

½ teaspoon oregano
½ teaspoon rosemary
Salt and pepper to taste
1 teaspoon brown bouquet sauce
1 cup sour cream
Cooked wild rice

Arrange meat in a large baking dish; do not crowd. Sauté onion in butter. Add remaining ingredients, except sour cream and wild rice. Pour mixture over meat. Cover lightly with foil. Bake at 325 degrees for 1 hour, turning meat occasionally. Add sour cream; stir into sauce. Bake, uncovered, an additional 20 minutes. Spoon over wild rice.
Mrs. Marshall C. Dunaway (Linden)

BREAKFAST QUAIL, DOVE OR SQUIRREL

6 quail, 6 doves, 2
   squirrels or combination
   of quail and dove
Salt
Pepper

Flour
Cooking Oil
Worcestershire sauce
Milk or water

Salt, pepper and generously flour pieces. Preheat ¼ inch cooking oil in heavy cast iron skillet on medium high heat. Fry until golden brown or about 10-15 minutes, usually turning once. Remove and drain on paper towels. Brown equal amounts of flour and pan drippings in skillet, stirring constantly to prevent lumping. Add 1 cup water or milk very gradually to each 2 tablespoons of flour used. Cook until thickened. Make enough to cover game. Correct seasonings with salt, pepper and Worcestershire sauce. Add game and simmer 1 hour or more, especially for squirrel. Serve over grits.
Mrs. Jack V. Allen, Jr. (Rebecca)

CHICKEN IMPERIAL

4 whole large chicken breasts,
   halved
All-purpose flour
½ cup butter or margarine
1 pound small mushrooms,
   quartered

1 tablespoon onion, minced
1 cup heavy or whipping
   cream
¼ cup dry sherry
1½ teaspoons salt
⅛ teaspoon pepper

With sharp knife, remove skin from chicken breasts. On wax paper, coat chicken breasts with ¼ cup flour. In 12-inch skillet over medium heat, in hot butter or margarine, cook chicken, a few pieces at a time until lightly browned on all sides. Set chicken aside. In drippings in skillet, over medium heat, cook mushrooms and onions five minutes, stirring frequently. Stir in cream, sherry, salt, and pepper. Blend well. Return chicken to skillet. Reduce heat to low. Cover skillet and let simmer 20 minutes or until chicken is fork tender. Remove chicken to warm platter. In cup blend 1 tablespoon flour with 2 tablespoons water. Gradually add to pan liquid, stirring constantly. Cook until mixture is thickened. Serve sauce over chicken. Serves 8.
Mrs. Fred Murphy, III (Dawn)

CALICO CHICKEN IN WINE

8 chicken breasts   Salt and pepper

Salt and pepper 8 chicken breasts. Place in greased baking dish, skin side down. Preheat oven to 375 degrees. Cover chicken with sauce and bake covered for 1 hour. After 30 minutes turn chicken. Baste while cooking. Remove cover last 10 minutes of baking.

SAUCE:

1 cup dry white wine   ¼ cup green onion tops, chopped
1 teaspoon lemon juice   ¼ cup parsley, chopped
¼ teaspoon pepper   ¼ cup butter, melted
½ teaspoon paprika   Lots of fresh mushrooms,
⅛ teaspoon powdered oregano   if desired
1 tablespoon salt

(If mushrooms are used, increase wine to 1½ cups and butter to ½ cup). Mix all together.
Mrs. Heywood Mason (Edie)

LILY'S CHINESE CHICKEN

6 chicken breasts   Cashews or macadamia nuts
1 clove garlic, crushed   Butter
Salt and pepper

Skin and bone chicken breasts. Sauté in foaming butter with garlic, salt and pepper. Put in oven-proof plate in oven and cover with the following sauce:

SAUCE:

2 tablespoons cornstarch   1 tablespoon oyster sauce
¼ cup pineapple juice   1 tablespoon vinegar
1 cup pear or plum preserves   1 cup water
1 tablespoon soy sauce

Dissolve cornstarch in pineapple juice and bring to a boil. Add remaining ingredients and cook over low heat until thickened. Spread over chicken breasts and sprinkle with chopped nuts. Heat in slow oven until piping hot.
Miss Maury Flowers

BAKED CHICKEN BREASTS WITH CASHEWS

4 whole chicken breasts,
  split
Garlic salt to taste
¼ cup butter, melted
1 tablespoon paprika
1 tablespoon lemon juice
1 3-ounce can mushrooms

½ teaspoon Worcestershire
  sauce
¼ cup sherry
½ cup cashew halves
2 tablespoons flour
¼ cup sour cream

Season chicken with garlic salt. Combine butter, paprika and lemon juice. Dip chicken into mixture. Place in shallow baking dish with skin side up. Bake at 350 degrees for 30 minutes. Mix mushrooms, Worcestershire sauce and wine. Spoon over chicken. Sprinkle with cashews. Bake for 30 minutes longer. For extra tender chicken, cover with foil and bake for 30 additional minutes. Remove chicken; thicken sauce with flour. Stir in sour cream. Serve over chicken breasts. Serves 6-8.
Mrs. Tom Faircloth (Janice)

CASHEW CHICKEN

3 whole chicken breasts
1 package frozen pea pods,
  partially thawed
½ pound mushrooms, sliced
4 green onions
1 small can sliced bamboo
  shoots, drained
1 cup chicken broth

¼ cup soy sauce
2 tablespoons cornstarch
½ teaspoon sugar
½ teaspoon salt
¼ cup salad oil
1 4-ounce package cashew
  nuts

Skin and bone chicken breasts. Slice horizontally in ⅛-inch slices, then cut in one-inch squares. Cut green part of onion in one-inch lengths and white parts in ¼-inch slices. Mix together soy sauce, cornstarch, sugar, and salt. Before cooking begins, have all ingredients measured and chopped ready to add to the wok. (If wok is not available, recipe can be cooked in regular skillet on high heat; however it must be cooked and stirred very quickly.) Heat 1 tablespoon oil and add nuts all at once. Cook one minute or until toasted and remove from pan. Add remaining oil to pan. When hot add chicken all at once. Stir fry until opaque. Add peas, mushrooms, and broth; cover and cook 2 minutes. Add bamboo shoots and onions. Stir the soy sauce mixture into the pan juices and cook until sauce is thickened. Stir constantly for 1 minute. Sprinkle with nuts. Serve immediately. Serves 6.
Mrs. Lee Mayfield (Patricia)   *Covington, Georgia*

CHICKEN BREASTS FLORENTINE

2 cups medium white sauce
  with 1 cup grated Cheddar
  cheese added
1 tablespoon butter
½ cup onion, chopped
½ pound mushrooms, chopped
2 10-ounce packages frozen
  spinach, chopped

¼ teaspoon dried leaf basil
⅛ teaspoon nutmeg
1½ teaspoons salt
¼ teaspoon pepper
2 teaspoons lemon juice
4 whole chicken breasts,
  deboned and halved

In large skillet, melt butter. Add onion and mushrooms and cook until tender. Add spinach; cover and cook 5 minutes. Stir in basil, nutmeg, salt, pepper, and lemon juice. Turn into a shallow 3-quart baking dish. Top with chicken breasts and pour cheese sauce over all. Bake uncovered in 375 degree oven for 45 minutes until chicken is tender. Serves 8.
The Editors

STUFFED CHICKEN BREASTS SAVANNAH

4 whole chicken breasts,
  skinned, boned, and halved
4 thin slices ham, cut in half
4 thin slices Swiss cheese,
  cut in half
½ cup all-purpose flour,
  divided
1 egg, slightly beaten
⅔ cup fine dry bread crumbs
½ cup plus 2 tablespoons butter,
  melted

1 cup dry white wine
¼ cup onion, finely chopped
½ teaspoon salt
Pepper to taste
1 cup milk
1 cup half and half cream
Chopped fresh parsley
Hot cooked rice or noodles

Flatten chicken breasts with meat mallet. Place a slice of ham and cheese on each chicken breast. Roll up and secure with toothpick. Dredge each roll in ¼ cup flour, dip in egg, and coat well with bread crumbs. Lightly brown on all sides in ¼ cup butter. Add wine. Simmer, covered, 20 minutes. Place rolls in shallow baking dish, reserving drippings. Sauté onion in 6 tablespoons butter until tender, stirring occasionally. Blend in ¼ cup flour, salt, and pepper. Gradually add milk and cream stirring constantly until smooth and thickened. Pour sauce over rolls; bake, uncovered, at 325 degrees for 20 minutes. Garnish with parsley and serve over rice or noodles. Serves 8.
The Editors

COQ AU VIN

10-inch electric skillet
2½ pounds chicken, cut up
Salt and pepper
1 bay leaf
16-20 small white onions
3 tablespoons flour
4 cups fresh mushrooms,
  quartered
2-3 tablespoons butter
  (optional)

½ cup fresh fat pork strips
  (¼ by ½ inch)
2 or more tablespoons oil
¼ cup Cognac
¼ teaspoon thyme
2 cups red wine
2 cups brown chicken stock
  or beef bouillon
2 cloves garlic, minced
1 tablespoon tomato paste

Sauté pork in 2 tablespoons oil until lightly browned. (Bacon can be used.) Remove to side dish and leave fat in pan. Heat to moderately hot and add chicken. Turn chicken to brown on all sides. Pour in Cognac, shake pan until bubbling hot, then ignite with match. Let flame a minute or two and then extinguish with a pan cover. Season chicken with salt and pepper; add bay leaf and herbs. Place onions around chicken. Cover pan and cook slowly for 10 minutes, turning once. Uncover pan and sprinkle on the flour, turning chicken and onions so flour is absorbed; cook 3-4 minutes turning once or twice. Remove from heat. Gradually stir and swirl in the wine and enough stock or bouillon to almost cover chicken. Add browned pork strips, garlic, and tomato paste. Cover pan and simmer 25-30 minutes or until tender. Add mushrooms and simmer 4-5 minutes. Sauce should be just thick enough to coat chicken and vegetables lightly. If too thin, boil down rapidly to concentrate. If too thick, thin out with spoonfuls of bouillon. To serve immediately, arrange chicken and vegetables on platter. Swirl optional butter into sauce and spoon over chicken. If serving later or freezing, baste chicken with its sauce and let cool, uncovered, to room temperature; then cover and refrigerate or freeze. To reheat, cover chicken and simmer slowly for about 6-8 minutes. Baste and turn chicken until thoroughly warmed but do not overcook. Serves 4-6.
The Editors

CHICKEN DIVAN

8 chicken breasts
3 10-ounce packages broccoli
   spears
3 teaspoons curry
¼ cup onions, diced
¼ cup celery, diced
Salt to taste

3 tablespoons lemon juice
2 cans cream of chicken soup
1 cup mayonnaise
1 cup Cheddar cheese, grated
Buttered bread crumbs
   (Pepperidge Farm)

Simmer breasts with onion and celery for 45 minutes. Cool in stock. When cool, bone and skin. Cook broccoli and season to taste. Layer broccoli in bottom of buttered casserole. Put breasts on spears of broccoli. Mix mayonnaise, soup, lemon juice and curry. Pour over casserole. Sprinkle with cheese. Top with crumbs. Bake for 30 minutes at 350 degrees.

Mrs. Jasper Davis (Marthalene)
Similar recipes submitted by Mrs. Linda Pinckney and Mrs. Elizabeth Roberson.

CHICKEN BREASTS IN SOUR CREAM

2 packages chipped beef
6 medium-size chicken breasts,
   boned and cut in half
1 10¾-ounce can cream of
   mushroom soup

1 cup sour cream
6 strips bacon
Salt and pepper to taste

Season chicken pieces lightly with salt and pepper; wrap each piece with half strip of bacon, securing with toothpick, if desired. Blend soup and sour cream. Line up chicken pieces in large, shallow, buttered baking dish, putting 3 or 4 slices of chipped beef under each piece of chicken. Top with soup-sour cream mixture and bake, uncovered, in 300 degree oven for 2½ to 3 hours. Serves 12 ladies or 6 men.

Mrs. Jack Sanford (Sue)
Mrs. Randolph Jones (Nancy)

CHICKEN VIRGINIA WITH GRAPE SAUCE

3 chicken breasts, boned
  and halved
4 tablespoons butter, melted
  and divided

12 fresh mushrooms
6 slices Virginia ham or
  country-cured ham,
  thinly sliced

Preheat broiler and line broiler pan with foil. Place chicken in single layer, skin side down, and brush with butter. Broil 3 to 4 inches from heat for 15 minutes, then turn chicken over and brush skin side with butter. Lower pan to 7 to 8 inches from heat. Broil 10 to 15 minutes longer, or until chicken is done. Sauté whole mushrooms in remaining butter. Serve each half of chicken breast on a slice of ham. Spoon Grape Sauce over the meat, and garnish with sautéed mushrooms.

GRAPE SAUCE:

¼ cup butter
¼ cup all-purpose flour
½ teaspoon salt
2 cups chicken stock or
  canned chicken broth

2 tablespoons lemon juice
2 tablespoons sugar
2 cups seedless grapes

Melt butter in saucepan and blend in flour and salt. Stir until smooth. Gradually add stock, stirring constantly until smooth and thick. Stir in lemon juice and sugar. Add grapes just before serving. Makes 3 cups, enough to serve 6. This is served at the Kings Arms Tavern in Williamsburg.
Mrs. Maurice Tanner (Peggy)

CHICKEN WITH CHERRIES

3 chicken breasts, halved
1 8-ounce bottle Italian
  dressing
6 ounces blackberry jelly
  (or currant)

½ 6-ounce can frozen orange
  juice concentrate
1 16-ounce can pitted Bing
  cherries, undrained

Marinate chicken in Italian dressing overnight. Drain off dressing and place chicken on roasting pan skin side up. Bake uncovered in 350 degree oven for 2 hours. Cover only if chicken is getting too brown. While chicken is baking, melt jelly in saucepan and blend in orange juice concentrate and cherries. Pour sauce over chicken and continue baking for 15 minutes at 325 degrees. Serves 6.
Mrs. Ken Beverly (Mary Jo)

CHICKEN ORANGE

1 whole fryer, cut, or
   3 whole breasts, split
⅓ cup oil
¼ cup wine vinegar
2 tablespoons crystallized
   ginger, chopped

1 scant cup orange
   marmalade
3 tablespoons water
1 envelope Italian
   dressing mix

Put chicken into an open roasting pan. Mix all ingredients together and spread over chicken. Bake uncovered 1½-2 hours at 300 degrees. Serves 6.
Mrs. Lawson Neel (Josie)

ORANGE CHICKEN BREASTS

8 boneless chicken breasts,
   lightly floured
Salt
Pepper

Butter, melted
½ cup water

Season chicken well with salt and pepper and dip into butter. Put chicken in upright position in baking pan. Add ½ cup water and bake for 30 minutes, covered, at 375 degrees. Remove cover and continue baking until tender, about 1½ hours total time. Place 1 orange slice on each breast. Pour hot sauce over breasts and serve.

SAUCE:

1 tablespoon cornstarch
⅔ cup sugar
1 cup orange juice
½ teaspoon salt

½ teaspoon cinnamon
½ teaspoon cloves
4 teaspoons orange peel,
   grated

Mix all ingredients together. Cook in double boiler until thick and clear.
Mrs. William Z. Bridges (Mary)

OVEN-BAKED CHICKEN

2 chickens (2½-3 pounds each), cut into eighths
1¾ teaspoons salt
¼ teaspoon ground black pepper
1 15-ounce can tomato sauce
1½ cups water
2 tablespoons onion powder

2 tablespoons parsley flakes
1½ tablespoons flour
1½ teaspoons marjoram leaves, crumbled
1 teaspoon sugar
¾ teaspoon garlic powder

Sprinkle both sides of chicken with salt and black pepper. Place chicken pieces skin side up, in 18 x 11½ x 2-inch roasting pan; set aside. Combine remaining ingredients. Pour over chicken. Bake, uncovered, in a preheated hot oven at 425 degrees until chicken is tender, about 50 minutes, basting occasionally. Serves 8.
Mrs. Kenneth L. Miller (Kathryn)

BARBECUED CHICKEN

1 fryer, cut up
2 teaspoons tomato catsup
2 teaspoons white vinegar
2 teaspoons Worcestershire sauce
4 teaspoons water
1 teaspoon mustard

2 teaspoons butter
2 teaspoons lemon juice
1 teaspoon paprika
1 teaspoon chili powder
½ teaspoon red pepper
Well-greased paper bag

In large bowl mix all ingredients. Salt and pepper chicken and dip into sauce. Place in well-greased paper bag and tie tightly with a string. Place in baking pan. Cook in 375 degree oven for 1 hour and 15 minutes. Serves 2 to 4.
Mrs. Harry Park (Mary)

CHICKEN COUNTRY CAPTAIN

12 halves of chicken
   breasts
Flour
Oil
1 large onion, sliced
2 green peppers, sliced
1 stick margarine

4 No. 2 cans tomatoes
1½ teaspoons salt
1½ teaspoons pepper
½ box seedless raisins, plumped
   in hot water for an hour
1 cup sliced almonds, toasted
   in butter

Flour and brown chicken breasts in oil. Place in a single layer in a large flat pan. Cook onion and green pepper in margarine. Add tomatoes, salt and pepper. Cook together for 5 minutes. Pour over chicken breasts, adding the fat in which chicken was browned. Bake covered in 300 degree oven for 2 hours. Cover large platter with cooked rice. Place chicken breasts on rice. Spoon sauce over chicken. Drain raisins and place over chicken. Sprinkle with almonds. Serves 12.
The Editors

COCA-COLA CHICKEN

In electric skillet, bring to a boil:
1 king-size Coca-Cola
1 cup catsup

¼ cup Worcestershire sauce
1 fryer, cut

Rub salt and garlic salt into fryer. Add chicken parts to cola mixture. Cover and simmer for 1 hour, turning occasionally. Serve with rice.
Mrs. Langdon Flowers (Bobbie)
Mrs. Vance Watt (Mercer)

CHICKEN POT PIE

5 pounds chicken, cut up
6 cups water
1 large onion
1 large carrot, peeled and
    cut into 2-inch pieces
1 large stalk celery with
    leaves, cut into 2-inch pieces
1 tablespoon salt
½ teaspoon dill weed
2 whole cloves

¾ pound carrots, peeled and
    cut into 1-inch pieces
½ pound small white onions,
    peeled
1 10-ounce package frozen
    green peas
¼ cup butter
½ cup all-purpose flour
¼ teaspoon pepper
1 cup milk or light cream

Bring chicken and water to a boil in a large pot. Add onion, 1 carrot, celery, salt, dill weed and cloves. Cover pot; cook 1 hour on low heat. Remove chicken from broth and cool. Bring stock to boil and let boil until reduced to 3 cups, about 25 minutes. Meanwhile, slip skin from chicken, debone and cut into bite-size pieces. Reserve. Strain broth and return to pot. Add remaining carrots and onions. When mixture boils, reduce heat; cover and let simmer 10 minutes. Add peas and simmer 5 minutes longer or until vegetables are tender. Add chicken. Melt butter in small saucepan. Add flour and pepper. Cook until bubbly. Stir in milk. Cook, stirring, until thickened. Pour over chicken and vegetables. Cook 2 minutes or until heated through. Spoon chicken filling into individual casseroles or an 8-cup shallow casserole. Cover with Biscuit Topping. Bake at 425 degrees for 25 minutes. Let stand 15 minutes before serving. Serves 10.

BISCUIT TOPPING:

2 cups all-purpose flour
1 tablespoon baking powder
½ teaspoon salt

¼ cup butter
¾ cup milk

Sift flour, baking powder, and salt together. Cut in butter with pastry blender until mixture is crumbly. Stir in milk with a fork just until dough holds together. Turn out on floured board and knead until smooth. Roll out dough to 1 inch larger than top of casserole. Cut several slits near center to allow steam to escape. Place on top of filling, fold edges under and flute. Brush top with milk, if you wish.
Mrs. A. B. Wight, Jr. (Carolyn)

CHICKEN TETRAZZINI CREPES

CREPES:

1 egg, slightly beaten
1 cup milk

1 cup flour
1 tablespoon butter, melted

Combine egg, milk, flour and butter with rotary beater until smooth. Heat oil in skillet until water dances on surface. Pour 2 tablespoons batter into skillet. Brown on one side only. Makes 14 crepes.

FILLING:

2 whole chicken breasts
    or 1 fryer, cooked and
    diced (2 cups)
1¼ cups chicken stock
5 ounces fresh mushrooms,
    sliced and sautéed
6 tablespoons margarine

⅓ cup flour
¾ cup light cream
⅓ cup dry sherry
1 cup (4 ounces) Cheddar
    cheese, shredded
2 tablespoons Parmesan cheese

Melt 3 tablespoons margarine. Stir in flour and 1¼ cups chicken broth and cream. Cook and stir over low heat; then add cheese and sherry. Add 1 cup of cheese sauce to chicken and mushrooms. Fill crepes and place in baking dish. Pour remaining sauce over filled crepes and sprinkle with Parmesan cheese. Bake at 375 degrees for 20 minutes. If refrigerated, bake 30 minutes.
Mrs. Ken Beverly (Mary Jo)

CREPES CHICKEN DIVAN

CREPES:

2 eggs, beaten
1 cup milk
1 cup all-purpose flour,
    pre-sifted

1 tablespoon butter, melted
Pinch of salt

In mixing bowl, add milk to beaten eggs. Gradually pour in the flour, stirring constantly with a wire whisk or fork until mixture is smooth. Add butter and salt and mix until smooth. The batter should have the consistency of fresh cream. Preheat greased crepe griddle or pan over medium-high heat. (Test temperature by sprinkling pan with a few drops of water. If drops bounce and sputter, pan is ready.) Cook each crepe 20-30 seconds. (A brown ring and some curling around the edge should be apparent.) Stack cooked crepes browned-side-up and cover with fry-pan lid or damp towel to preserve moisture. Note: Crepes may be wrapped and stored in refrigerator for several days before using. Yield: Approximately 16 5 to 6-inch crepes.

FILLING:

4-5 whole chicken breasts,
    cooked and boned
4 10-ounce packages frozen
    broccoli, cooked and drained
3 cans cream of chicken soup,
    undiluted

2 cups mayonnaise
2 teaspoons lemon juice
½ teaspoon curry powder
1 cup sharp cheese, grated

Arrange cooked broccoli in baking dish. Sprinkle boned chicken over broccoli. Make sauce by combining soup, mayonnaise, lemon juice and curry powder, and pour on top of chicken. Sprinkle with grated cheese. Bake at 350 degrees for 30 minutes. Yield: enough to fill 32 crepes. NOTE: This recipe may be prepared several days ahead and stored in refrigerator or freezer.

SERVING:

Place crepe, browned-side-down, on plate. Center a large spoonful of filling on it. Fold one side of crepe across filling. Then fold the other side across the filling. (NOTE: There should be enough filling so that it spills out the ends, but not so much that the crepe will not stay folded.) Place folded crepes on a buttered baking sheet and top with more grated cheese. Bake at 350 degrees until heated and cheese is melted. Serve immediately. Allow 2 crepes per person.

Mrs. Tom Faircloth (Janice)

CHICKEN AND WILD RICE CASSEROLE

1 cup wild rice
½ cup onion, chopped
½ cup margarine
¼ cup flour
1 6-ounce can mushrooms,
    sliced
Chicken broth
1½ cups skim milk

3 cups chicken, cooked and
    diced
¼ cup pimento, diced
2 tablespoons parsley, snipped
1½ teaspoons salt
¼ teaspoon pepper
½ cup blanched almonds,
    slivered

Cook the rice (Uncle Ben's white and wild rice combination may be substituted) and set aside when done. Cook the onion in margarine until tender but not brown. Remove from heat; stir in flour. Drain mushrooms, reserving liquid. Add enough chicken broth to mushroom liquid to measure 1½ cups; gradually stir into flour mixture. Add milk. Cook and stir until mixture thickens. Add the rice, mushrooms, chicken, pimento, parsley, salt and pepper. Place in casserole dish. Sprinkle with almonds. Bake at 350 degrees for 30 minutes; or after placing in casserole, it can be covered with heavy foil and put in the freezer until needed.
Mrs. Charles Watt (Julie)

FAMILY-STYLE CHICKEN CASSEROLE

1 whole chicken or small hen,
    cooked and cut into bite-
    sized pieces
2 10¾-ounce cans cream of
    chicken soup
1 10¾-ounce can of cream of
    mushroom soup
1 4-ounce can mushrooms, cut
    into small bits
½ cup of cooking sherry
1 cup celery, finely chopped

¼ cup slivered almonds or
    pecans, finely chopped
2 teaspoons onions, finely
    chopped
½ cup of mayonnaise
1 8-ounce carton of sour
    cream
1 large package of Pepperidge
    Farm Cornbread Dressing Mix
    (Reserve half for topping)

Combine all ingredients, and add ½ package of the dressing mix. Mix lightly, place in buttered casserole dish, and top with the other half of the dressing mix. Bake at 350 degrees for about 30 minutes.
Mrs. R. Franklin Smith (Alma)

TURKEY OR CHICKEN LOAF WITH SAUCE

4 cups turkey or 5-pound
   hen, cooked and cut up
1 cup rice, cooked
2 cups fresh bread crumbs
1¾ cups broth
4 raw eggs
1½ cups milk

1 10¾-ounce can cream of
   mushroom soup
Small jar pimento (¼ cup)
2 tablespoons onion, grated
½ cup almonds
2 cups celery, chopped
Dash Accent

Soak bread crumbs in broth. Add other ingredients. Bake in loaf or casserole
1 hour at 350 degrees. Serve with sauce.

SAUCE:

¼ cup butter
¼ cup flour
2 cups broth
¼ cup canned milk

1 4-ounce can mushrooms,
   sliced
Paprika
1 teaspoon parsley, chopped
1 teaspoon lemon juice

Cook until thick. Serves 10-12.
Mrs. Harry Tomlinson (Corrie)
Similar recipe submitted by *Mrs. Lloyd Megahee (Frances).*

CHICKEN BRUNSWICK STEW

1 hen, cooked and boned
1 16-ounce can cream-style
   corn
1 16-ounce can tomatoes
1 large onion, chopped
1 8-ounce bottle chili sauce
2 tablespoons Worcestershire
   sauce

¼ cup vinegar
1 teaspoon dry mustard
¼ stick butter or margarine
1 pint chicken broth
Salt and pepper to taste

Combine all ingredients and simmer 1½ hours. Serve over cooked rice.
Mrs. Woody Faircloth (Millie)

CHICKEN MOUSSE — HAVANA, CUBA

3 cups chicken, minced
⅓ cup mayonnaise
2 envelopes gelatin
½ cup cold water
2 cups chicken stock

2 teaspoons salt
6 egg yolks
2 cups cream (Measured
  when whipped)
1 cup blanched almonds

Beat egg yolks and add to stock. Add salt and cook in top of double boiler for 8-10 minutes. Add chicken, mayonnaise and gelatin that has been dissolved in cold water. When mixture is cold, add whipped cream and almonds. Pour into greased loaf mold and set in refrigerator for at least 2 hours. This can be made the day before. Serves 10.
Mrs. Cyrus Helm (Fran)

CHICKEN AND DUMPLINGS

Boil one three-pound fryer until tender. Cool and take meat off of bone.

DUMPLINGS:

2 cups self-rising flour
2 whole eggs

1 tablespoon of butter or
  cooking oil

Mix flour, egg and butter. If necessary, add enough water to make stiff dough. Roll thin and cut into small strips. Put chicken back into boiling stock. Drop strips of dumplings into stock and boil for 15 minutes.
Mrs. Arthur Taylor (Thelma)

CHICKEN TETRAZZINI

1 hen (4 or 5 pounds), cooked and cut into small pieces.

SAUCE:

3 cups chicken stock
1 cup whipping cream
(not whipped)
16 ounces sharp American
process cheese

¼ pound butter or margarine
(1 stick)
8 level tablespoons flour

Mix all ingredients and cook until thick and creamy. Remove from heat and add:

3 tablespoons onion, finely
chopped
3 tablespoons green pepper,
finely chopped
3 tablespoons celery, finely
chopped

1 8-ounce can pitted ripe
olives
1 8-ounce can mushrooms,
sliced
Almonds

Now combine cut-up chicken and sauce. Set aside. Cook in salted water until tender one 12-ounce package of medium noodles. Drain. In bottom of a casserole dish, place cooked noodles and pour sauce on top. Sprinkle almonds over sauce. Just before serving put casserole into 350 degree oven for about 30 minutes or until mixture is hot through and almonds are slightly browned. Serves 12 or 14.
Mrs. Robert G. Lauder (Annelle)

SHERRIED CORNISH HENS

3 Cornish hens, halved
Cooking sherry
3 cups bread crumbs
1½ cups Parmesan cheese
1½ cloves garlic, crushed
¼ teaspoon pepper

3 teaspoons salt
1 teaspoon parsley flakes
¾ cup almonds or pecans,
chopped
1½ sticks butter, melted

Marinate hens in sherry for 2 hours. Combine bread crumbs, cheese, garlic, salt, pepper, parsley and nuts. When mixed, add ⅔ of the melted butter and stir. Drain the hens and dip each half in remaining ⅓ of butter; then roll in crumb mixture. Place pieces in uncovered 9 x 13-inch pan. Put small amount of butter on each piece. Bake at 350 degrees for 1 hour. Garnish with parsley.
Mrs. Ken Beverly (Mary Jo)

CORNISH HENS WITH CHINESE GLAZE

4 Cornish game hens
(about 14 ounces each)
1 teaspoon salt
1 large onion, cut into
large pieces

2 stalks celery, cut into
1-inch pieces
4 medium carrots, cut into
½-inch pieces
2 tablespoons butter or
margarine, melted

Rub hens inside and out with salt and pepper. Stuff with vegetables. Place breast side up on rack in shallow pan; brush with butter or margarine. Roast uncovered in moderate oven (350 degrees) for 30 minutes. Remove from oven; brush with glaze. Return to oven and roast another 30 minutes or until tender. Baste occasionally. Serves 4.

CHINESE GLAZE:

Use a prepared Chinese duck sauce or make your own as follows: Cook ½ cup dried apricots as directed on package; drain. Press through wire strainer or food mill. Add 1½ teaspoons grated orange rind, ¼ cup orange juice, 1 tablespoon light corn syrup, 1 tablespoon vinegar, 1½ teaspoons soy sauce and a dash of ground ginger. Bring slowly to boil, stirring often.
Mrs. Ralph Neel, Jr. (Katherine)

BAKED CORNISH HENS

8 Cornish hens
Salt and pepper
8 small whole onions
¾ cup butter or margarine

¼ cup Kitchen Bouquet
1 8-ounce jar orange
marmalade

Clean and dry hens. Season inside and out with salt and pepper; refrigerate overnight. When ready to bake, insert whole onion in cavity of each hen and place in open roasting pan, leaving space between each. In a small saucepan combine butter, Kitchen Bouquet and orange marmalade. Heat together until butter has melted and mixture is blended. Spoon over the hens and bake at 325 degrees until hens are tender, about 1½ hours, basting often. If sauce cooks down before hens are tender, add a little hot water to the pan to assure having some of the delicious sauce to accompany the hens. If hens appear to be getting dry during the baking, place a piece of foil loosely over the pan to retard the browning. Serves 8. Note: When entertaining guests, the onions should be removed before serving; however, the family will enjoy leaving them in.
Mrs. Albert Stringer (Regina)

ROCK CORNISH HENS WITH APPLE AND RAISIN STUFFING

4 to 6 rock Cornish hens, thawed
1 tablespoon flour
1 small onion, sliced

2 tablespoons currant jelly,
    melted

STUFFING:

½ cup celery, chopped
1 tablespoon onions, chopped
½ cup raisins
2 cups tart cooking apples,
    coarsely chopped

2 tablespoons parsley, chopped
1 7-ounce package prepared
    stuffing, croutons or crumbs
1 Brown-In-Bag

Preheat oven to 350 degrees. Shake 1 tablespoon flour in empty Brown-In-Bag and place in pan. Place celery tops and onion slices in bottom of bag. To prepare stuffing, melt butter in large skillet. Add celery, onions, raisins and apples. Cover skillet with aluminum foil and cook until just soft. Add parsley and crumbs to skillet; combine mixture lightly. Moisten with water so stuffing sticks together. Stuff hens and truss with string. Brush hens with soft shortening and season with salt and pepper. Place hens in bag. Cook for 1 hour. Remove from oven. Slit bag open and turn bag back to cover drippings. Brush hens with currant jelly. Return to oven for 15 minutes or until hens are golden brown. Serves 6 to 8.
Mrs. Linda Pickney

CANTONESE CHICKEN LIVERS À LA OUTRIGGER

2 pounds chicken livers
4 garlic sections
1 7-ounce can water chestnuts
1 7-ounce can mushrooms, sliced
2 cups chicken stock
⅓ cup toasted almonds, sliced

2 cups soy sauce
2 bay leaves
1 tablespoon Burgundy
1 tablespoon corn starch
6 toast wedges

Marinate livers in soy sauce, bay leaves, and garlic for 4 to 5 hours. Sauté livers until browned. Add sliced chestnuts, mushrooms, and Burgundy. Add chicken stock thickened with corn starch. Bring to a boil until livers are cooked. Serve in casserole on toast wedges. Garnish with toasted sliced almonds. Serves 6.
Mrs. William Luckie (Patty)

CHICKEN LIVER CASSEROLE

1 cup rice, uncooked
2 tablespoons butter
1 pound chicken livers
1 4-ounce jar mushrooms,
    sliced
1 10¾-ounce can mushroom
    soup

⅓ cup milk
Dash pepper
2 tablespoons white wine
Few sprigs parsley or
    parsley flakes
¼ cup toasted almonds, chopped

Preheat oven to 350 degrees. Cook rice until tender and drain. Melt butter and brown livers quickly. Add mushrooms and liquid, soup, milk, pepper, parsley and wine. Cook until hot and smooth. Add rice and pour into a 2-quart casserole. Top with almonds and bake 30 minutes.
Mrs. Vance Watt (Mercer)

CHICKEN LIVERS PAPRIKASH

1 pound chicken livers
1 medium onion
3 tablespoons margarine
½ teaspoon salt
½ teaspoon pepper

1 tablespoon sweet paprika
1 clove garlic, sliced in half
½ teaspoon thyme
1 tablespoon flour
¼ cup sour cream

Clean livers, removing all fats and connecting tissue. Heat margarine in 10-inch skillet and in it sauté onions until soft and bright yellow, but not brown. Add livers and brown on all sides. Sprinkle with salt, pepper, and paprika; sauté for about 2 minutes until paprika loses raw smell. Add 1 cup water or just enough to half cover livers. Add garlic and thyme and simmer, covered 15 or 20 minutes, or until livers are done. Blend flour into sour cream, stir into skillet and simmer 3 or 4 minutes. Adjust seasoning to serve. Serves 4.
Mrs. William Blackburn (Connie)

Meats

SAUSAGE CREPES

16 crepes (See Crepes)
1 pound hot pork sausage
¼ cup onion, chopped
½ cup Cheddar cheese, grated

1 3-ounce package cream cheese
1 cup sour cream
1 tablespoon milk
4 tablespoons butter, softened

Cook sausage and onion until brown. Drain. Stir in the Cheddar cheese and the cream cheese. Mix well. Add ¾ cup sour cream and 1 tablespoon milk. Place 2 tablespoons sausage mix down center of each crepe. Roll crepes up. Arrange in a shallow baking dish. Combine the butter and ¼ cup sour cream. Spread over center of crepes. Bake, covered, at 375 degrees for 20 minutes. Serves 6.
Mrs. Fred Cooper (Helen)

SAUSAGE AND WILD RICE CASSEROLE

1 pound hot bulk sausage
2 medium onions, chopped
2 3-ounce cans mushrooms
¼ cup flour
½ cup half and half cream
2½ cups condensed chicken broth

1 teaspoon monosodium glutamate
½ teaspoon poultry seasoning
1 tablespoon salt
2 6-ounce packages long grain
  and wild rice, cooked
½ cup toasted almonds, slivered

Sauté sausage. Drain on paper towel. Break into small pieces. Sauté onion in sausage drippings. Add mushrooms and cooked sausage. Mix flour with cream, add chicken broth, and cook until thickened. Add seasonings. Combine all ingredients except almonds and pour into casserole. Bake 25-30 minutes at 350 degrees. Sprinkle with almonds when ready to serve. Serves 12.
The Editors
Similar recipes submitted by *Mrs. J. D. Hall (Willene) and Mrs. Bill Oliver (Noami).*

SAUSAGE AND CHEESE ENCHILADAS

1 package frozen tortillas
in a boilable bag
8 ounces cream cheese,
softened
2 tablespoons green onion, finely
chopped (use the green ends)
4 ounces sour cream
1 teaspoon salt
1 cup Cheddar cheese, grated

1 pound pork sausage, mild or
hot according to preference
1 medium onion, chopped
1 large clove garlic, chopped
1 1-pound can tomatoes, chopped
1 4-ounce can green chilies
½ teaspoon cumin
2 teaspoons sugar
1 chicken bouillon cube

Prepare the tortillas according to package directions. You will use 10-12 of the softened tortillas. To make sauce: Brown the pork sausage and pour off almost all of the grease. Add the chopped onion and garlic and cook until the onion is soft. Add the can of tomatoes with their liquid, green chilies, cumin, sugar, bouillon cube and ½ teaspoon salt. Cook the sauce covered for 20 minutes. Keep hot. To make the filling: Thoroughly mix the softened cream cheese with the green onions, sour cream and ½ teaspoon salt. Cover the bottom of a baking dish with several tablespoons of the sausage mixture. Place 3 tablespoons of cheese filling on each of the 10-12 tortillas. Roll each tortilla up and place seam side up on sausage mixture in baking dish. Spoon remainder of sausage mixture over top of the tortillas. Bake in 350 degree oven for 30 minutes. After the first 15 minutes, sprinkle the grated Cheddar cheese over top and continue to bake. Serve each enchilada on shredded lettuce. Serves 4-8.

Mrs. Thomas H. Vann, Jr. (Janine)

SKEWERED LAMB

1 lamb shoulder (4-6 pounds)

Have the butcher bone and roll the lamb shoulder. Make marinade and pour over the rolled shoulder. Marinate it for at least two hours. When ready to cook, run a skewer through the meat and place on the rotisserie. Cook for two hours, basting occasionally with the reserved marinade.

MARINADE:

1 cup red wine
½ cup olive oil
1 teaspoon salt
⅛ teaspoon pepper

1 teaspoon oregano
1 teaspoon spearmint
1 clove garlic, pressed

Mix all ingredients together and pour over rolled lamb shoulder.
Mrs. John L. Turner, III (Anne)

LAMB CHOPS

6 lamb chops
6 orange slices
6 onion slices

1 10-ounce can beef consommé
2 tablespoons butter

In skillet brown lamb chops in butter. Secure orange slice and onion slice on each chop with toothpick. Return to skillet. Add consommé. Cook lamb chops, uncovered, over very low heat for about 1½ hours. Consommé should not be allowed to evaporate until cooking time has ended. Should chops appear to be drying out, cover. (An electric skillet is ideal to use because the temperature can be controlled.) If it is necessary to add more liquid, add more consomme' or a little water.
Mrs. Ken Beverly (Mary Jo)

JANE HERNDON'S OLD SOUTHERN COUNTRY HAM

For whole or half ham put in deep pot and cover, barely, with water. Add to water a chopped onion, 1 cup brown sugar and 1 cup vinegar. Boil very slowly for 15-20 minutes per pound, covered. Leave in water to cool overnight. To serve, drain and brown in hot oven for 20-30 minutes or until browned. This is absolutely the moistest ham you can imagine. To fry slices: put slice in cold skillet with nothing else. Cook on LOW, uncovered, until ham begins to brown. Turn and brown on other side. Remove ham and make red-eye gravy the usual way. The ham is very tender and juicy.
Mrs. Michael Herndon (Jane)   *Columbus, Georgia*

TO BAKE COUNTRY HAM

Rinse ham well in cold water; scrub off mold and excess salt with cloth or brush. Cover with cold water and soak overnight. Bake uncovered in 325 degree oven until small bone in hock will move a little bit. Remove from oven. Increase heat to 375 degrees. Remove skin from ham and glaze with mixture of brown sugar and peach pickle juice. Stud with cloves. Put back in oven for about 20 minutes. Cool completely before slicing very thinly.
Mrs. Richard Hackney (Mary)

SLICE OF HAM, PLANTATION-STYLE

1 center cut slice of ham,
2 inches thick

1 cup brown sugar
1 teaspoon dry mustard

Mix the sugar and mustard; rub mixture into both sides of ham until most of it is absorbed. Place the ham slice in a roasting pan and sprinkle the top with any leftover sugar-mustard mixture. Cover and bake at 350 degrees for 50-60 minutes or until tender, basting occasionally with the pan juices. Remove to a hot platter; garnish with parsley and orange slices.
Mrs. William A. Lardin (Sharon)

GLAZED PORK LOIN

4 pound pork loin roast
2 garlic cloves, mashed
2 teaspoons salt
1 teaspoon sage
½ teaspoon pepper

½ teaspoon nutmeg
¼ cup currant jelly
1 teaspoon dry mustard
Cloves to stud top

Have butcher cut through the bone at the back of a pork loin roast. Combine garlic, salt, sage, pepper and nutmeg. Rub the mixture well into the meat. Put meat, fat side up in roaster. Splash water over meat and roast uncovered 1½ hours at 325 degrees. Take meat out. Criss-cross fat with a sharp knife about 1½ inches apart. Combine jelly and mustard and spread over meat. Stud with cloves. Roast 1 hour more. Serves 6.
Mrs. Gerald Muller (Emmy)

HAM LOAF

1 pound lean pork, ground
1 pound ham, ground
2 eggs, beaten
½ cup bread crumbs

½ cup milk
Salt
½ can tomato soup

Mix all ingredients except soup and form into loaf. Place in greased pan and pour tomato soup on top. Bake at 375 degrees for 1½ hours.
Mrs. Elliott McCollum (Lorna)

HAM BALLS

1½ pounds pork steak
1½ pounds ham ends
2 eggs
1 cup milk

2 cups dried bread crumbs
(Herb stuffing or cereal,
crushed)

Have the grocer grind the pork and ham together. Make a mixture of the meats, eggs, crumbs, and milk and form into good size balls. This will make about 18 balls.

SAUCE:

1 cup brown sugar
1½ cups vinegar

½ teaspoon dried mustard
½ cup water

Mix sauce ingredients together and pour over meat balls. Cook two hours at 350 degrees. Baste occasionally. This dish is cooked covered for the first hour and cooked uncovered for the second hour.
Mrs. Ames Watkins Kindred

SWEET AND SOUR PORK

1½ pounds lean pork shoulder,
 cubed
2 tablespoons salad oil
¼ cup water
1 large can pineapple chunks
¼ cup brown sugar
2 tablespoons cornstarch

¼ cup vinegar
1 tablespoon soy sauce
½ teaspoon salt
½ cup green pepper strips
¼ cup thinly sliced onion
Rice or chow mein noodles

Brown pork in oil. Add water, cover and simmer 1 hour. Drain pineapple, reserve juice. Combine juice, brown sugar, cornstarch, pork and let stand 10 minutes or more. (May be put in refrigerator at this point and reheated before serving). Add green pepper, onion, and pineapple chunks. Cook until hot, 3-4 minutes. Serve over rice or chow mein noodles. Serves 3 to 4.
Mrs. Scott Rich (Peggy)

SOUTH PACIFIC CASSEROLE

1-1½ cups ham, cubed
1 cup rice, uncooked
½ cup green pepper, chopped
½ cup onion, chopped
1-1½ teaspoons curry powder

1 teaspoon salt
2 tablespoons brown sugar
1½ cups orange juice
 (or to taste)

Cook rice, salting according to directions. Sauté green pepper and onion until tender. Add brown sugar, curry powder and ¼ cup orange juice. Cook until ingredients are well mixed and sugar is melted. Add rice, ham, salt and remaining orange juice. Place in casserole dish. Bake at 350 degrees for 30 to 40 minutes.
Mrs. Rudolph Fletcher (Barbara)

BRAISED PORK CHOPS WITH TOMATO AND GARLIC SAUCE

6 pork chops, cut 1 to 1½
 inches thick
4 tablespoons olive oil (or 2
 tablespoons olive oil and 2
 tablespoons vegetable oil
 blended)
1 heaping teaspoon garlic,
 finely chopped
1 teaspoon dried oregano
½ teaspoon dried thyme
1 bay leaf
½ teaspoon salt

½ teaspoon sugar
½ cup dry red wine
1 cup canned tomatoes,
 drained and pressed through
 a sieve
1 tablespoon tomato paste
½ pound (about 1½ cups)
 peppers, seeded and cut into
 strips
½ pound fresh mushrooms,
 sliced

Cook the chops in 2 tablespoons of the oil until they are lightly browned, then transfer them to a plate. Pour off almost all of the fat. In the same pan cook the garlic, oregano, thyme, bay leaf and salt for 30 seconds, stirring constantly. Add the wine and boil briskly until it is reduced to about ¼ cup, scraping in any bits of meat or herbs in the pan. Stir in the tomatoes, tomato paste, and sugar; return the chops to the skillet. Baste with the sauce, cover, and simmer over low heat, basting once or twice, for 40 minutes. Meanwhile, heat the remaining 2 tablespoons of oil in another skillet. Fry the green peppers for about 5 minutes, stirring frequently. Add the mushrooms and toss them with the peppers for a minute or two; remove the skillet from the heat. When the chops are tender, add the green peppers and mushrooms to them; cover and simmer for 5 minutes. Uncover and simmer, stirring occasionally, until the vegetables are tender (5-10 minutes) and the sauce is thickened. (If the sauce is too thin, remove chops and vegetables and boil over high heat, stirring constantly.) Serve the chops with the sauce and vegetables spooned over them. Serves 4-6.
The Editors

PORK CHOPS WITH CREAM AND MUSTARD SAUCE
Côtés de Porc Braisées à la Moutarde

6 large pork chops, cut
    1 to 1½ inches thick
Salt
Freshly ground black pepper
Flour
2 tablespoons butter
2 tablespoons vegetable oil
1½ cups onions, sliced
4 tablespoons wine vinegar

Bouquet garni, made of 2 parsley
    sprigs and 1 bay leaf
¾ cup heavy cream
2 teaspoons Dijon-style-
    prepared mustard
A few drops of lemon juice
4 tablespoons chicken broth
    (may be made with a bouillon
    cube)

Season the chops generously with salt and pepper, dip them in flour, then shake off all but a light dusting. Melt the butter and oil over moderate heat. When the foam subsides, brown the chops on each side until they are a rich golden brown. As the chops brown, remove them from the skillet and keep warm. After all the chops are browned, pour off all but a thin film of fat from the skillet. Add the onions and cook over moderate heat, stirring frequently, until they are soft and lightly browned. Stir in the wine vinegar; bring to a boil and scrape in any browned bits that cling to the skillet. Cook the vinegar almost away then add the bouquet garni and the chicken broth; stir to blend. Add the chops, cover, and simmer slowly until tender. Baste once or twice with the skillet juices and turn the chops once during this cooking period. When the chops are tender, remove the chops to a serving platter and keep warm. Tip the skillet and skim as much fat as possible from the surface of the drippings. Remove the onions and bouquet garni from the drippings and place into a fine sieve. Hold directly over skillet and press down hard on the onions with the back of a spoon to remove all the juices, then discard pulp. Pour in the cream and bring to a boil over high heat, stirring constantly. When the sauce has thickened enough to lightly coat the back of a spoon, remove the skillet from the heat and stir in the mustard and lemon juice. Pour over chops, garnish with parsley. Serves 4-6.
Mrs. Thomas H. Vann, Jr. (Janine)

BRAISED PORK CHOPS IN WINE

Pork chops
Salt and pepper
2 tablespoons butter
1 small onion, chopped
1 rib celery, chopped
½ to 1 cup white wine
  (or dry vermouth)

1 cup water
1 chicken bouillon cube
1 clove garlic, chopped
Pinch each of thyme and
  rosemary
1 tablespoon cornstarch
¼ cup water

Brown chops in frying pan. Remove; salt and pepper chops. In same pan, melt the butter and sauté the onion and celery until soft. Add remaining ingredients except cornstarch and water. Add chops and cook over low heat for 45 minutes. Thicken sauce with cornstarch and water mixed. Good with noodles.

Mrs. Patrick Fenlon (Renie)

ORANGE-BAKED PORK CHOPS

6 pork chops,
  ¾ inches thick
½ cup orange juice
1 teaspoon salt

¼ teaspoon pepper
½ teaspoon dry mustard
¼ cup brown sugar

Cut fat from chops, if necessary. Place chops in large shallow baking dish (they do not need to be browned). Combine remaining ingredients, pour over chops and bake at 350 degrees for about an hour, depending on thickness of chops. Baste occasionally during baking.

Mrs. Fred E. Murphy, Jr. (Vi)

APPLE STUFFED PORK CHOPS

6 large pork chops,
  cut at least 1 inch thick
1 cup apples, minced
1½ cups bread crumbs
¼ cup onion, chopped
¼ cup celery, chopped

½ teaspoon poultry seasoning
  or sage
1 teaspoon salt
½ teaspoon pepper
1 tablespoon sugar
2 or 3 tablespoons milk

Make a pocket in each pork chop. Combine apples, bread crumbs, onions, celery, salt, pepper, sage and sugar. Add only enough milk to moisten. Use dressing to stuff pockets. Secure pockets with toothpicks. Place chops in shallow baking dish. Bake at 350 degrees for 1 hour and 30 minutes. Baste occasionally with drippings. Cover during last 30 minutes of baking time. Serves 6.

Mrs. Ken Beverly (Mary Jo)

BARBECUED PORK CHOPS

6 large pork chops
½ teaspoon chili powder
¼ cup wine vinegar
½ cup brown sugar
1 teaspoon prepared
   mustard
¼ teaspoon dry mustard

½ cup catsup
1 tablespoon Worcestershire
   sauce
½ teaspoon Accent
1 cup water
1 medium onion, sliced

Salt and pepper pork chops and fry in small amount of fat until well browned. Mix the rest of the ingredients and pour over the chops. Top with a sliced medium onion and let simmer for 45 minutes to 1 hour.
Mrs. Randy Malone (Mary)

CHINESE BARBECUED SPARERIBS

1 10-ounce jar damson plum
   jelly
⅓ cup dark corn syrup
⅓ cup soy sauce
¼ cup green onion, chopped

2 cloves garlic, minced
2 teaspoons ground ginger
2 pounds spareribs, cut up
   (baby ones if available)

Heat all ingredients for sauce until well blended. Pour over ribs in pan. Cover and marinate for several hours in refrigerator until ready to cook. Bake for 1 hour at 350 degrees, basting several times.
The Editors

OVEN BARBECUED RIBS

3-4 pounds spareribs or loin
   back ribs, cut in pieces
1 lemon, thinly sliced

1 large onion, thinly sliced
Salt

Salt ribs; place in a shallow roasting pan with the meaty side up. Roast for 30 minutes in a 450 degree oven. Drain the excess fat from pan. Top each piece of rib with a slice of unpeeled lemon and a slice of onion. Pour sauce over the ribs. Lower the temperature of the oven to 350 degrees. Bake until well done, about 1½ hours. Baste ribs with the sauce in the pan every 15 minutes. If the sauce gets too thick, add more water.

BASTING SAUCE:

1 cup catsup
⅓ cup Worcestershire sauce
1 teaspoon chili powder

2 dashes Tabasco
1 teaspoon salt
1½ cups water

Combine ingredients and bring to a boil. Pour over ribs. Serves 4.
Mrs. W. J. Becknell (Gwen)

BAR-B-QUE CHUCK

5 pounds lean chuck,
cut in slabs
2 tablespoons pickling spices
(tied in bag)

1 large onion

Place above ingredients in skillet and cover a little more than half with water. Simmer 5-6 hours. After cooking, remove from skillet; shred meat with fingers or fork. (Save liquid for soup, if desired.) Make sauce; pour over meat and simmer one hour longer. Serve over rice.

SAUCE:

3 large onions
3 green peppers
¼ cup olive oil
2 1-pound cans stewed
tomatoes, puréed in blender
1 4-ounce can enchilada sauce
1½ teaspoons dry mustard
¼ cup vinegar
Pinch oregano

¼ cup brown sugar
Salt
Pepper
3 tablespoons Worcestershire
sauce
Dash Tabasco
½ clove garlic
1 teaspoon Kitchen Bouquet

Put onions and green peppers in blender; reduce to purée. Sauté onions and peppers in olive oil; add remaining ingredients and blend well.
Mrs. Ken Beverly (Mary Jo)

AUNT KITTY'S BAR-B-Q

¾ cup chili sauce
(12-ounce bottle)
¾ cup water (use chili sauce
bottle)
1 tablespoon Worcestershire
1 tablespoon vinegar

⅛ teaspoon red pepper
⅛ teaspoon chili powder
1 tablespoon salt
⅛ teaspoon black pepper
2 Bermuda onions, sliced
2 pounds lean ground beef

Bring all ingredients except meat to boil; simmer. Shape meat balls or hamburgers, brown, and add to sauce. Simmer 3 hours or more. Serve on rice, buns, or noodles. Try sauce on ribs, hot dogs or chicken. Variation: Red and black pepper and chili powder can be increased to ¼ or ½ teaspoon if you like a hot sauce, but ½ teaspoon of each makes it pretty hot!
Mrs. Al Zavaleta (Pat)

BARBECUED BEEF

1½ pounds stewing beef	4 teaspoons Worcestershire sauce
1 cup catsup	1 onion, diced
3 teaspoons mustard	⅛ cup sugar
3 tablespoons vinegar	

Cook beef 2½ hours, adding water as needed. When the beef is tender drain and shred. Add remaining ingredients and heat. Serve on a bun. Makes 6 sandwiches.
Mrs. Frederick Jefferson (Marilyn)

CAPTAIN McGOWAN'S EASY ROAST

1 5 to 8 pound roast (works well for almost any weight)	Salt and pepper to taste

Before 11:00 a.m. preheat oven to 375 degrees. Put roast in oven and cook for 1 hour. Turn off oven, leaving roast inside. Do *not* open oven door! At 6:00 p.m. turn on oven again (without opening door). Heat to 375 degrees and cook: 15 minutes for rare, 20 minutes for medium, 25 minutes for well-done. Don't start to time cooking until oven reaches 375 degrees. When desired degree of doneness is reached, remove from oven and serve. Delicious!
Mrs. Henry Pepin (Sara)

ROAST BEEF

This recipe is for people who like their roast beef rare to medium rare. Use a very good cut of beef for roasting, any size. Season the roast as you usually do. Preheat your oven to 500 degrees. Place roast inside and cook for 6 minutes per pound; then turn oven off and do not open the oven door. Leave the door closed for 2 hours after you turn oven off.
Mrs. Thomas H. Vann, Jr. (Janine)

CAMERON STEAK CASSEROLE

6 servings round steak
Salt and pepper
1 6-ounce can tomato paste
1 1-pound can whole
   tomatoes

1 small box elbow macaroni,
   cooked and drained
10 ounces Longhorn cheese,
   grated

Salt, pepper, and flour steak; then fry in small amount of shortening in thick skillet. When brown on both sides, add tomatoes and tomato paste, plus one tomato paste can of water. Stir until smooth around steak. Cover and simmer for 1 hour. Remove steak from sauce and set aside. Layer macaroni, sauce, and grated cheese in 2½-quart casserole. Top with steak. Place in warm oven until ready to serve. Freezes well.
Mrs. Daniel Autry (Janice)

MUGGS' STEW

2 pounds beef, cubed and chopped
1 cup onions, chopped
1 cup green pepper, chopped
1 cup carrots, sliced
1 No. 2 can tomatoes

1 tablespoon salt
1 teaspoon pepper
3 tablespoons tapioca
¼ cup red wine
Potatoes (optional)

Combine all ingredients. Bake, covered, for 4 hours at 300 degrees.
Mrs. Elliott McCollum (Lorna)

LOUISIANA BEEF

3 tablespoons flour
1 teaspoon salt
½ teaspoon celery salt
¼ teaspoon garlic salt
½ teaspoon black pepper
½ teaspoon ginger
3 pounds chuck, cubed
2 tablespoons bacon fat

1 1-pound can tomatoes
3 medium onions, sliced
⅓ cup red wine vinegar
½ cup molasses
6-8 carrots, cut in
   1-inch pieces
½ cup raisins

Combine the first 6 ingredients and sprinkle onto meat. Brown meat in hot bacon fat. Add next 4 ingredients and ½ cup water. Bring to boil, cover and simmer about 2 hours. Add carrots and raisins and simmer 30 minutes more. Serve over rice.
Mrs. Lawrence Harmon (Kaki)

PEPPER STEAK AND RICE

1 pound round steak,
   ½ inch thick
1 tablespoon paprika
2 tablespoons margarine
2 cloves garlic, crushed
1½ cups beef broth
1 cup green onions, chopped,
   using green tops also

2 green peppers, cut into
   strips
¼ cup water
¼ cup soy sauce
2 fresh tomatoes, cut into
   ⅛-inch slices
3 cups rice, cooked

Cut meat into ¼-inch wide strips and sprinkle with the paprika. Let the meat stand ½ hour. Using a large skillet, brown the meat strips in the margarine. Add the garlic and broth. Cover and simmer 30 minutes or until tender. Stir in the onions and green peppers; cover and simmer 10 minutes more. Pour in the water and soy sauce. Stir and cook 5 minutes. Add the tomatoes and stir gently. Serve over hot rice. Serves 5-6.
Mrs. Howard Carnes (Henrietta)

STEAK AND BACON TOURNEDOS

1-1½ pounds beef flank steak
Instant meat tenderizer
½ pound bacon
1 teaspoon garlic salt

½ teaspoon pepper
2 tablespoons parsley, chopped
Béarnaise Sauce (See Sauces)

Pound flank steak to ½-inch thickness. Use meat tenderizer according to directions on bottle. Meanwhile, cook bacon until almost done but not crisp. Sprinkle steak with garlic salt and pepper. Score steak diagonally, making diamond shapes. Place bacon strips lengthwise on steak. Sprinkle with parsley. Roll steak up and skewer at 1-inch intervals with toothpicks or small skewers. Cut into 1-inch slices. Grill 15 minutes, turning once. Prepare Béarnaise Sauce. Serve sauce over pinwheels. Serves 8.
Mrs. Elliott McCollum (Lorna)

SEASONED BROILED STEAK

½ cup butter
¼ cup fresh parsley, chopped
¼ cup onion, minced
½ teaspoon dry mustard

½ teaspoon black pepper,
   freshly ground
2 teaspoons Worcestershire sauce
Steak

Melt the butter; add seasonings, parsley, onions and Worcestershire sauce. Cook 1 minute. Brush sauce on steak and broil to taste, basting once during broiling time.
The Editors

STEAK WITH TOMATOES AND GARLIC
Bistecca alla Pizzaiola

4 tablespoons olive oil
2 teaspoons garlic, finely
   chopped
2 cups canned tomatoes,
   chopped, and liquid
1 scant teaspoon sugar

2 teaspoons dried oregano
½ teaspoon salt
Freshly ground black pepper
A 3-pound T-bone, porterhouse or
   sirloin, cut 1 to 2 inches
   thick

Heat 2 tablespoons of the oil until a light haze forms over it. Remove the pan from the heat; add the garlic and stir it around for about 30 seconds. Add the tomatoes and liquid, oregano, salt, sugar and a few grindings of pepper; cook over moderate heat, stirring frequently. Cook until about half the liquid has boiled away. Remove the pan from the heat. In a heavy skillet, heat the remaining 2 tablespoons of oil, again until a light haze forms over it. Over high heat, brown the steak in the hot oil for 1 or 2 minutes on each side. Lower the heat to moderate and spoon the tomato sauce over and around the meat. Cover and cook for 6-10 minutes, or until the steak is done to your taste. To serve, scrape the tomato sauce off the top of the steak into the skillet and transfer the steak to a carving board. Simmer the sauce left in the skillet for 1 or 2 minutes, scraping in any browned bits. Taste for seasoning. Carve the steak and spoon the sauce over the slices. Serves 4.
Mrs. Thomas H. Vann, Jr. (Janine)

STEAK MARCHAND DE VIN

2½ pounds sirloin or better
   steak, 2 inches thick
2 tablespoons butter
1 tablespoon shallots, chopped
1 teaspoon flour
1 beef bouillon cube, dissolved
   in 2 tablespoons hot water

1 cup dry red wine
1 teaspoon lemon juice
Salt
Freshly ground pepper
1 tablespoon cream
1 teaspoon parsley,
   chopped

Sauté the chopped shallots in butter. Blend in flour and add beef bouillon, wine, lemon juice, and salt and pepper to taste. Simmer down to ½ cup, stir in cream, and simmer a few seconds longer. Broil steak to desired doneness and cover with sauce to serve. Sprinkle with chopped parsley. Serves 4.
The Editors

BEEF BURGUNDY

1½-2 pounds stewing beef,
  cubed
2 tablespoons oil
1 large Bermuda onion, chopped
Generous pinch each of thyme
  and marjoram

Salt and pepper to taste
2 tablespoons flour
2 cups beef stock or broth
2 cups dry red Burgundy wine
1 pound fresh mushrooms

Sauté beef cubes in oil until very brown. Remove the beef from the pan. Sauté the chopped onion in the same pan, adding more oil if necessary. Remove onions from pan and set aside. Place meat cubes back in the pan and sprinkle with the thyme, marjoram, salt and pepper. Sprinkle flour over the meat and spices and stir until it is absorbed. Add the beef stock and wine to cover meat. Simmer, covered, for 3-4 hours, adding more wine and stock as necessary. Add the mushrooms and sautéed onions and simmer for 30 minutes more. If desired, this can be thickened with cornstarch dissolved in water. Serves 6.
Mrs. Marshall C. Dunaway (Linden)
Similar recipe submitted by *Mrs. Fred Allen (Winnie).*

Variation: 4 cups of wine may be used instead of half wine and half broth.

BEEF STROGANOFF I

1½ pounds round steak, cut
  in thin strips
¼ cup flour
Dash pepper
1 can sliced mushrooms
  (about 1 pound, drained)
½ cup onion, chopped

1 small garlic clove, minced
1 10¾-ounce can beef broth or
  consommé
1 cup sour cream
3 cups noodles or rice,
  cooked

Flour and brown steak. Remove meat from skillet and pour off most of the grease. Add mushrooms, garlic, and onion; brown slightly. Return meat to skillet and add beef broth. Cover and cook 1 hour or until meat is tender. Gradually add sour cream and cook over low heat for 5 minutes. Serve over noodles or rice. Serves 4-6.
Mrs. Max E. Beverly (Clara)

Variation: Add ¼ teaspoon oregano, 2 bay leaves (remove before serving), and 2 tablespoons of sherry wine.
Mrs. Elliott McCollum (Lorna)

BEEF STROGANOFF II

1½ pounds sirloin or round
    steak, cut in strips
3 tablespoons butter
1 onion, chopped
1 clove garlic, chopped
½ teaspoon salt
1 large can mushrooms, drained
1 tablespoon butter

Flour
1 cup sour cream
½ teaspoon salt
2 tablespoons catsup
2 beef bouillon cubes
½ teaspoon white pepper
Paprika for color

Heat 3 tablespoons of butter in iron or heavy skillet. Sauté onion and garlic. Add meat and ½ teaspoon salt; sear. Cover and cook approximately 30 minutes, turning occasionally. Add mushrooms and transfer mixture to a double boiler. In separate skillet melt butter and blend in flour. Add the remaining ingredients with enough paprika to get desired color. Cook until smooth, stirring constantly. Mix with meat mixture in double boiler. Cook an additional 15 minutes. Serve over rice.
Mrs. Heeth Varnedoe, Jr. (Jackie)
Similar recipes submitted by *Mrs. Sara Shipp and Mrs. R. F. DeLamar, III (Peggy).*

CORNED BEEF BRISKET WITH MUSTARD SAUCE

5 pounds corned beef brisket
1 onion, halved
1 clove garlic, halved
6 whole cloves

8 peppercorns
2 bay leaves
4 stalks celery, sliced

Cover corned beef with cold water. Add remaining ingredients and bring to a boil. Cover and simmer 3½ to 4 hours, or until tender. Cool slightly before slicing. Serve with English Mustard Sauce.

ENGLISH MUSTARD SAUCE:

1 tablespoon flour
1 teaspoon dry mustard
½ teaspoon salt
⅛ teaspoon pepper

½ cup water
1 tablespoon vinegar
1 tablespoon butter
1 tablespoon prepared mustard

Combine dry mustard, flour, salt and pepper in saucepan. Gradually add water and vinegar. Cook, stirring constantly, until boiling. Continue to cook 2 minutes. Remove from heat. Stir in butter and prepared mustard. Serve hot.
Miss Josephine Craig

SAUERBRATEN

1 large bottom round,
   top round, or chuck roast
2 cups vinegar and/or
   cooking wine
2 cups water
2 medium onions, sliced
6 whole cloves

4 bay leaves
1 tablespoon salt
6 peppercorns
1 tablespoon sugar
⅓ cup gingersnap crumbs
2 tablespoons sugar
2 tablespoons flour

Bring vinegar and/or wine, water, onions, cloves, bay leaves, peppercorns, and 1 tablespoon sugar to boil. Pour over roast in large bowl or pot. Refrigerate 4 days, turning once each day. Remove meat from marinade, pat dry, coat with flour, and brown well. Reserve 3 cups marinade strained. Drain all fat from meat, add 1 sliced onion, 6 cloves, 1 bay leaf and 3 cups of marinade. Simmer 4 hours or until done. (Can be roasted, covered, in 325 degree oven.) Add gingersnap crumbs, flour and sugar to marinade for sauce. Good served with potato pancakes.
Mrs. Al Lookabaugh (Diana)

CHILI

1½ pounds of ground beef
2 onions, chopped
½ large bell pepper, chopped
Salt and pepper to taste
2 tablespoons chili powder
1 16-ounce can stewed tomatoes

1 6-ounce can tomato paste
2 tablespoons Worcestershire
   sauce
1 16-ounce can kidney beans,
   drained

Brown ground beef and add onions and bell pepper. Add remaining ingredients, except beans, and simmer for 2 hours. Stir in beans.
Mrs. Randolph Jones (Nancy)
Similar recipes submitted by *Mrs. Joe Beverly (Mary) and Mrs. Warren Garrard (Dottie).*

REAL TEXAS CHILI

3 pounds boneless chuck,
cut into 1-inch cubes
2 tablespoons vegetable oil
2 to 3 cloves garlic,
chopped
4-6 tablespoons chili powder
2 teaspoons ground cumin
3 tablespoons flour
1 tablespoon leaf oregano

2 13¾-ounce cans beef
broth
1 teaspoon salt
¼ teaspoon pepper
1 15-ounce can pinto beans,
optional
1 cup dairy sour cream
1 lime, cut into wedges

Heat oil in 4-quart kettle or heavy-bottom pan over medium heat. Add beef, stirring frequently with a wooden spoon until meat changes color but does not brown. Lower heat; stir in garlic. Combine chili powder, cumin seed and flour. Sprinkle meat with chili mixture, stirring until meat is evenly coated. Crumble oregano over meat. Add 1¼ cans of the broth and stir until liquid is well-blended. Add salt and pepper. Bring to a boil, stirring occasionally. Reduce heat; simmer, partially covered, over low heat for 1½ hours. Stir occasionally. Add remaining broth; cook for 30 minutes longer, or until meat is almost falling apart. Cool thoroughly. Cover; refrigerate overnight to ripen flavor. Reheat chili in top part of double boiler placed over boiling water. If using beans, heat them, drain, and stir into chili. Garnish chili with sour cream and add wedges of lime to squeeze over each portion. Serves 8.
Mrs. A. B. Wight, Jr. (Carolyn)

JOE MAZOTTI

1½ pounds lean ground
pork
8 large onions, sliced
¼ cup cooking oil
1 can tomato paste
2 cups water
4 tablespoons butter
1 large bunch celery,
diced

2 green peppers,
finely chopped
1 pound fresh mushrooms
Juice of ½ lemon
1 pound sharp New York
cheese, cubed
Salt and pepper to taste
1 package wide noodles, cooked

Sauté meat and add onions. Fry until softened and golden brown. Add tomato paste and water and simmer. In separate skillet, sauté the celery, pepper and chopped mushrooms in the butter until wilted. Mix with the meat mixture; add the lemon juice and cubed cheese. Mix cooked noodles with the sauce and bake one hour in 350 degree oven in an open dish with tiny cubes of cheese sprinkled on top. Serve with hard rolls or French bread. Garlic bread is excellent! Serves 8.
Mrs. Cyrus Helm (Fran)

218

MEAT LOAF

2 pounds ground beef
2 garlic cloves, finely
  chopped
1 teaspoon salt
1 crumbled bay leaf
1 teaspoon green peppers,
  chopped
6-8 slices bacon

1 pound ground pork
1 large onion, finely
  chopped
1 teaspoon pepper
½ teaspoon thyme
½ cup dry bread crumbs
2 eggs

Mix all ingredients except bacon. Knead until mixture is blended. Arrange 3 or 4 slices of bacon on bottom of loaf pan; add meat mixture. Place 3 or 4 slices of bacon on top of loaf. Bake in 350 degree oven for 45 to 55 minutes. Remove from oven and unmold onto hot platter. Let stand 10-15 minutes before serving. Serves 6-8.
Mrs. William A. Lardin (Sharon)

Variation: Canned tomato sauce can be poured over the meat loaf to bake. Similar recipes submitted by *Mrs. Richard Miller (Charlotte), Mrs. Dan Bain (Sally) and Mrs. James Pringle (Mae).*

HUNGARIAN GOULASH

2½ pounds beef round steak,
  cut in ½-inch cubes
1 cup onion, chopped
1 clove garlic, minced
¼ cup all-purpose flour
1½ tablespoons paprika
1½ teaspoons salt

¼ teaspoon pepper
¼ teaspoon thyme
2 bay leaves
1 No. 2½ can tomatoes
  (3½ cups)
1 cup dairy sour cream

Brown meat, half at a time in ¼ cup hot fat. Reduce heat. Add onion and garlic; cook until onion is tender but not brown. Blend in flour and seasonings. Add tomatoes. Cover simmer, stirring occasionally, until meat is tender, about 1 hour. Stir often toward end of cooking. Stir in sour cream. Serve at once over hot noodles. Serves 8.
Mrs. A. B. Wight, Jr. (Carolyn)

Variation: 1 teaspoon of caraway seed makes a delicious addition.

VEAL SCALLOPINI

¼ cup flour
½ cup Parmesan cheese,
   grated
1 teaspoon salt
⅛ teaspoon pepper
1½ pounds veal cutlets, sliced
   ¼ inch thick and cut into
   2-inch strips

2 tablespoons olive oil
1 clove garlic
½ cup dry white wine
½ cup consommé or stock
1 tablespoon lemon juice
Parsley

Mix flour, cheese, salt and pepper together. Wipe meat dry; sprinkle with flour mixture and pound it into meat with a potato masher. Heat olive oil with garlic, and brown meat lightly on both sides. Remove garlic; add wine, stock, and lemon juice. Cover and simmer slowly for about 30 minutes. Sprinkle with chopped parsley to serve. Serves 4-6.
Mrs. Fred Cooper (Helen)

VEAL WITH LEMON
Veal Scaloppine al Limone

1½ pounds veal scallops,
   cut ½ inch thick and
   pounded until ¼ inch thick
Salt
Freshly ground black
   pepper
Flour
2 tablespoons butter

3 tablespoons olive oil
¾ cup beef stock, fresh or
   canned
6 thin lemon slices
1 tablespoon juice
2 tablespoons butter,
   softened

Season the veal scallops with salt and pepper; then dip them in flour and shake off the excess. In a heavy skillet, melt 2 tablespoons of butter with the olive oil over moderate heat. When the foam subsides, add the veal, 4 or 5 scallops at a time, and sauté them until they are golden brown. Transfer the veal to a plate. Pour off most of the fat from the skillet. Add ½ cup of the beef stock and boil it briskly for 1 or 2 minutes, stirring constantly and scraping in any browned bits in the pan. Return the veal to the skillet and arrange the lemon slices on top. Cover the skillet and simmer over low heat for 10 to 15 minutes, or until veal is tender. To serve, transfer the scallops to a heated platter. Add the remaining ½ cup beef stock to the juices in the skillet and boil briskly until the sauce is like a syrupy glaze. Add the lemon juice and cook, stirring, for 1 minute. Remove the pan from the heat; stir in the 2 tablespoons of soft butter and pour the sauce over the scallops. Serves 2-4.
Mrs. Thomas H. Vann, Jr. (Janine)

VEAL PARMESAN
Scaloppine di Vitella alla Parmigiana

1½-2 pounds veal round steak
(cutlet), cut about ½ inch
thick
1⅓ cups (4 slices) fine,
dry bread crumbs
⅓ cup Parmesan cheese, grated
3 eggs, well beaten
1 teaspoon salt

¾ teaspoon monosodium
glutamate
¼ teaspoon pepper
⅓ cup olive oil
2 cups Tomato Meat Sauce
(Leftover spaghetti sauce
is great!)
6 slices (3 ounces) mozzarella
cheese (1 slice per cutlet)

Pound veal and cut into 6 pieces. Set aside. Mix bread crumbs and grated cheese. Set aside. Combine eggs, salt, monosodium glutamate and pepper. Dip cutlets into egg mixture and then into crumb mixture. Heat ⅓ cup olive oil in skillet. Brown cutlets on both sides. Arrange cutlets in 11x7x1½-inch baking dish. Pour 2 cups sauce over cutlets and top with cheese. Bake at 350 degrees for 15-20 minutes or until cheese is melted and lightly browned. Serves 4-6.

TOMATO MEAT SAUCE:

¼ cup olive oil
1 medium onion, chopped
1 medium green pepper,
chopped
1 3-ounce can mushrooms,
stems and pieces
1 pound ground beef
1 1-pound can tomatoes (or
tomato sauce with tomato bits)

1 6-ounce can tomato paste
1 tablespoon salt
1 bay leaf
Garlic to taste
1 teaspoon basil
1 teaspoon oregano
1 tablespoon parsley,
chopped

Sauté onion, pepper and mushrooms in olive oil until tender. Remove and set aside. In same pan cook ground beef until brown, stirring occasionally. To meat, add cooked mushrooms, onions, pepper, tomatoes, salt, garlic, bay leaf and other spices. Cover and simmer over low heat at least 1 hour. If sauce becomes too thick, add ½ cup water. Makes approximately 4 cups sauce.
Mrs. Tom Faircloth (Janice)

HEARTY MANICOTTI

1 pound Italian sausage
1 pound ground beef
1 medium onion, chopped
2 16-ounce cans tomato purée
1 6-ounce can tomato paste
1¾ teaspoons basil
Salt
1 teaspoon sugar
½ teaspoon pepper

1 8-ounce package manicotti
  shells (16 shells), cooked
2 15- or 16-ounce containers
  ricotta or cottage cheese
1 8-ounce package mozzarella
  cheese, diced
2 tablespoons parsley,
  chopped
Parmesan cheese, grated

In covered Dutch oven over medium heat, cook sausage in ¼ cup water for 5 minutes. Uncover; brown sausage well and drain on paper towels. Discard fat from Dutch oven. Over medium heat, brown ground beef and onion well; stir in tomato purée, tomato paste, 1 teaspoon basil, salt, sugar, pepper, and 1 cup water. Simmer, covered, 45 minutes. Cut sausage into bite-size pieces and add to mixture. Cook 15 minutes, stirring occasionally. Preheat oven to 375 degrees. In large bowl, combine ricotta and mozzarella cheese, parsley, ¾ teaspoon basil, and ½ teaspoon salt. Stuff into cooked shells. Spoon half of meat sauce into one 13 x 9-inch or two 9 x 9-inch baking dishes. Arrange half of stuffed shells over sauce in one layer. Spoon remaining sauce, except ¾ cup, over shells; top with remaining shells in one layer. Spoon reserved meat sauce over top. Sprinkle with Parmesan cheese. Bake 30 minutes at 375 degrees. Serves 8.

Mrs. A. B. Wight, Jr. (Carolyn)

LASAGNE

1 pound ground beef
1 medium onion, chopped
2 6-ounce cans tomato paste
2 cups water
1 teaspoon parsley
1 teaspoon paprika
1 teaspoon oregano
1 teaspoon garlic salt
½ teaspoon salt

½ teaspoon pepper
1 pound mozzarella cheese
1 pound American cheese
Grated Parmesan cheese
6-8 lasagne noodles
2 eggs
¾ pound creamed
  cottage cheese

Brown ground beef and onion; add the seasonings, water and tomato paste. Simmer 1 hour. In separate bowl stir together the eggs and cottage cheese. Set aside. Add lasagne noodles to boiling salted water. Cook 15 to 20 minutes and drain. Arrange noodles in buttered baking dish. Cover them with some of the sauce, then with sliced mozzarella cheese. Then arrange triangles of American cheese with points together over the mozzarella. Cover with thin layer of egg mixture. Continue layering ingredients in this order, ending with egg mixture. Cover with grated Parmesan cheese. Sprinkle with paprika. Bake at 375 degrees for 30 minutes. Let set 5-10 minutes before slicing. May be prepared ahead of time and refrigerated until 1 hour before baking. Serves 6-8.

Mrs. Rocky Ivey (Mickie)

RIGATONI

1½ pounds mixed ground beef,
 veal, and pork
¼ cup onion, chopped
4 8-ounce cans tomato sauce
1 3-ounce can tomato paste
2 tablespoons Italian seasoning
1 pound rigatoni shells
½ cup spinach, cooked and
 chopped

¼ cup Parmesan cheese,
 grated
1 large clove garlic, pressed
1 egg
1 teaspoon salt
½ teaspoon pepper

First make tomato sauce by sautéing ½ pound of the mixed ground meats with the chopped onion until meat is brown and the onion tender. Add tomato sauce, tomato paste, Italian seasoning and salt and pepper to taste. Simmer for 30 minutes, stirring occasionally. Pour ½ of this tomato sauce into the bottom of a buttered baking dish. Boil rigatoni shells according to directions on the package. While shells are cooking, combine in a bowl the remaining pound of raw meat and the spinach, cheese, garlic, egg, salt and pepper. Mix well. Drain the rigatoni shells in a colander and rinse under running water. Stuff each rigatoni shell with the raw meat-spinach mixture and place shell on top of the tomato sauce. Pour remaining tomato sauce over the rigatoni shells, sprinkle with more Parmesan, and bake uncovered for 35 minutes in a 350 degree oven. If recipe is made the day before, bake 20 minutes at 350 degrees. Refrigerate. Reheat 15 minutes at 350 degrees. Cover and heat 20 minutes more. Serves 6-8.

Mrs. Lee Mayfield (Patricia)   *Covington, Georgia*

HERBED SPAGHETTI

3 medium onions, chopped
2 carrots, pared and
 shredded
2 cloves garlic, crushed
¼ cup butter or margarine
1½ pounds ground beef
1 pound ground pork
10 medium tomatoes, peeled
 and coarsely chopped

1 15-ounce can tomato sauce
½ cup fresh basil leaves,
 snipped, or 2 tablespoons
 dried basil
1 teaspoon dried oregano leaves
1 cup dry red wine or
 tomato juice
Spaghetti noodles, cooked

Cook and stir onions, carrots and garlic in butter in Dutch oven until onions are tender. Stir in beef and cook until light brown. Stir in remaining ingredients, except spaghetti. Heat to boiling, reduce heat. Cook over medium heat, stirring occasionally until thickened, about 1 hour. Refrigerate at least 8 hours. Skim off fat. Serve sauce over hot spaghetti. Can be frozen for 3 months.

Mrs. Bolling Jones, III (Connie)

MARY CALLAHAN'S SAUCE FOR SPAGHETTI

1 No. 2 can tomatoes
1 tablespoon salt
¼ teaspoon Tabasco
2 tablespoons Worcestershire
  sauce
1 small can (5 or 6-ounce)
  tomato paste
3 or 4 dashes black pepper
½ teaspoon chili powder

2 large white onions,
  thinly sliced
2 bell peppers, chopped
3 or 4 stalks celery,
  chopped
1½ pounds ground round
  steak
3 or 4 tablespoons
  bacon drippings

Place the first seven ingredients into a heavy saucepan and keep covered over low heat. Brown the onions, bell pepper and celery in the bacon drippings. Add the browned vegetables to the tomato sauce mixture. Fry the 1½ pounds of ground round steak in bacon drippings or butter until well done. Add the meat to the tomato sauce mixture and let simmer for 1½ or 2 hours, the longer the better. Serve over spaghetti which has been cooked according to directions on the package.
Mrs. E. C. Oliver (Clancy)

SPAGHETTI CASSEROLE
Family Style

3 cups onion, chopped
3 pounds ground beef
4 tablespoons salad or olive
  oil
Black pepper, salt, garlic salt,
  chili powder, Worcestershire
  sauce to taste

4 8-ounce cans tomato
  sauce
2 3-ounce cans sliced
  mushrooms, drained
2 8-ounce packages long,
  thin spaghetti, cooked
2 cups Cheddar cheese, grated

Brown beef and onions in oil in heavy pot. Add mushrooms, tomato sauce and seasonings. Stir well; cover and simmer 15 minutes. Pour over cooked spaghetti; mix well. Pour into 2 3-quart casseroles. (Can be frozen at this point, or refrigerated until next day). Allow to return to room temperature before baking. Sprinkle cheese on top. Bake 30 minutes at 300 degrees. Recipe can be easily halved.
Mrs. Al Zavaleta (Pat)

Variation: For spicier sauce, one may add chopped green pepper and chopped celery; also, oregano, basil, cayenne pepper, and sugar to taste.
Mrs. Jasper Davis (Marthalene)

Vegetables

SCALLOPED ARTICHOKES

10 small butter crackers	1 egg
1 small onion, finely chopped	¾ cup sour cream
½ medium green pepper,	¼ teaspoon salt
finely chopped	Dash of Tabasco, optional
2 tablespoons vegetable oil	⅛ teaspoon each: thyme,
8 cooked artichoke hearts	sweet basil or rosemary
(fresh, frozen or canned)	(optional)

Cook onion and green pepper in oil until soft, but not browned. Turn into 1½-quart casserole and add artichoke hearts. Beat egg slightly and combine with sour cream. Add seasonings. Pour over artichoke hearts. Crush crackers and sprinkle on top. Bake in a 350 degree oven for 20-25 minutes. Serves 4.
Mrs. Thomas Williams (Marguerite)

MRS. COBB'S ASPARAGUS-ARTICHOKE CASSEROLE

2 14-ounce cans colossal	2 cups New York State sharp
green asparagus	cheese, grated
2 15-ounce cans hearts of	½ cup sherry
artichokes	Pinch of nutmeg
2 small cans water chestnuts	Salt
½ pound butter	Pepper
1 cup flour	Accent
Juice from vegetables	Toasted almonds

Melt butter. Brown flour slowly in butter. Add juices from vegetables. If needed, add a little water. Sauce should be thick. Add grated cheese and sherry. Season to taste. Layer vegetables in casserole dish. Top with sauce. Bake at 350 degrees for 20 to 30 minutes or until bubbly and hot throughout. Sprinkle with almonds.
Mrs. Maurice Tanner (Peggy)
Similar recipe submitted by *Mrs. Chris CoCroft (Katie).*

ASPARAGUS SOUFFLÉ

1 large can asparagus	1 cup Cheddar cheese, grated
1 stick butter	½ to 1 cup almonds
2 tablespoons flour	½ teaspoon salt
1 cup milk	

Melt butter. Stir in flour and milk. When well-combined and slightly thickened, add cheese and salt. When cheese is melted, remove from heat. In casserole alternate layers of asparagus, cheese sauce and almonds. Bake at 400 degrees for 20 to 30 minutes. Serves 3-4.
Mrs. Scott Rich (Peggy)
Similar recipe submitted by *Mrs. William Smitha (Helen).*

WALNUT-MUSHROOM ASPARAGUS

4 small green onions,
    chopped
3 cups fresh mushrooms,
    sliced
6 tablespoons butter or
    margarine

½ cup toasted walnuts, coarsely
    ground
Salt to taste
3 pounds fresh asparagus, cooked;
    or 2 1-pound cans, drained; or
    1 10-ounce package, frozen

Sauté onions and mushrooms in butter until tender, but not brown. Add walnuts and salt. Spoon over hot cooked asparagus spears that have been drained well.
Mrs. Albert Stringer (Regina)

ASPARAGUS VINAIGARETTE

1 10-ounce package frozen asparagus
    sprouts, cooked and drained
½ teaspoon sugar
⅛ teaspoon salt
⅛ teaspoon paprika

⅛ teaspoon black pepper
3 tablespoons sweet pickle
    relish
1 tablespoon vinegar
1 pimento

Place asparagus in casserole dish. Combine other ingredients and pour over asparagus. Reheat and serve.
Mrs. Lewis Hall Singletary (Mildred)

FRENCH GREEN BEAN CASSEROLE

3 boxes frozen French-cut
    green beans
1 large onion, chopped
1 stick butter
½ pound mushrooms
2 cans mushroom soup

½ pound sharp cheese
Juice of 1 lemon
¼ cup sherry
1 French-fried onions
or topping

Cook onion and mushrooms transparent. Mix with cooked beans and other ingredients. Blend well. Put into greased casserole and top with French-fried onions. Bake 10-12 minutes at 325 degrees. Serves 10 to 12.
Mrs. William Z. Bridges (Mary)
Similar recipes submitted by *Mrs. W. W. Gravely (Tan) and Mrs. Linda Pinckney.*

GREEN BEANS INDIA

8 slices bacon, crumbled
½ cup sugar
½ cup vinegar
½ medium onion, diced

2 cans French-style
   green beans
3 tablespoons India relish

Preheat oven to 275 degrees. Fry bacon and remove from pan. Sauté sugar, onions and vinegar in bacon drippings. Place green beans in casserole and pour sugar mixture over beans. Crumble bacon and mix with relish. Top beans with this mixture and cover. Bake at 275 degrees for 1½ hours.
Mrs. Thomas Lear (Ann)

BROCCOLI PUFF

1 pound cottage cheese
½ teaspoon onion powder
1 teaspoon salt
3 eggs
½ pound Cheddar cheese,
   grated

2 packages frozen, chopped
   broccoli, thawed
¼ cup butter or margarine,
   melted
½ to ¾ cup bread
   crumbs

Combine cottage cheese, onion powder, salt, eggs, Cheddar cheese and broccoli in large bowl. When mixed well, pour into 9 x 12-inch baking dish. Make topping of melted butter and crumbs. Sprinkle on top of broccoli mixture. Bake at 350 degrees for 1 hour, or until knife inserted comes out clean. Let set for 10 minutes before serving.
Mrs. Maureen Otis Adams

BROCCOLI CASSEROLE I

2 packages frozen
   broccoli spears
2 tablespoons butter
2 tablespoons flour
2 cups milk
¾ cup cheese, grated

1 teaspoon salt
¼ teaspoon pepper
¼ cup almonds, slivered
4 slices crisp bacon
½ cup bread crumbs,
   buttered

Cook broccoli with salt; drain. Make white sauce with butter, flour and milk. Then stir in cheese and almonds. Add seasonings. Place broccoli in casserole and pour sauce over top. Crumble bacon and crumbs over casserole. Bake at 350 degrees for 20 minutes.
Mrs. Bernard Lanigan (Kathy)

BROCCOLI CASSEROLE II

2 tablespoons butter or
    margarine, melted
2 tablespoons all-purpose
    flour
1 3-ounce package cream cheese,
    softened
1-ounce bleu cheese, crumbled
    (¼ cup)

1 cup milk
2 10-ounce packages frozen
    chopped broccoli, cooked
    and drained
⅓ cup Ritz crackers, crushed
    (about 10 crackers)

In a large saucepan, blend butter, flour, cream cheese and bleu cheese. Add milk; cook and stir until mixture bubbles. Stir in cooked broccoli. Turn into a 1-quart casserole. Top with cracker crumbs. Bake at 350 degrees for 30 minutes. Makes 8 to 10 servings.
Mrs. Dilworth Mills (Mary)

BROCCOLI CASSEROLE III

3 packages frozen chopped
    broccoli
¾ cup water chestnuts,
    chopped
1½ cans cream of mushroom soup
1½ sticks Kraft garlic
    cheese roll

½ cup almonds, toasted
1 large onion, chopped
1 stick butter
Bread crumbs

Sauté onions in butter. Add frozen broccoli to skillet and let thaw. When broccoli is heated add mushroom soup, cheese, almonds and water chestnuts. Put in buttered casserole. Top with bread crumbs. Bake at 300 degrees for 1 hour.
Mrs. Marshall C. Dunaway (Linden)

Variation: 1 small can sliced mushrooms may be added.
Mrs. E. C. Oliver, Jr. (Jerreann)

CARROTS AND BEANS

2 tablespoons margarine
1 tablespoon flour
1 tablespoon sugar
1½ teaspoons salt
⅛ teaspoon dry mustard
½ teaspoon celery salt
⅛ teaspoon horseradish

1½ tablespoons Worcestershire
 sauce
1½ cups chili sauce
2 cups green beans, cooked
1½ cups carrots, cooked
 and cut into strips

Cook beans and carrots until just tender. Melt margarine over low heat. Add flour and stir to form a smooth paste. Add all other ingredients and heat, but do not boil. Arrange beans in serving dish with carrots nested in center. Pour sauce over vegetables and serve. Serves 8-10. (This recipe belonged to my mother-in-law. She always served it with Thanksgiving and Christmas dinners.)
Mrs. Tom Vann, Jr. (Ann)

COPPER PENNY CARROTS

2 pounds or 16-18 carrots
2 green peppers, sliced
1 large onion, sliced
1 can tomato soup
½ cup vegetable or salad
 oil

¾ cup vinegar
1 cup sugar
1 teaspoon prepared mustard
1 teaspoon Worcestershire
 sauce
Salt and pepper to taste

Cut carrots into slices and boil until tender with 1 teaspoon of the sugar added. Drain and cool. Alternate layers of carrots with slices of green peppers and onions. Blend well the remaining ingredients and pour over the vegetables. Refrigerate for at least 24 hours before serving.

Served chilled, this dish counts as salad, vegetable, or relish. It is perfect for a covered-dish dinner because you can make it ahead, and it keeps indefinitely in the refrigerator.
Mrs. Terry Rouse (Bobbie)
Similar recipes submitted by *Mrs. Rudolph Bell (Sarah) and Mrs. Marshall Woodson (Betty).*

CELERY CRUNCH

2 cups celery, chopped
½ cup blanched almonds,
    chopped
⅔ cup Cheddar cheese,
    grated
Cornflakes, crushed

Cracker crumbs
1 egg, beaten
½ cup milk, scalded
1 10½-ounce can cream
    of celery soup

Cover chopped celery with boiling water. Boil until tender. Grease a 1½-quart casserole with butter or margarine. Put 1 cup celery, ¼ cup almonds, ⅓ cup cheese into casserole. Cover with cracker crumbs. Add remainder of celery, another ¼ cup almonds, ⅓ cup cheese. Cover with cracker crumbs mixed with crushed cornflakes. Just before baking, mix egg, milk, and cream of celery soup. Pour over casserole. Heat in 350 degree oven until bubbly.
Mrs. Fred Scott, Jr. (Mary)

PARMESAN CAULIFLOWER

1 head cauliflower
Dash Parmesan cheese

2 tablespoons butter

Cook cauliflower in boiling water about 15 minutes. Remove from water and drain. Divide into flowerets and top with Parmesan cheese and butter. Serve hot. Serves 3-4.
Mrs. Fred Allen (Winnie)

CAULIFLOWER À LA POLONAISE

1 medium-sized head
    cauliflower
Boiling salted water, or
    use steamer
½ cup butter or margarine,
    melted

⅓ cup dry bread crumbs or
    Pepperidge Farm Herb Stuffing
2 hard-cooked eggs, chopped
Salt and pepper to taste

Cut out thick core from cauliflower; break into flowerets and wash. Cook until just tender; drain. To the cauliflower add butter, eggs, salt and pepper and mix well. Add bread crumbs and mix lightly. Garnish with parsley, if desired. Serve at once. Serves 4.
Mrs. Maureen Otis Adams

CORN BAKE

2 packages frozen cream-
    style corn or 1 No. 2 can
    cream-style corn
1 6-ounce can evaporated
    milk
1 egg, beaten
2 tablespoons onion,
    chopped
2 tablespoons bell pepper,
    chopped
½ teaspoon dried parsley or
    fresh parsley

Pinch marjoram
Salt and pepper to taste
1 cup Cheddar cheese,
    shredded
½ cup herb-seasoned
    bread crumbs
1 tablespoon margarine, melted
Paprika

If using frozen corn, cook in cup of boiling salted water three to four minutes. Combine corn with milk, egg, onion, green pepper, salt, herbs, and pepper. Then add ¾ cup of the Cheddar cheese. Mix well. Turn into small casserole dish. Toss bread crumbs with melted margarine. Add remaining cheese. Sprinkle over corn. Top with paprika and bake 25-30 minutes in 350 degree oven. Garnish with parsley and green pepper rings. Serves 4-6.

Mrs. Ed Kelly (Pat)
Similar recipes submitted by *Mrs. Huddie Cheney (Ann), Mrs. Stephen Eckels (Beth), Mrs. James Mason (Trudy), Mrs. Elliott McCollum (Lorna), Susan J. Murray, Mrs. Frank Neel (Frances) and Mrs. Lewis Hall Singletary (Mildred).*

FRESH CORN FRITTERS

¼ cup all-purpose flour
1 teaspoon salt
½ teaspoon baking powder
2 egg yolks
1½ cups fresh corn,
    cut off cob

¼ teaspoon pepper
1 tablespoon salad oil
2 egg whites
Shortening

Combine flour, salt and baking powder. Beat egg yolks in medium-size bowl; stir in corn, pepper, and flour mixture. Blend in salad oil. Beat egg whites until they stand in soft peaks; fold into mixture. Drop from tablespoon into skillet containing 1 inch of hot shortening. Cook until golden brown, turning once. Yield: 1½ dozen.
The Editors

EGGPLANT PARMESAN
Parmigiana di Melanzane

1½ pounds eggplant, peeled
and cut in ½-inch slices
Salt
Flour
¼ to ½ cup olive oil

2 cups Tomato Sauce
(see below)
8 ounces mozzarella cheese,
thinly sliced
½ cup freshly grated
imported Parmesan cheese

Preheat the oven to 400 degrees. Choose a shallow 1½ to 2-quart baking dish that is attractive enough to serve from and rub it with oil. Sprinkle both sides of the eggplant slices with salt (to draw out their moisture) and spread them out in one layer on a platter or board. After 20-30 minutes, pat the eggplant dry with paper towels. Dip each slice in flour and shake or brush off the excess. In a heavy 10-12 inch skillet, heat ¼ cup of olive oil until a light haze forms over it and brown the eggplant slices a few at the time, working quickly to prevent them from soaking up too much oil. If the oil cooks away, add more. As the eggplant browns, transfer the slices to fresh paper towels to drain. Now pour ¼ inch of the tomato sauce into the oiled baking-and-serving dish. Spread the drained eggplant slices over the sauce, top them with a layer of mozzarella cheese, and sprinkle over it part of the grated Parmesan cheese. Repeat with 1 or 2 more layers (depending on the capacity of the baking dish), but be sure to finish up with layers of the tomato sauce, mozzarella and Parmesan. Cover the dish snugly with foil and bake on the middle shelf of the oven for 20 minutes longer. Remove the foil and bake uncovered for 10 minutes. Optional: Put the dish under a hot broiler for a few seconds to brown the cheese on top, but do not overcook it or the cheese will become rubbery. Serve directly from the baking dish. Serves 4.

TOMATO SAUCE:

2 tablespoons olive oil
½ cup onions, finely chopped
2 cups Italian plum or
whole-pack tomatoes, coarsely
chopped but not drained
3 tablespoons tomato paste

1 tablespoon fresh basil,
finely cut, or 1 teaspoon dried
basil
1 teaspoon sugar
½ teaspoon salt
Freshly ground black pepper

Using a 2- to 3-quart enameled or stainless-steel saucepan, heat the olive oil until a light haze forms over it. Add the onions and cook them over moderate heat for 7-8 minutes, or until they are soft but not browned. Add the tomatoes, tomato paste, basil, sugar, salt and a few grindings of pepper. Reduce the heat to very low and simmer, with the pan partially covered, for about 40 minutes. Stir occasionally. Press the sauce through a fine sieve (or a food mill) into a bowl or pan. Taste for seasoning and serve hot. Makes about 1½ cups.
The Editors

EGGPLANT CASSEROLE

1 medium eggplant,
    peeled and cubed
1 egg, beaten
1 cup Pepperidge Farm
    Stuffing
2 tablespoons green pepper,
    chopped

1 medium onion, chopped
1 cup canned tomatoes
1 cup cream-style corn
½ cup American cheese,
    grated
½ teaspoon pepper

Cover cubed eggplant with water and add some salt. Cover and cook 8 minutes or until tender. Drain. Add remaining ingredients except cheese. Put into a greased casserole and cover the top with the cheese. Bake 30 minutes at 350 degrees. Serves 6-8.
Mrs. Marshall Woodson (Betty)

EGGPLANT AND TOMATO SOUFFLÉ

1 large eggplant
2 medium tomatoes
2 eggs
2 tablespoons cream

Salt and pepper
Bread crumbs
Butter

Place eggplant on plate on its flattest side and cut a long thin slice from top, leaving all of the green stem. Scoop out inside of eggplant, leaving ⅛-inch wall all around shell. Cut up the eggplant you removed from shell and boil in salted water to cover. While this is cooking, peel and slice tomatoes and let them drain thoroughly. When eggplant is soft, remove from stove and drain. Do not mash. When completely drained, add the 2 eggs, cream, salt and pepper. Put half of this mixture in eggplant shell and cover with a layer of drained tomato slices. Salt slightly. Add another layer of eggplant, then another layer of tomato slices. Salt slightly again and cover with a layer of dry bread crumbs. Dot with butter and sprinkle with paprika. Cook in 325 degree oven for 1 hour or until a silver knife inserted in middle comes out clean. Place on platter and garnish with parsley.
Mrs. Martin Cooper (Peggy)

FRIED EGGPLANT

Eggplant
Salt and pepper
Corn meal

Parmesan cheese
Oil

Peel eggplant and slice in fingers ½ inch thick and 2 inches long. Lay the eggplant out in a single layer on paper towel and salt very well. Let the eggplant sit for 10-15 minutes; then blot off the moisture which is on top. Salt and pepper the fingers and shake in corn meal. Fry in hot oil until brown. Drain and serve hot. Sprinkle with Parmesan cheese.
The Editors

MUSHROOMS IN SOUR CREAM

1 pound fresh mushrooms,
 sliced
1 large onion, sliced
5 tablespoons butter

1 cup sour cream
Salt and pepper
Fresh parsley, chopped

Sauté sliced mushrooms and onions in butter until limp, about 3 minutes. Remove from heat and stir in sour cream, which is at room temperature. Sprinkle with salt and pepper and serve, garnished with fresh parsley. Serves 4-6.
The Editors

MUSHROOM CASSEROLE

1 pound fresh mushrooms
8 tablespoons butter
8 slices white bread,
 buttered and cubed, with
 crusts cut off
½ cup onion, chopped
½ cup green pepper, chopped
½ cup celery, chopped
½ cup mayonnaise

¼ teaspoon salt
¼ teaspoon pepper
3 eggs, beaten
½ cup milk
¼ cup cheese
 (sharp or Parmesan)
1 can cream of mushroom
 soup

Sauté mushrooms in butter. Place three slices cubed bread, onion, celery, peppers, salt and pepper in 2-quart casserole. Place mushrooms over this; then 3 more slices cubed bread. Combine eggs and milk. Pour over casserole. Let stand in refrigerator overnight. One hour before serving spoon soup over top and spread with remainder of bread cubes. Sprinkle with cheese. Bake 1 hour at 325 degrees. Serves 10-12.
Mrs. Donald Davis (Sara)

MACARONI CASSEROLE WITH MUSHROOMS

1 8-ounce package macaroni
¾ cup cheese, grated
¼ cup pimento, chopped
¼ cup green pepper,
 . chopped

1 cup mushrooms, undrained
1 cup mushroom soup
¾ cup mayonnaise
Cracker crumbs

Cook macaroni until just tender. Mix with all remaining ingredients except cracker crumbs. Pour into a casserole; cover with crumbs. Bake 30 minutes at 350 degrees. Serves 8-10.
Mrs. Paul L. Sampson (Katherine)

NOODLE AND MUSHROOM CASSEROLE
Good with chicken!

2 cups fine noodles	½ teaspoon paprika
¾ pound fresh mushrooms	½ cup butter, melted
⅛ pound butter	2 tablespoons parsley flakes
1 large onion, diced	¼ teaspoon salt
4 eggs, separated	1 cup whipping cream

Cook noodles, rinse in cold water and drain thoroughly. Remove stems from mushrooms, chop stems and set aside. Brown mushroom caps slightly in ⅛ pound butter. Remove caps and add stems and diced onions. Sauté until onion is soft and caps are tender. Add mushrooms and onions to noodles in large bowl. Beat egg yolks, paprika, melted butter and parsley flakes together and pour over noodle mixture. Whip 4 egg whites with 1 teaspoon salt until stiff. Whip 1 cup cream. Fold egg whites and cream into noodle mixture lightly. Bake in well-greased casserole or a ring mold with smooth sides. Set casserole in a pan of water so that water reaches halfway up sides of casserole. Bake at 350 degrees until firm, about ½ hour or longer for large ring mold.
Mrs. Thomas Hawkins (Harriet)

BAKED ONIONS

Peel onions (Big Spanish) and flatten the tops. On top of each onion put a pinch of brown sugar, salt and pepper and a pat of butter. Wrap in foil and bake in a 325 degree oven for 40 minutes.
Mrs. Huddie Cheney (Ann)

TWICE-BAKED POTATOES

6 baking potatoes	2 eggs
6 tablespoons butter	1 cup sharp Cheddar cheese,
1½ teaspoons salt	grated
½ teaspoon Tabasco	

Bake potatoes in 450 degree oven for 1 hour. Immediately cut slice from top of each and scoop out potato. Mash well. Add butter, salt, Tabasco, eggs and half of the cheese. Beat until smooth and creamy. Spoon into shells and top with remaining cheese. Bake at 425 degrees for 20 minutes. May be made in advance, but do not add eggs to the mixture. Right before the second baking, add eggs and spoon into shells. Serves 6.
Mrs. Fred Cooper (Helen)

POTATO CASSEROLE

6-8 potatoes, cooked and
diced
Small container cottage cheese

8 ounces sour cream
½ medium onion, chopped
8 ounces Cheddar cheese

Mix above ingredients. Bake in medium oven for 30-40 minutes.
Mrs. Lewis Hall Singletary (Mildred)

SCALLOPED HAM 'N POTATOES

2 tablespoons enriched
flour
1½ teaspoons salt
¼ teaspoon pepper
1 can condensed cream of
mushroom soup
½ cup milk

6 cups potatoes, sliced
Ham, sliced as desired
¼ cup onion, chopped
¼ cup pimento, chopped
¼ cup green pepper,
chopped

Combine flour, salt and pepper. Slowly stir in soup and milk and heat to boiling. In a greased 2-quart casserole, alternate layers of potatoes, ham, onion, pepper and pimento. Pour soup mixture over contents of casserole and with a fork make holes for soup to seep through. Bake covered in 350 degree oven for 45 minutes. Uncover and bake 45 minutes longer. Garnish with hot canned mushrooms, if desired. Serves 6-8.
Mrs. Rudolph Davis (Anne)

SWEET POTATOES AND APRICOTS

1 1-pound, 1-ounce can
whole sweet potatoes,
halved lengthwise
1¼ cups brown sugar
1½ tablespoons cornstarch
¼ teaspoon salt
¼ teaspoon cinnamon

1 teaspoon orange peel,
grated
1 1-pound can or 2 cups
apricot halves
2 tablespoons butter
½ cup pecan halves

Place sweet potatoes in greased 10 x 6 x 1½-inch baking dish. In saucepan, combine brown sugar, cornstarch, salt, cinnamon and orange peel. Drain apricots, reserving syrup. Stir 1 cup apricot syrup into cornstarch mixture. Cook and stir over medium heat until boiling. Boil 2 minutes. Add apricots, butter, and pecan halves. Pour over potatoes. Bake at 375 degrees for 25 minutes. Serves 6.
Mrs. Jack Sanford (Sue)

SWEET POTATO SOUFFLÉ I

3 pounds raw sweet potatoes
   or 2 pounds, cooked
¾ cup sugar
¾ cup orange juice
½ teaspoon salt

1 egg, beaten
3 tablespoons butter
1 teaspoon vanilla
¼ cup coconut
Marshmallows

Cook sweet potatoes. Peel and mash while hot. Add all ingredients. If mixture seems dry, add more orange juice. Pour into 1½-quart casserole. Bake at 350 degrees for 30 minutes. Top with marshmallows and return to oven until they have browned. Serves 8.
Mrs. Robert Sullivan (Sally)

Variation: For a spicier soufflé, add nutmeg and cinnamon to taste.
Mrs. Robert Braswell (Sandra)

SWEET POTATO SOUFFLÉ II

4-5 cups sweet potatoes,
   cooked, drained and mashed
1 stick margarine, softened
5 eggs
1 teaspoon vanilla

1½ cups sugar
½ teaspoon allspice
½ teaspoon cinnamon
1 can sweetened condensed milk
1 cup pecans, chopped

Stir softened margarine into hot mashed potatoes. Beat together the eggs, vanilla, sugar, allspice, cinnamon, milk and nuts. Stir mixture into potatoes and mix well. Pour into a 9 x 13-inch baking dish and bake at 350 degrees for 30 minutes. Remove from oven and add topping.

TOPPING:

½ stick margarine
1½ cups brown sugar

1¼ cups pecans, chopped

Mix topping ingredients together and sprinkle over top of casserole. Return to oven and bake at 325 degrees for 20 minutes or until a toothpick inserted comes out clean. Note: Squash or pumpkin may be substituted for the sweet potatoes.
Mrs. Woody Faircloth (Millie)
Similar recipe submitted by *Mrs. Kenneth L. Miller (Kathryn)*.

SWEET POTATO-HONEY BALLS

2½ cups sweet potatoes,
   cooked and mashed, or
   canned
¾ teaspoon salt
Dash pepper
5 tablespoons butter,
   melted and divided

½ cup miniature
   marshmallows
½ cup honey
1 cup pecans, chopped

Combine potatoes, salt, pepper and 2 tablespoons butter; stir in marshmallows. Chill. Shape potato mixture into balls, using ¼ cup for each. Combine 2 tablespoons butter and honey in small heavy skillet; add potato balls one at a time, quickly coating each with glaze. Roll potato balls in chopped nuts and place in a greased shallow casserole dish. Drizzle with remaining butter. Bake at 350 degrees for 15-20 minutes.
Mrs. Chip Coffin (Sheila)

Similar recipe submitted by *Mrs. Gene Walker (Hilda)*.

WILD RICE CASSEROLE

1½ cups boiling water
1 package Uncle Ben's Wild
   Rice and Herbs
1 can chicken with
   rice soup
1 small can mushrooms and
   liquid
½ cup water
1 teaspoon salt

1 bay leaf
¼ teaspoon each of celery
   salt, garlic powder, pepper,
   onion, salt, paprika
3 tablespoons onion, chopped
3 tablespoons oil
¾ pound lean ground
   beef

Pour boiling water over rice and herbs. Simmer, covered, 15 minutes. Place rice in a 2-quart casserole. Add soup, mushrooms with liquid, water and seasonings. Mix and let stand. Sauté onions in oil until glossy and add to casserole. Brown meat in frying pan and add to rice mixture. Refrigerate. When ready to bake, cover and bake 2 hours at 325 degrees. Serves 4-6.
Mrs. Al Lookabaugh (Diana)

WILD RICE WITH MUSHROOMS

4 tablespoons butter
2 tablespoons carrots,
    scraped and finely diced
2 tablespoons celery,
    finely diced
2 tablespoons onion,
    finely chopped
1 cup wild rice
1 teaspoon salt

2 cups chicken stock, fresh
    or canned
½ pound fresh mushrooms,
    coarsely chopped
2 tablespoons fresh parsley,
    finely chopped
¼ cup pecans,
    finely chopped

In a heavy 2-quart saucepan melt 2 tablespoons butter over moderate heat. When the foam subsides add the carrots, celery and onions. Cover and cook for 10 to 15 minutes, stirring occasionally, until the vegetables are soft but not brown. Stir in the cup of rice and the salt and cook for 2 to 3 minutes, uncovered, stirring to coat the rice thoroughly with the butter. In a small saucepan bring the stock to a boil and pour over rice mixture. Bring to a boil again, cover tightly and reduce heat to its lowest point. Cook undisturbed for 25 to 30 minutes or until the rice is tender and has absorbed all the stock. Meanwhile, over moderate heat melt the remaining 2 tablespoons of butter in enameled or stainless steel skillet. When foam subsides, add the mushrooms and parsley; cook, stirring, for 5 minutes. Add the pecans and cook for 2 to 3 minutes more. With a fork stir the contents of the skillet into the finished rice. Taste for seasoning and serve.
Mrs. Robert W. Jackson (Beverly)

MUSHROOM RICE

1 cup raw rice
1 can onion soup
1 4-ounce can sliced
    mushrooms

1 can beef consommé
1 stick butter

Melt butter in 2-quart baking dish. Add remaining ingredients. Bake uncovered for 50 minutes at 400 degrees. Serves 4-6.
Mrs. J. M. Hancock (Leafy)
Similar recipes submitted by *Mrs. Alex Crittenden (Chris), Mrs. Joe Beverly (Mary), Mrs. Fred Murphy (Vi), Mrs. Richard Atwell (Libby).*

CHARLESTON RED RICE

1 can or 2 cups stewed
   tomatoes
1 can tomato paste
½ can water (paste can)
2 onions, finely chopped
3 teaspoons salt
3 teaspoons sugar

4 strips bacon, cubed
8 tablespoons bacon
   drippings
Dash of pepper
2 cups raw rice (with 2
   teaspoons salt)

Fry bacon; remove from pan. Sauté onions in 8 tablespoons of bacon drippings. Add stewed tomatoes, tomato paste, water, salt, sugar and pepper. Slowly cook sauce, uncovered, about 10 minutes; then add it to rice in top section of steamer. Steam for ½ hour; then add crumbled bacon and stir with fork. Cook 30-45 minutes longer. Serves 6-8. Always good with ham. If there's any left it can be reheated in steamer for lunch next day.
Mrs. Al Zavaleta (Pat)

SKILLET SPANISH RICE

¼ cup cooking oil
1 medium onion, chopped
½ medium green pepper,
   chopped (optional)
1 cup long grain rice,
   uncooked
1 pound ground beef
½ pound mild, pure pork
   fresh sausage

1 15-ounce can tomato
   sauce
1¾ cups hot water
1 teaspoon prepared
   mustard
1 teaspoon salt

Brown ground beef and sausage in hot cooking oil. Add onion, green pepper, and rice. Stir well. Add tomato sauce, water, and spices. Bring quickly to a boil. Cover and simmer 25 minutes or until rice is done. More water may need to be added to prevent sticking. Serves 8 people. Note: Grated cheese may be sprinkled over top before serving.
Mrs. Bryant Harvard (Kathy)

ORANGE RICE

3 tablespoons butter
1 cup celery, diced
2 tablespoons onion,
    chopped
2 tablespoons seedless raisins
1 cup raw rice

2 tablespoons orange rind,
    grated
1 cup orange juice
1½ cups water
1½ teaspoons salt

Melt butter in heavy pan. Add celery and onions and cook until tender. Stir in raisins, orange rind, juice, water and salt. Bring to rolling boil; then slowly add 1 cup raw rice. Cover; let simmer for 25 minutes, stirring occasionally. Serve with pork or poultry. Serves 6.
Mrs. Carl Zinn (Louise)

SPINACH ROCKEFELLER

3 packages frozen spinach
1 cup bread crumbs
1 small onion, chopped
3 eggs, slightly beaten
½ cup sharp cheese, grated
½ teaspoon Accent

½ tablespoon garlic salt
¼ tablespoon thyme
½ teaspoon pepper
⅛ teaspoon red pepper
Parmesan cheese
8 medium tomatoes

Salt and pepper spinach to taste; cook, drain and set aside. Mix together all ingredients except tomatoes, spinach and Parmesan cheese. Add spinach to mixture. Place spinach mixture into tomatoes which have been scooped out. Sprinkle cheese on top. Place in buttered casserole dish. Bake at 350 degrees for 15 minutes.
Mrs. Lewis Hall Singletary (Mildred)

SPINACH RING

2½ cups spinach,
    cooked and chopped
1 cup milk
3 tablespoons butter
3 tablespoons flour

⅓ teaspoon nutmeg
1 teaspoon onion, grated
1 tablespoon lemon juice
2 eggs, well beaten
1 teaspoon salt

Mix all ingredients and pour into a well-greased 1-quart ring mold. Place in a hot water bath and bake at 375 degrees until firm. Unmold and fill center with creamed vegetable, seafood or chicken.
Mrs. Bolling Jones, III (Connie)

SPINACH CASSEROLE

2 10-ounce packages
    frozen chopped spinach
½ pint commercial sour
    cream
1 1½-ounce envelope dehydrated
    onion soup

Dash of Tabasco
Salt and pepper to taste
¼ cup pecans, chopped

Cook spinach as directed on package. Drain well. Mix spinach, sour cream, soup mix, Tabasco, salt and pepper. Refrigerate. When ready to bake, place spinach, uncovered, in 350 degree oven for 20 minutes. Sprinkle nuts on top and bake 15 minutes more. Serves 4.
Mrs. Heyward Vann (Mildred)
Similar recipe submitted by *Mrs. L. G. Hardy (Cile)*.

ANNE'S SPINACH CASSEROLE

2 packages chopped spinach
1 8-ounce package cream cheese
1 can artichoke hearts,
    drained, or 1 package
    frozen artichoke hearts

1 tablespoon lemon juice
1 stick butter
Bread crumbs
Butter

Cook spinach and drain. Melt butter, cream cheese, and lemon juice in pan. Add spinach and mix well. Line bottom of casserole dish with artichoke hearts and top with spinach mixture. Sprinkle top with bread crumbs and dot with butter. Bake 20 minutes at 350 degrees. Serves 6-8.
Mrs. Chris Cocroft (Katie)
Similar recipe submitted by *Mrs. Lewis Hall Singletary (Mildred)*.

SQUASH SOUFFLÉ

2 cups squash, cooked
2 eggs, beaten
1 cup milk
1 cup Ritz cracker
    crumbs
4 tablespoons margarine
½ cup onions, chopped

¼ cup green pepper
⅛ teaspoon salt
⅛ teaspoon black pepper
Ritz cracker crumbs for
    topping
Butter
Paprika

Cook squash and drain. Heat milk and margarine. When margarine is melted, add beaten eggs, onions, green pepper, salt and pepper; then add 1 cup cracker crumbs. Add squash. Pour into well-greased casserole. Top with additional cracker crumbs, dot with butter, and sprinkle with paprika. Bake at 350 degrees for 30 minutes.
Mrs. Tom Boyle (Iris)

SQUASH SUPREME

2 cups yellow squash,
    fresh, frozen or canned
1 can cream of chicken
    soup
1 cup sour cream
3 carrots, grated

½ package Pepperidge Farm
    Herb Seasoned Stuffing
1 medium onion, grated
½ stick butter, melted
Salt and pepper to taste

Cook and mash squash. Add onion, soup, sour cream, carrots, salt and pepper. Butter casserole. Sprinkle layer of crumbs in bottom. Add squash mixture and cover with light layer of crumbs. Pour melted butter over top. Bake at 350 degrees for 30 minutes.
Mrs. Tom Lear (Ann)
Similar recipes submitted by *Mrs. Paul Hjort (Frances), Mrs. Richard Atwell (Libby), Mrs. Gene Walker (Hilda), Mrs. Raymond Waits (Barbara), Mrs. Gerald Muller (Emmy), and Mrs. Theo Clark (Katie).*

BUTTERNUT SQUASH CASSEROLE

2 cups squash, cooked
    and sieved
⅓ cup orange juice
½ cup raisins (optional)
1 stick butter or
    margarine, melted

1 cup sugar
⅓ cup powdered milk
2 eggs
Salt to taste

Combine all ingredients and mix well. Pour in greased baking dish. Bake at 350 degrees for 1 hour.
Lambuth Inn   *Lake Junaluska, North Carolina*

SQUASH FRITTERS

1 cup squash, grated
    (small yellow, unpeeled)
1 teaspoon onion, grated
½ teaspoon salt
Few grains of pepper

1 teaspoon sugar
3 tablespoons flour
1 egg, beaten
1 teaspoon melted fat
    or cooking oil

Combine all ingredients and mix well. Drop by tablespoon on greased griddle. Fry on both sides until a delicate brown. Serve with roast chicken or eat with maple syrup.
Mrs. Hilton S. Read (Kathryn)

SAUTÉED ZUCCHINI

3 tablespoons butter
½ yellow onion, peeled
    and finely chopped
1½ teaspoons fresh sweet
    marjoram (if you use dried
    sweet marjoram, remember it
    will be 3 times as strong
    as fresh)

1 pound small zucchini,
    unpeeled, thinly sliced
½ teaspoon salt

Heat the butter in a large, heavy skillet. Add the onion and brown lightly over a high heat. Mix the minced herb with the zucchini. Add to the skillet and stir-fry for one minute. Cover with a lid (preferably spatter or ventilated). Reduce heat and simmer for five minutes. Sprinkle with salt just before serving. Serves 4.

Mrs. Leon Neel (Julie)

SQUASH AND CORN PUDDING

2 cups fresh corn,
    cut and stewed (or 1 No.
    303 can cream-style corn)
2 cups summer squash, sliced
    and steamed with 1 large
    sliced onion
1 green pepper, slivered

1 egg
½ cup milk
2 tablespoons butter
¼ cup flour
1 tablespoon sugar
½ teaspoon salt
Pinch of mace

Melt butter in saucepan. Sauté slivered green pepper until just soft. Add flour and stir until well blended with the butter. Beat egg and milk together. Combine with pepper-flour mixture and add the sugar, salt and mace. Fold in the corn and drained, mashed squash. Turn into baking dish and bake at 350 degrees for 30 minutes or until slightly brown on top.

Mrs. William M. Searcy, Jr. (Emily)

TOMATO DELIGHT

1 medium tomato, sliced
   ½ inch thick
4 slices bacon, cooked and
   crumbled
2 ounces natural Muenster
   cheese or soft white cheese

Mayonnaise
Oregano
Salt and pepper

Place tomato slices on baking sheet. Sprinkle with salt, pepper and oregano. Put a small amount of mayonnaise on each slice. Sprinkle with bacon and cover with cheese. Broil in hot oven for about 3 minutes or until cheese melts and begins to brown. Serve as a side dish. Good for leftover bacon or prepare extra bacon while cooking breakfast. Serves 2.
Mrs. Julian Neel (Phoebe)

VEGETABLE CASSEROLE

1 10-ounce package frozen
   English peas
1 10-ounce package frozen
   Lima beans
1 10-ounce package frozen
   green beans
1 green pepper, chopped

1 small can mushrooms,
   sliced
1 3-ounce can Parmesan
   cheese
½ pint whipping cream,
   whipped
1 pint mayonnaise

Cook peas and beans separately in salted water according to package directions. Drain. Arrange vegetables alternately in casserole with a mixture of the pepper, mushrooms and cheese, reserving some of the cheese for topping. Top casserole with a mixture of whipped cream and mayonnaise. Sprinkle with cheese and bake at 350 degrees for approximately 20 minutes or until brown and bubbly.
Mrs. Jasper Davis (Marthalene)
Similar recipes submitted by *Miss Ophelia Smith and Mrs. James Carico (Helen)*.

APPLE CASSEROLE
Absolutely Delicious!

6 medium apples, peeled,
  cored and cut into wedges
1 cup brown sugar, plus
  enough for topping

Butter
3 or 4 slices of lemon
Cinnamon
Bread squares, small

Mix apples and 1 cup brown sugar. Arrange in baking dish, rotate with butter and lemon slices. Sprinkle with cinnamon. Bake at 350 degrees until tender. Dip bread squares in melted butter and arrange on top of apples. Sprinkle with brown sugar. Place in oven and cook until bread is toasted. Serves 4-6.
Mrs. John T. King (Mary)
Mrs. R. F. DeLamar, III (Peggy)

ALICE'S FRUIT LOUISE

1 No. 2½ can peeled apricots,
  pits removed
1 can sliced Elberta
  peaches, same size can
1 can black Bing cherries,
  same size

1 lemon, juice and
  grated rind
Dark brown sugar
Cinnamon

Drain fruit and arrange in flat casserole dish. Bake uncovered for 1 hour in preheated oven at 325 degrees. Remove from oven. Top with grated lemon rind, lemon juice, brown sugar and cinnamon. Bake for 10 minutes more. Serve hot or cold dotted with whipped cream. Serves 6-8.
Mrs. Chris CoCroft (Katie)

CURRIED FRUIT

1 can pears
1 can apricots
1 can peaches
1 can pineapple chunks

1 cup margarine
¾ cup brown sugar
1 teaspoon curry powder

Drain fruit and arrange in a casserole. Melt together margarine, brown sugar and curry powder. Pour over fruit. Dot with cherries. Bake for 1 hour at 325 degrees. Good to serve with fowl or wild rice casserole. Serves 6-8.
Mrs. Al Lookabaugh (Diana)

Accompaniments

PEACH PICKLES

6 pounds peaches, peeled	1 tablespoon ginger
3 pounds sugar	2 tablespoons whole
1 pint vinegar	crushed cloves
1 pint water	4 sticks cinnamon

Blanch and peel peaches. Drop in cold salt and vinegar-water solution (2 tablespoons salt, 2 tablespoons vinegar, 1 gallon water) immediately to prevent discoloration. Put vinegar into preserving kettle with hot water, boil and skim; add spices (tied in cloth bag). Drain peaches well; drop into boiling syrup and cook about 1 minute, until they can be pierced with a straw but are not too soft. Remove from fire and pack in spiced vinegar. Seal and process 20 minutes at simmering in hot water bath.

The Editors

CAULIFLOWER PICKLES

2 medium heads of cauliflower	2 teaspoons turmeric
2 cups tiny white onions	2 tablespoons mustard seed
¾ cup of salt	1 tablespoon celery seed
Ice cubes	Dash of hot sauce, if
2 quarts white vinegar	desired
1¼ cups sugar	

Divide cauliflower into flowerets. (There should be 2 quarts.) Scald and peel onions. Add salt to vegetables and mix with ice cubes. Cover with more ice cubes and let stand for 3 hours. Drain. Mix remaining ingredients in large boiler and bring to a boil, stirring to dissolve sugar. Add onions and cauliflower. Cook 10 minutes until tender but not soft. Pack in hot sterilized pint jars. Reheat liquid to boiling and pour over vegetables and seal. Yield: 5-6 pints.

Mrs. Martin Cooper (Peggy)

PICKLED OKRA

Okra
2 quarts water

1 quart vinegar
¾ cup salt

PER PINT JAR:

1 clove garlic
1 small piece celery
½ hot pepper

½ teaspoon dill seed
½ teaspoon mustard seed

Combine water, vinegar and salt and heat for 5 minutes. Wash okra and trim stems off. Pack in pint jars. To each jar add garlic, celery, pepper, dill seed and mustard seed. Pour heated mixture over contents of each jar. Seal tightly. Place in refrigerator to chill before serving.
Mrs. Lloyd Eckberg (Maxine)

SQUASH PICKLES

8 cups squash, sliced
2 cups onions, sliced
1 tablespoon salt
    (not iodized)
1 cup green pepper, diced

2 cups cider vinegar
3½ cups sugar
1 teaspoon celery seed
1 teaspoon mustard seed

Combine squash and onion. Sprinkle with salt and let stand 1 hour. Combine green pepper, vinegar, sugar and seeds; bring to a boil. Pack squash and onion into hot sterilized jars. Cover with vinegar mixture and seal. Yield: 4 pints.
Mrs. Ophelia Smith

WATERMELON RIND PICKLES

1 large watermelon with
    thick rind
3 tablespoons slaked lime or
    1 cup pure granulated salt
1 lemon, washed, quartered
    and seeds removed
2 sticks cinnamon, each
    about 2½ inches long

2 tablespoons cracked dried
    ginger root
1 tablespoon mustard seed
1 quart white vinegar
8 cups sugar

Cut washed watermelon in half lengthwise, then in 1-inch slices crosswise. Using vegetable peeler, peel off dark skin and cut off pink meat (use for other purposes). Cut rind into 1-inch pieces and measure 4 quarts. Put in large mixing bowl. Dissolve lime (or salt) in 2 quarts water and pour over rind. If necessary add additional water to cover rind. Let stand in cool place 2 hours if lime is used or 6 hours if salt is used. Drain; then rinse well. Put in large kettle and cover with water. Bring to boil, cover and simmer 15 minutes or until tender; drain. Tie lemon wedges, cinnamon, ginger root and mustard seed in cheesecloth bag. Put spice bag, vinegar, sugar and 1 quart water in kettle, bring to boil and simmer, covered, 10 minutes. Add rind, bring to boil and simmer, uncovered, about 2 hours or until rind is translucent and syrup is thickened. If syrup becomes thick before rind is ready, a small amount of water may be added. Remove spice bag. Pack at once into hot sterilized jars, filling to within ½ inch of top. Seal at once, then process in boiling-water bath 10 minutes for pints or half-pints. Makes 4-6 pints.

Note: Slaked lime (calcium hydroxide) is essential to make pickles crisp and to insure a large yield. Salt makes a softer pickle and a smaller yield.
The Editors

GREEN TOMATO PICKLES I

1½ pounds large white
    onions, peeled and sliced
1 peck stark green tomatoes, sliced
2 pounds sugar
2 boxes ground ginger
2 boxes celery seed
6 red hot peppers,
    finely chopped

Salt
3 quarts vinegar
8 small boxes of ground mustard
1 box cinnamon
1 box turmeric
1 heaping tablespoon black
    pepper

In large bowl alternate layers of sliced tomatoes and sliced onions, salting each layer of tomatoes with about ¼ cup of salt. Let set overnight. In the morning drain juice, squeezing it out of handfuls of tomatoes and onions. In a large preserving kettle put tomatoes and onions and add remaining ingredients. Boil until tender, but not falling to pieces (about one hour), stirring often to prevent sticking. Seal in hot jars immediately. Makes 16 or more pints.
Miss Emily R. Jerger

GREEN TOMATO PICKLES II

7 pounds small green
   tomatoes, sliced ¼-inch
   thick
2 gallons water
1 cup lime
3 quarts vinegar
5 pounds sugar
1 teaspoon salt

1 teaspoon ground cloves
1 teaspoon ground
   ginger
1 teaspoon allspice
1 teaspoon ground
   cinnamon
1 teaspoon celery seed

Prepare tomatoes and soak 24 hours in water to which lime has been added. Water must cover tomatoes in crock container. Stir occasionally. After 24 hours drain and rinse thoroughly. Soak in fresh water 4 hours, changing water every 2 hours. Drain. Mix and bring to boil vinegar, salt, sugar and spices. Pour mixture over tomatoes and let stand overnight. Next morning boil tomatoes and vinegar mixture for 1 hour until tomatoes are transparent and the vinegar is a light syrup. Put into jars and seal.

Mrs. David Stowers (Lynn)
Similar recipe submitted by *Mrs. Theo Clark (Katie)*.

SWEET PICKLES

Cucumbers, washed and
   sliced
Pickling spices to taste

1 cup vinegar
2 cups sugar

Prepare cucumbers and cover with boiling water. Let stand 25 minutes. Drain and towel dry. Pack in jars. Mix vinegar, sugar and spices and bring to boil. Pour boiling mixture over contents of jars and seal. Chill before serving.

Mrs. Theo Clark (Katie)

CRISP CUCUMBER PICKLES

7 pounds cucumbers,
   cut crosswise
3 cups lime
1½ quarts vinegar
4½ pounds sugar

1 teaspoon ground cinnamon
1 teaspoon celery seed
1 teaspoon allspice
1 teaspoon mace
1 teaspoon ginger

First day: Soak cucumbers for 24 hours in 2 gallons of water to which 3 cups of lime have been added. Remove from lime water and soak in clear water 4 hours, changing water every hour. Second day: Make syrup with remaining ingredients and bring to a boil. Pour mixture over cucumbers and let set for 24 hours. Third day: Put cucumbers and syrup on stove and simmer for 1 hour. Pack in hot jars and seal.

Mrs. Leroy B. Edwards (Sarah Martha)

PEPPER JELLY

¾ cup jalapeño peppers, chopped
¾ cup bell pepper, chopped
1½ cups vinegar

6½ cups sugar
1 6-ounce bottle Certo
Several drops green food coloring

Wear rubber gloves to seed and chop peppers. Put coarsely chopped peppers and vinegar into the blender to grind. Put peppers, vinegar and sugar into a boiler. Stir until the sugar is dissolved. Bring to a rolling boil and boil for 8 to 10 minutes. Remove from heat. Add Certo and 2 or 3 drops of food coloring. Pour into jars and seal. Serve with meat, or serve over a block of cream cheese with crackers as an hors d'oeuvre.
Mrs. Michael Herndon (Jane)   *Columbus, Georgia*

PEAR RELISH

2 quarts pears (hard), cut in small cubes
6 bell peppers, cut small
1 quart onions, cut small
1 quart brown vinegar
2 cups sugar

1 cup flour
1 teaspoon turmeric
1 teaspoon celery seed
1 tablespoon dry mustard
1 tablespoon salt

Mix all ingredients and boil for 5 minutes. Stir. Seal in jars. Excellent served with pork.
Mrs. David Stowers (Lynn)

MOTHER'S PRESERVED KUMQUATS

Kumquats (round, rather than oblong, if available)

Baking soda
Sugar

Soak kumquats in water to which baking soda has been added to clean and brighten skin of fruit. Halve kumquats and remove seeds. Cover, just barely, the bottom of a large pan with water. Put kumquats in and cover completely with sugar. Cook slowly, carefully stirring the fruit on the bottom to keep it from scorching. After sugar melts and syrup has formed, heat may be slightly increased. Stir gently, occasionally. Check syrup for thickening process. When suitably thickened, put in fruit jars. This, traditionally, is served with Thanksgiving and Christmas dinners in our family.
Mrs. Chris CoCroft (Katie)

CHRISTMAS RELISH

20 sweet green peppers
20 sweet red peppers
20 small onions

1 quart vinegar
1 pint sugar
3 tablespoons salt

Remove seeds, grind, and pour boiling water over peppers. Let stand 5 minutes. Drain and pour boiling water over peppers again. Let stand 10 minutes. Drain. Mix vinegar, sugar, salt and add peppers. Bring to boil and cook 5 minutes. Seal.
Mrs. T. R. Sample (Nell)

PEACH CHUTNEY

1 gallon peaches
2 onions
1 clove garlic
1 cup raisins
5 cups vinegar

¼ cup white mustard seed
2 tablespoons ginger
1 hot red pepper
1 cup brown sugar
2 teaspoons salt

Chop peeled peaches, onions, garlic and raisins. Add ½ the vinegar. Cook until soft. Add all other ingredients and cook until thick. Pour into hot jars and seal at once.
Mrs. A. B. Wight, Jr. (Carolyn)

SPICED GRAPES
From my mother's cookbook

5 pounds fruit
3 pounds sugar
1½ cups apple cider
  vinegar

1 tablespoon cinnamon
1 tablespoon allspice
1 teaspoon cloves,
  ground

Pulp grapes and boil pulps in small amount of water until broken and tender. Rub through colander to remove seeds. Boil hulls until tender in just enough water to cover them. Mix fruit. Add sugar, vinegar and spices. Cook until thick as jam. Seal in jars while hot. Makes delicious pies. Good with meats!
Mrs. Sydney Fleming (Mabel)

CRANBERRY CONSERVE

2 cups cranberries
½ cup orange juice
1½ cups sugar
1 cup raisins

1 teaspoon orange rind,
   grated
½ cup almonds or pecans,
   chopped

Wash and pick cranberries. Add orange juice to berries and cook over low heat until skins pop. Rub berries through rough sieve. Add sugar and boil slowly 10 minutes, adding raisins, nuts and orange peel during the last 5 minutes.
Mrs. Sydney Fleming (Mabel)

PEAR BUTTER

¾ pint sugar per pint
   pear pulp
1 small can crushed pineapple
   per 8 pints

Ground cinnamon

Peel pears and cook until tender. Grind pulp. Add sugar, pineapple, and cinnamon to taste. Cook mixture a few minutes and then put into jars.
Mrs. T. R. Sample (Nell)

ORANGE MARMALADE
From my mother's cookbook

1 lemon
3 oranges

2 cups sugar

First day: Grind or finely chop fruit. Add 3 cups of water and set mixture aside overnight. Second day: Boil mixture vigorously for 10 minutes. Set aside overnight. Third day: Gradually add sugar to fruit mixture and cook to jelly stage. Makes 6 glasses.
Mrs. Sydney Fleming (Mabel)

PEACH-ORANGE PRESERVES

Sugar
24 fresh peaches

4 oranges

Peel and slice peaches. Slice whole oranges thinly and cut slices in half. Place fruit in heavy pan. Add a cup of sugar for each cup of fruit. Cook until thick. The preserves will be a dark color. Seal in jars.
Mrs. Fred Cooper (Helen)

STRAWBERRY BUTTER

1 box frozen strawberries   1 cup confectioners' sugar
1 cup of butter or margarine

Blend ingredients well and use on muffins, waffles, toast, etc.
Mrs. Lawson Neel (Josie)

STRAWBERRY PRESERVES

2 quarts strawberries   6 cups sugar

Cover strawberries with boiling water and let mixture stand 2 minutes. Drain well. Add 4 cups sugar to strawberries and boil for 2 minutes. Remove from heat and stir in 2 more cups sugar. When mixture has quit bubbling and has cooled, return to heat and boil for 5 minutes. Pour into shallow pan 1½ inches high and let stand overnight. Then seal in jars.
Mrs. T. R. Sample (Nell)

BLUEBERRY PANCAKE SYRUP

2 tablespoons cornstarch   1 6-ounce can frozen
½ cup sugar   concentrated raspberry-lemon
1 15-ounce can blueberries,   juice, thawed
   packed in water   ¼ cup butter or margarine

Mix cornstarch and sugar in saucepan. Drain syrup from blueberries and stir in raspberry-lemon juice. Add enough water to make 3 cups. Gradually stir liquid into cornstarch. Add butter or margarine. Cook over low heat, stirring constantly, until sauce thickens. Fold in blueberries and spoon hot syrup over pancakes. Yield: 3½ cups.
Mrs. Tom Vann, Jr. (Ann)

HOT MUSTARD

Combine and refrigerate overnight:

3 small cans dry
   mustard

1 cup apple cider
   vinegar

Beat well and add to above:

4 eggs

1 cup sugar

Cook in double boiler until thickened. Keep refrigerated. Use sparingly!
Mrs. Paul McCollum (Nancy)
Mrs. Gerald Wolsfelt (Vicki)

CHILI SAUCE

14 pounds ripe tomatoes
10 or 12 green peppers
2 small hot peppers
6 large onions
½ cup salt

2 cups sugar
5 cups vinegar
2 teaspoons allspice
2 teaspoons cinnamon
2 teaspoons cloves

Scald tomatoes and remove skins. Finely chop peppers and skinned onions. Put remaining ingredients in big pot and bring to boil. Add the vegetables and let simmer slowly about 3 hours. Bottle and seal. One and a half times the above makes 8 quarts.
Mrs. Wallace Hicks (Margaret)   *Jacksonville, Florida*

BARBECUED CHICKEN SAUCE

1 cup butter or margarine
2 tablespoons A.1. Sauce
1 tablespoon Worcestershire
   sauce
Juice of 2 lemons

1 teaspoon onion salt
1 teaspoon poultry seasoning
1 teaspoon Accent
1 teaspoon black pepper
1 teaspoon paprika

Before putting on grill, rub chickens with lemon juice. For sauce, mix all ingredients together; let simmer for 5 minutes. Cool and then stir in 1 beaten egg.
Mrs. M. T. Shiver (Maxine)

TERIYAKI MARINADE

¾ cup oil
½ cup soy sauce
½ cup honey

1½ teaspoons ginger
2 garlic cloves
1 cup green onion, chopped

Combine the above ingredients and pour over meat. Recipe marinates up to 5 pounds of beef, chicken, or shrimp.
Mrs. Joe Griffin (Ginger)

VENISON MARINADE

1 cup water
1 cup red wine
1 bay leaf
1 tablespoon whole cloves

1 onion, sliced
1 tablespoon peppercorns
Grated peel of one lemon

Cover meat with marinade and place covered in refrigerator for 1-2 days turning occasionally.
Mrs. Jack V. Allen, Jr. (Rebecca)

WINE-MUSHROOM SAUCE

24 mushrooms, sliced
2 sticks margarine
1 tablespoon onion, chopped
½ teaspoon black pepper
2 tablespoons lemon juice
½ cup cornstarch

½ tablespoon salt
1 tablespoon Worcestershire
  sauce
1 tablespoon parsley flakes
2 cups water
2 cups Burgundy wine

Sauté and brown mushrooms in mixture of margarine, onion, pepper, salt, lemon juice, Worcestershire and parsley. Remove mushrooms from pan. Add to pan drippings, water and wine. When mixture boils, add cornstarch dissolved in small amount of water to make gravy of desired thickness. A thin consistency is better. Return mushrooms to pan. More wine may be added just before serving for more zip!
Mrs. Jasper Davis (Marthalene)

ALICE'S SAUCE FOR WILD DUCK

1 6-ounce jar of currant
  or wild plum jelly

4 ounces port wine
Rind of an orange, grated

Heat and serve.
Mrs. Chris CoCroft (Katie)

BLENDER HOLLANDAISE SAUCE

2 egg yolks
2 teaspoons lemon juice
Dash cayenne pepper

Salt to taste
1 stick butter,
  melted and bubbling

Combine egg yolks, lemon juice, cayenne pepper, and salt in blender at high speed until mixed well. With blender on high speed, slowly pour in bubbling butter and blend until mixed. Sauce will not separate and can sit in blender for little while until ready to serve. Can be refrigerated in covered container until ready to use. Heat up in pan of hot water.
Mrs. A. B. Wight, Jr. (Carolyn)

MRS. MARTIN'S HOLLANDAISE SAUCE

4 egg yolks
Juice of 1 lemon
½ teaspoon salt
Pepper

1 stick margarine
Dash of Tabasco or
  red pepper
2 tablespoons boiling water

Boil water in bottom of double boiler. In cold top of boiler combine egg yolks, lemon juice, salt, pepper, margarine and Tabasco. Beat well. Slowly add 2 tablespoons boiling water. Place mixture over boiling water and beat until thick. Remove from heat and set aside until used. If sauce cools too much, the hot vegetable over which it is served will warm it up. *Never* reheat sauce. Place leftover sauce in refrigerator for future use, but never reheat.
Miss Mary Harris

Cakes

ITALIAN CREAM CAKE

1 stick margarine
½ cup vegetable shortening
2 cups sugar
5 egg yolks
2 cups flour
1 teaspoon vanilla

1 cup buttermilk
1 small can coconut
1 cup nuts, chopped
5 egg whites, stiffly
    beaten
1 teaspoon soda

Cream margarine and shortening. Add sugar and beat until mixture is smooth. Add egg yolks and beat well. Combine flour and soda and add to mixture alternately with buttermilk. Stir in vanilla. Add coconut and nuts. Fold in egg whites. Pour into 3 9-inch greased and floured cake pans. Bake at 350 degrees for 25 minutes or until done.

FROSTING:

8 ounces cream cheese
1 stick butter or margarine

1 box confectioners'
    sugar
Chopped pecans

Cream butter and cream cheese. Gradually beat in powdered sugar. Continue beating until smooth and creamy. Garnish with chopped nuts.
Mrs. Joe Whittemore (Pat)

TIPSEY CAKE

3 layers of Basic
    1-2-3-4 Cake, baked in
    square pan and cooled (See
    Cakes)
⅓ cup sherry
Whole almonds
1 large fresh coconut,
    grated
Whipped cream

Custard:
1½ quarts milk
6 eggs
1 cup sugar
1 tablespoon sherry

Prepare custard by combining ingredients and cooking until mixture becomes the consistency of thick custard. Set aside to cool. Pour sherry into top of dripolator and sprinkle each cake layer until surface of layer is slightly moist. Over moist surface thickly sprinkle whole almonds; then spoon a layer of custard over almonds. On top of custard sprinkle freshly grated coconut. Stack layers. When complete, ice whole cake with whipped cream to which sherry has been added. Serve in squares with an extra pitcher of custard which has been thoroughly chilled.
Mrs. Ralph Neel, Jr. (Katherine)

RUM CAKE

1 box yellow cake mix
1 package instant vanilla
    pudding
½ cup light rum

½ cup water
½ cup shortening
4 eggs
Chopped nuts

Mix all ingredients except nuts. Do not beat over two minutes. Butter a tube pan. Line bottom with chopped nuts. Pour in batter. Bake at 325 degrees for 55 minutes.

FROSTING:

½ cup light rum
1 cup sugar

¼ cup water
1 stick margarine

Mix ingredients and pour over hot cake, piercing to allow mixture to permeate.
Mrs. Jasper Davis (Marthalene)

MERINGUE CAKE

2 tablespoons butter
⅔ cup sugar
4 eggs, separated
1 cup flour
1 teaspoon baking powder

4 tablespoons milk
1 cup sugar
½ pint whipped cream
Strawberries or peaches

Cream butter; add ⅔ cup sugar and beat in yolks. Fold in flour and baking powder alternately with milk. Pour into two layer pans. Beat egg whites stiffly. Add one cup sugar and spread over cake mixture in pans. Bake in 325 degree oven 30 minutes. To serve, top with fruit and whipped cream.
Mrs. Harry L. Hershey (Patti)

FIVE DAY COCONUT CAKE

1 box yellow cake mix
2 cups sugar

1½ cups sour cream
2 packages frozen coconut

Bake cake mix in two layers and freeze. On the same day prepare filling by mixing the sugar, sour cream and coconut. Put in a tight container in the refrigerator. On the second day, split frozen layers in half and ice. Put cake in tight container and refrigerate. Serve after five days.
Mrs. Jack Herring (Rosalyn)

LEMON CHEESE CAKE

1 cup butter
2 cups sugar
3 cups plain flour
3 eggs
½ teaspoon soda

1 teaspoon vanilla
1 teaspoon lemon
 flavoring, if desired
1 cup buttermilk

Cream butter and sugar. Add eggs one at a time, beating after each addition. Alternately add sifted flour and soda with buttermilk. Bake in four 9-inch pans at 350 degrees about 25 minutes or until lightly brown. While still warm frost with Lemon Cheese Frosting.

LEMON CHEESE FROSTING:

1½ cups sugar
3 lemons, juice and
 grated rind

2 tablespoons butter
4 eggs

Beat eggs slightly and add other ingredients. Place in top of double boiler and cook over boiling water until thick, stirring constantly. NOTE: Use sparingly between layers if 4 layers are used.
Mrs. Tom Faircloth (Janice)

SHERRY CUSTARD CAKE

5 egg yolks
¾ cup sherry
¼ cup sugar
2½ pints whipping cream
½ cup sugar

1 envelope unflavored gelatin
½ cup water
1 large angel food cake
Whipping cream and pecans
 or almonds for garnish

Beat egg yolks well. Cook egg yolks, sherry and ¼ cup sugar in the top of a double boiler until it is a thick custard. Soak gelatin in ½ cup water. Fold gelatin mixture into warm custard. Whip 2½ pints whipping cream with ½ cup sugar. When custard mixture is cool, fold in whipped cream. Break 1 large angel food cake into chunks about the size of an egg. Alternate cake and custard in tube pan. Congeal in refrigerator. Unmold. Ice with whipped cream and garnish with toasted pecans or almonds.
Mrs. Huddie Cheney (Anne)

BUTTERNUT CAKE

2 sticks margarine
4 eggs
3 cups flour
2 cups sugar

1 cup milk
1 teaspoon baking powder
1 tablespoon butternut
 flavoring

Mix margarine and sugar thoroughly. Add eggs, one at a time, mixing well after each. Sift flour and baking powder 3 times. After eggs, sugar, and margarine are creamy, add flour and milk alternately. Add flavoring. Pour into well-greased and floured cake pans. Bake at 350 degrees for 30 minutes.

FROSTING:

2 sticks margarine
1 box confectioners' sugar
1 egg

1 cup toasted pecans,
 chopped
1 tablespoon butternut
 flavoring

Cream until fluffy margarine, sugar and egg. Add flavoring, blend, and add nuts. Spread on cake.
Mrs. Gene Walker (Hilda)

ALTERNATE FROSTING:

1 box confectioners' sugar
1 8-ounce package cream
 cheese, softened

1 stick butter, softened
2 tablespoons butternut flavoring
1½ cups pecans, chopped

Cream cheese and butter. Add sugar, beat until smooth, and add flavoring. Add nuts. Spread on cake.
Mrs. Ken Beverly (Mary Jo)

BASIC 1-2-3-4 LAYER CAKE

1 cup butter
2 cups sugar
3 cups flour
4 eggs, separated
1 scant cup milk

2 teaspoons baking powder
½ teaspoon lemon
 flavoring
½ teaspoon vanilla
 flavoring

Cream butter, sugar and egg yolks. Sift baking powder with flour. Add alternately with milk. Add flavoring. Fold in stiffly beaten egg whites. Bake in 3 greased and floured layer pans at 300 degrees until done, about 25 to 30 minutes.
Mrs. Curtis F. Culpepper (Bonnie)

CARROT CAKE

4 eggs
2 cups sugar
1½ cups salad oil
3 cups carrots, grated

2 cups cake flour
1 teaspoon salt
2 teaspoons baking soda
2 teaspoons cinnamon

Cream the eggs, sugar and salad oil. Add remaining ingredients. Bake in 3 greased and floured cake pans at 350 degrees for 25 to 30 minutes. Cake will feel very moist. Carrots may be puréed in blender instead of grated. If blender is used, cut up carrots and add about 3 carrots at a time with almost enough water to cover them. Purée in blender, then pour off excess water and dry carrots in several layers of paper towels.

ICING:

1 8-ounce package
    cream cheese
½ stick butter

⅔ box confectioners' sugar
1 teaspoon vanilla
Pecans, chopped

Have cheese and butter at room temperature. Mix all ingredients together and frost cake.

Mrs. Robert Sullivan (Sally)

PEACH CAKE

2 cups sugar
1 cup shortening
3 eggs
1 cup nuts, chopped
2 teaspoons soda
1 teaspoon salt
2 cups flour

2 teaspoons cinnamon
1 teaspoon cloves
2 teaspoons allspice
1 teaspoon nutmeg
7 tablespoons buttermilk
1 No. 2 can peaches,
    drained

Cream sugar and shortening; add eggs and nuts. Sift together flour, soda, salt, and spices and add to first mixture. Add buttermilk and peaches. Beat well in mixer until peaches are mashed and blended into batter. Pour into greased and floured tube pan. Bake at 350 degrees for 40 minutes. Ice with your favorite icing.

Mrs. T. R. Sample (Nell)

LINDY'S CHEESECAKE

CRUST:

1 cup all purpose flour,
sifted
¼ cup sugar
1 teaspoon lemon peel,
grated

½ teaspoon vanilla extract
1 egg yolk
¼ cup butter, softened

Preheat oven to 400 degrees. Grease inside of 9-inch (3 inches high) spring-form pan. Remove side. To make crust, combine flour, sugar, lemon peel, and vanilla in medium bowl. Make well in center; with fork blend in yolk and butter. Mix with fingertips until smooth. On bottom of pan, form half of dough into ball. Place wax paper on top; roll pastry to edge of pan. Remove paper. Bake 6-8 minutes or until golden. Cool. Meanwhile, divide rest of dough into 3 parts. Cut 6 strips of wax paper strips, roll each part 2¼ inches wide and 9 inches long. Assemble spring-form pan with crust on bottom. Line inside of pan with pastry strips, overlapping ends. Remove waxed paper strips. Preheat oven to 450 degrees.

FILLING:

1¾ cups sugar
5 8-ounce packages cream
cheese, softened
3 tablespoons flour
2 teaspoons lemon peel,
grated
1½ teaspoons orange peel,
grated

¼ teaspoon vanilla
5 eggs, plus 2 egg yolks
¼ cup heavy cream
1 8-ounce carton sour
cream, for topping
Strawberries for garnish
(optional)

In large mixing bowl, blend cheese, sugar, flour, peels, and vanilla at high speed. Beat in eggs and yolks, one at a time; beat until smooth. Beat in cream. Pour into pan. Bake 10 minutes and lower oven to 250 degrees. Bake 1 hour longer. Remove to rack to cool for 2 hours. Put sour cream on top as glaze and refrigerate 3 hours or overnight. To serve, loosen pastry from side of pan with spatula. Remove side of spring-form pan. Cut into wedges. Garnish with strawberries. Serves 16.
The Editors

CHOCOLATE CHEESE CAKE

CRUST:

1½ cups graham crackers   ⅓ cup sugar
⅓ cup butter, melted

Mix ingredients and press into a 9-inch pie pan.

FILLING:

2 8-ounce packages   1¼ cups sugar
   cream cheese   ⅓ cup cocoa
1 teaspoon vanilla   2 eggs

Have cream cheese at room temperature. Mix in eggs with electric beater. Combine sugar and cocoa and add to cheese mixture. Add vanilla. Pour into pie shell and bake at 375 degrees for 35 minutes. Remove from oven immediately and spread on topping.

TOPPING:

1 cup sour cream   2 tablespoons sugar
1 teaspoon vanilla

Combine sour cream, sugar and vanilla and spread on baked filling. Chill several hours or overnight.
Mrs. T. R. Sample (Nell)

POUND CAKE

½ pound (2 sticks) butter   2 teaspoons vanilla
3 cups sugar   ½ teaspoon lemon flavoring
6 eggs, separated   3 cups flour, sifted
1 cup milk   1½ teaspoons baking powder

Cream butter and sugar. Add egg yolks. Beat well. Add milk, vanilla and lemon flavoring. Add sifted flour and baking powder. Mix until smooth. Beat egg whites until stiff and fold into batter. Pour into greased, floured tube pan. Bake at 325 degrees for 1½ hours or until golden and tester comes out clean.
Mrs. Genie Love Edelen

Similar recipes submitted by *Mrs. Prince E. Jinright, Jr. (Marjorie), Mrs. Bill Lawson (Diane), and Mrs. J. A. Stewart (Melba).*

SOUR CREAM POUND CAKE

3 cups sugar
½ pound (2 sticks) butter
1 cup sour cream
6 eggs, separated
3 cups flour

¼ teaspoon soda
¼ teaspoon salt
1 teaspoon vanilla
¼ teaspoon almond
    extract (optional)

Cream sugar and butter. Add egg yolks one at a time, beating well after each addition. Add sour cream and mix well. Add flavorings. Mix in 1 cup flour. Beat egg whites until they hold peak and fold them in. Add remaining dry ingredients. Turn into greased, wax paper-lined pan. Bake in 300 degree oven for 1¼ to 1½ hours.
Mrs. Henry Pepin (Sarah)

Similar recipe submitted by *Mrs. Fred E. Murphy, III (Dawn).*

CARAMEL NUT POUND CAKE

½ pound butter
½ cup Crisco
1 box light brown sugar
1 cup white sugar
5 large eggs
1 cup milk

3 cups flour
½ teaspoon salt
1 tablespoon vanilla
½ teaspoon baking powder
1 cup pecans, chopped

Cream butter and shortening. Add brown sugar a little at a time. Beat well. Add white sugar and beat until light and fluffy. Add eggs. Sift baking powder and salt with flour. Add to mixture alternating with milk. Add vanilla and nuts. Bake in tube pan for 1½ hours at 325 degrees. Cake may be frosted, if you wish.

FROSTING:

1 cup nuts, chopped and
    toasted in butter
½ stick margarine
½ box confectioners' sugar

1 teaspoon vanilla
Milk to make
    spreading consistency

Mix all thoroughly and spread on warm cake.
Mrs. John Wilson (Nell)

Similar recipes submitted by *Mrs. W. J. Vaughan (Virginia), Mrs. Oscar Mims (Candy), Miss Eunice Singletary, and Mrs. Roscoe Stewart (Eva).*

COCONUT POUND CAKE

2 sticks butter
1 stick margarine
1 8-ounce package
    cream cheese
3 cups sugar
6 eggs

3 cups flour
2 tablespoons cold water
2 teaspoons coconut
    flavoring
1 3½ or 4-ounce can
    coconut flakes

Cream butter, margarine, and cream cheese. Add sugar slowly, beating well. Add eggs one at a time, beating well. Add flour slowly to creamed mixture. Add cold water, coconut flavoring and coconut. Pour into well-greased and floured tube cake pan. Place into cold oven and cook at 275 degrees for 1½ hours.

Mrs. Tom Boyle (Iris)

Similar recipes submitted by Mrs. Curtis Culpepper (Bonnie), Mrs. Russell Fryar (Carole), and Miss Ophelia Smith.

CHOCOLATE POUND CAKE

½ pound butter
½ cup shortening
3 cups sugar
5 eggs
3 cups flour

½ teaspoon salt
½ teaspoon baking powder
4 tablespoons cocoa
1 cup milk
1 tablespoon vanilla

Cream butter and shortening and sugar. Add eggs one at a time. Sift flour, salt and baking powder. Add dry ingredients alternately with milk. Add vanilla and cocoa. Mix well. Bake at 325 degrees for 1 hour and 10 minutes in a well-greased and floured tube pan.

CHOCOLATE GLAZE (optional):

1 bar German's Sweet
    Chocolate (Baker's)
1 tablespoon shortening
¼ cup water

Dash salt
½ teaspoon vanilla
1 cup confectioners'
    sugar, sifted

Melt chocolate and shortening in water over low heat. Mix sugar and salt. Blend in chocolate and vanilla. Pour over cake.

Mrs. John Wilson (Nell)

Similar recipes submitted by Mrs. Bob Ausley (Ola) and Mrs. Dilworth Mills (Mary).

CREAM CHEESE POUND CAKE

1 8-ounce package cream cheese
3 sticks butter
2½ cups sugar
6 eggs

3 cups cake flour
1 teaspoon baking powder
1 teaspoon vanilla

Cream together butter and cream cheese. Beat in sugar and eggs, one at a time. Mix baking powder with cake flour, add to mixture and beat well. Add vanilla and pour into large Bundt pan or 4 8-inch layer pans. Bake at 300 degrees about 1 hour and 15 minutes. Great for wedding or party cake!
Mrs. Crawford Barrett (Agnes)

Similar recipes submitted by *Mrs. Eugene H. Driver (Carol) and Mrs. William A. Lardin (Sherry).*

CHOCOLATE SHEATH CAKE

2 cups flour
2 cups sugar
4 tablespoons cocoa
1 cup water
1 stick margarine

½ cup Crisco
2 eggs
1 teaspoon vanilla
1 scant teaspoon soda
½ cup buttermilk

Sift flour, sugar, and cocoa into a large bowl. Add 1 cup water and mix. Put margarine and Crisco in a saucepan. Bring to a rapid boil. Remove from heat, pour over flour mixture, and mix well. Add eggs, soda, vanilla and buttermilk. Mix well. Batter will be thin. Pour into a greased and floured 9 x 13-inch pan. Bake at 375 degrees for 25 minutes.

ICING:

1 stick margarine
4 tablespoons cocoa
6 tablespoons milk

1 box confectioners' sugar
1 teaspoon vanilla
½ cup nuts, chopped

Bring margarine, cocoa and milk to a boil and add the other ingredients. Beat until smooth. Spread on cake as soon as it comes from oven.
Mrs. E. P. McCollum (Louise)

Similar recipes submitted by *Mrs. Robert G. Lauder (Annelle), Mrs. Forrest Caldwell (Emily), and Mrs. Pat Fenlon (Renie).*

CHOCOLATE COCA-COLA CAKE

2 cups flour
2 sticks margarine
1 cup Coca-Cola
2 eggs, beaten
1 teaspoon soda

2 cups sugar
3 tablespoons cocoa
½ cup buttermilk
1 teaspoon vanilla
2 cups small marshmallows

Mix flour, soda and sugar. Heat margarine, Coca-Cola and cocoa over medium heat to boiling point. Pour over flour mixture and stir. Add buttermilk, eggs, vanilla and marshmallows. Batter will be thin. Bake in well-greased 3-quart Pyrex container (13½ x 8¾ x 1¾ inches). Bake for 35 minutes at 350 degrees.

FROSTING:

1 stick margarine
6 tablespoons Coca-Cola
1 cup pecans, chopped

3 tablespoons cocoa
1 box confectioners' sugar

Cook margarine, cocoa and Coca-Cola; bring to boiling point over medium heat. Pour over sugar and mix well. Add pecans. Ice cake while warm in pan.
Mrs. William King (Anne)
Mrs. E. C. Oliver (Clancy)

BLACK CHOCOLATE CAKE

4 eggs
¼ pound butter
1½ cups sugar
¼ teaspoon salt
2 squares unsweetened
    chocolate
¼ cup boiling water

1 cup sour cream
¼ cup cold water
2 cups cake flour
1 heaping teaspoon
    baking soda
1 teaspoon vanilla

Combine flour and baking soda and sift four times. Separate eggs. Put whites in a large bowl. Put yolks in a small bowl. With electric mixer beat yolks until thick and creamy. In large bowl cream butter and sugar. Add beaten egg yolks and salt. Melt chocolate squares in ¼ cup boiling water. Allow to cool but not harden. Add sour cream to butter and sugar mixture. Add ¼ cup cold water and chocolate mixture. Beat egg whites until stiff. Add flour and soda while beating on lowest mixer speed. Add vanilla. Fold in egg whites by hand. Bake in 2 layer pans (grease and flour sides; cut wax paper for bottom). Bake at 350 degrees for 20 minutes or until solid in the middle. Ice with White Sea-Foam Icing (See Icings).
Mrs. Thomas Hawkins (Harriet)

OLD FASHIONED DEVIL'S FOOD CAKE

¾ cup butter
2½ cups sugar
5 eggs
2 cups flour
2 teaspoons vanilla

1 teaspoon soda
1 tablespoon hot water
1 cup buttermilk
6 squares unsweetened
   chocolate, melted

Cream butter and sugar. Add eggs. Beat well. Add flour gradually. Add vanilla. Add soda dissolved in 1 tablespoon hot water. Add buttermilk and melted chocolate. Bake in three greased and floured pans for 25 to 30 minutes at 350 degrees.

CHOCOLATE FUDGE ICING:

6 squares unsweetened
   chocolate
1½ cups milk
3½ cups sugar

1 stick butter
Dash salt
2 tablespoons light corn
   syrup

Combine all ingredients except butter. Do not stir again. Cook until a soft ball is formed when a few drops are put in cool tap water. Remove from heat. Add butter. Beat until cool. Ice cooled cake.
Mrs. Robert Sullivan (Sally)

TUNNEL OF FUDGE CAKE

1½ cups of butter
6 eggs
1½ cups sugar
2 cups flour

1 package of Double Dutch
   Fudge Frosting Mix (Pillsbury)
2 cups walnuts or pecans,
   chopped

Butter a 10-inch tube pan or a Bundt pan. Cream butter in large mixer at high speed. Add eggs one at a time. Beat well. Gradually add sugar. Continue creaming at high speed until well mixed. Stir in flour, frosting mix, and nuts until well blended. Pour batter into greased pan. Bake at 350 degrees for 60 minutes. If you have a hot oven, lower rack and bake at 325 degrees for 50-55 minutes. Be sure not to overcook. Cool until just warm and then remove from pan.
Mrs. Gerald R. Wolfsfelt (Vicky)

MOSS CAKE

1 cup Crisco
2 cups granulated sugar
4 eggs
2 cups plain flour
2 teaspoons baking powder
½ teaspoon salt

1 cup milk
1 teaspoon vanilla
1 4-ounce package German's
   Sweet Chocolate, grated
1 4-ounce package semi-
   sweet chocolate, grated

Combine everything except the chocolate. Beat for 10 minutes on medium speed. Fold in grated chocolate. Bake 1 hour in 350 degree oven in a tube pan that has been greased and floured.
Mrs. Robert C. Brown (Frances)

GINGERBREAD WITH LEMON SAUCE

2 eggs
¾ cup brown sugar
¾ cup dark corn syrup
¾ cup cooking oil
2¼ cups plain flour
2½ teaspoons baking powder

¾ teaspoon soda
2 teaspoons ginger
1½ teaspoons cinnamon
½ teaspoon cloves
½ teaspoon nutmeg
1 cup boiling water

Beat eggs. Add sugar, syrup, and cooking oil. Blend well. Sift together dry ingredients and add to egg mixture. Stir in boiling water. Bake in 8 x 16 x 1½-inch pan at 375 degrees for about 25 minutes. Serve with lemon sauce.

SAUCE:

1 cup sugar
1 tablespoon cornstarch
¼ cup water
1 egg, beaten

3 tablespoons lemon juice
2 teaspoons lemon rind,
   grated
½ cup margarine

Mix sugar and cornstarch in small saucepan. Gradually stir in water, egg, lemon juice and rind, and margarine. Cook over medium heat, stirring, until mixture comes to a boil. Boil for 1 minute. Makes 1½ cups.
Mrs. Jack Kelly (Janis)

LEMON NUT CAKE

1 pound butter, softened
2½ cups sugar
6 eggs
4 cups flour
1 pound pecans
1 pound white raisins

1 pound cherries, candied
    or maraschino
1 teaspoon salt
1 teaspoon baking powder
4 ounces lemon extract

Dredge nuts, raisins and cherries in flour. Sift remaining flour with baking powder and salt. Cream softened butter with sugar. Add eggs one at the time alternating with dry ingredients. Then add nuts, fruit and lemon extract. Bake in greased and floured 10-inch tube pan or 3 8½ x 4½-inch loaf pans for 2 hours. Bake at 300 degrees for first hour and at 325 degrees for second hour.
Mrs. Bernard Lanigan (Kathy)

HOOTENHOLLER WHISKEY CAKE

½ cup butter
1 cup sugar
3 eggs
1 cup flour
½ teaspoon baking powder
¼ teaspoon salt
½ teaspoon nutmeg

¼ cup molasses
¼ teaspoon soda
1 pound raisins
2 cups pecans, chopped
¼ cup bourbon
¼ cup milk

Cream butter and sugar; beat in eggs. Sift flour once, then resift with baking powder, salt and nutmeg. Add dry ingredients alternately with milk. Mix together molasses and soda. Add to batter along with raisins, nuts and bourbon. Bake in large greased and brown paper-lined loaf pan at 300 degrees for two hours. Will keep indefinitely when wrapped and stored in refrigerator.
Mrs. J. Truman Holland, Jr. (Jimmie)

WHITE FRUIT CAKE

5 eggs
1 cup butter
1 cup sugar
1 tablespoon vanilla
1 tablespoon lemon extract

2 cups flour
4 cups nuts, whole pieces
1 pound candied cherries
¾ pound candied pineapple

Cream butter and sugar. Add eggs one at the time. Add extracts. Coat fruit and nuts with flour. Add to butter mixture. Spread in well-greased and floured 10-inch tube pan. Bake 1 hour at 350 degrees.
Mrs. William Z. Bridges (Mary)

POOR MAN'S FRUIT CAKE

1 pound seeded raisins
2 cups water
2 cups sugar
1 teaspoon salt
1 teaspoon cinnamon

1 teaspoon cloves
3 cups flour
1 teaspoon soda
1 tablespoon warm water
1 quart nuts, chopped

Boil the raisins, 2 cups water, sugar, salt, and spices and let cool thoroughly. Add 3 cups flour and the soda dissolved in 1 tablespoon warm water. Add the nuts and bake in a loaf pan for 2 hours at 250 degrees. A pan of water could be put in oven to help slow baking.
Mrs. Paul Hjort (Frances)

FRESH APPLE NUT CAKE

1½ cups cooking oil
2 cups sugar
4 eggs
3 cups self-rising
    or plain flour

1 teaspoon soda
1 teaspoon salt
2 teaspoons vanilla
3 cups apples, diced
1 cup pecans, chopped

Mix oil, sugar and eggs until creamy. Sift flour, soda, and salt together and add to mixture. Beat well. Add vanilla, apples and nuts. Pour into well-greased and floured tube pan. Bake at 325 degrees for 1½ hours.

GLAZE:

1½ sticks margarine
1 cup brown sugar

¼ cup milk
1 teaspoon vanilla

Mix everything except vanilla. Boil slowly for 10 minutes. Add vanilla. Cool and pour over cake.
Mrs. Lawrence Harmon (Kaki)
Mrs. J. C. Payne (Leola)

Variation: ½ teaspoon of cinnamon and ½ teaspoon nutmeg may be added to
    flour.
Mrs. Paul Hjort (Frances)

Similar recipes submitted by *Mrs. R. Rudolph Davis (Anne), Mrs. E. P. Mc-Collum (Louise), and Mrs. Arthur Taylor (Thelma).*

QUICK SAUCE FOR POUND CAKE

1 stick of margarine
1 cup light brown sugar

1 tablespoon flour
1 cup milk

Melt margarine in small saucepan. Add sugar and flour, then milk. Cook at medium heat ten minutes or until thickened.
Mrs. Fred Vonier (Mary Lou)

PUMPKIN CAKE

The day after Halloween put that Jack O' Lantern into a deliciously moist cake . . .

3 cups cake flour,
    unsifted
1 tablespoon baking powder
2 teaspoons ground cinnamon
1 teaspoon salt
4 eggs

2 cups sugar
1 cup corn oil
2 cups puréed pumpkin,
    fresh cooked or canned
1 cup walnuts or pecans,
    chopped

Sift together flour, baking powder, cinnamon and salt. In large mixing bowl with electric mixer at high speed, beat eggs until light and frothy. Gradually add sugar, beating until thick and ivory-colored. Slowly pour in corn oil, beating constantly. With mixer at low speed, add dry ingredients alternately with pumpkin, beginning and ending with dry ingredients. Beat until smooth after each addition. Stir in nuts. Pour into ungreased 10x4-inch tube pan. Bake in 325 degree oven 60-70 minutes or until cake tester inserted in center comes out clean. Cool cake in pan ½ hour; remove and cool completely on wire rack. Brush with glaze when cool. Also delicious served with ice cream or whipped cream.

GLAZE: (optional)

½ cup light corn syrup
½ teaspoon lemon rind, grated

½ teaspoon ginger, ground

In small saucepan, stir together light corn syrup, grated lemon rind and ground ginger. Bring to boil over medium heat. Remove from heat. Makes ½ cup.
Mrs. Robert Boissiere (Madeline)

NUT SPICE CAKE

3 eggs
2 sticks butter or
  margarine
1½ cups sugar
2 cups plain flour
1 box white seedless
  raisins

1 teaspoon baking powder
1 teaspoon allspice
½ teaspoon cinnamon
½ teaspoon nutmeg
2 cups pecans, chopped

Cream butter and sugar; add eggs one at a time and beat well. Fold in flour which has been sifted with other dry ingredients. Line greased pan, either tube cake pan or long loaf pan, with wax paper. Add raisins and nuts to dough which will be very thick. Press mixture into pan and bake at 275 degrees for 1½ to 2 hours or until straw comes out clean.
Mrs. Richard R. Ramsey (Elsie)

Similar recipe submitted by *Mrs. Genie Love Edelen.*

PRUNE CAKE

3 eggs
1 cup vegetable oil
1½ cups sugar
1 cup buttermilk
1½ teaspoons soda
1 teaspoon cinnamon
1 teaspoon nutmeg

1 teaspoon allspice
1 teaspoon vanilla
2 cups flour
1 cup prunes, cooked and
  chopped
1 cup nuts, chopped

Beat eggs; then add vegetable oil and sugar. Dissolve soda in buttermilk and add to mixture. Add spices and vanilla. Stir in flour, prunes and nuts. Mix well. Pour into greased 10-inch Bundt pan. Bake at 350 degrees for 45 to 50 minutes or until cake pulls away from pan. While cake is baking make icing.

BUTTERMILK ICING:

1 cup sugar
½ cup buttermilk
½ teaspoon soda

1 tablespoon white corn
  syrup
¾ stick margarine
½ teaspoon vanilla

Mix ingredients in saucepan and boil for 1 minute. Pour over cake while still warm.
Miss Ophelia Smith

FIG CAKE

4 eggs, beaten
¾ cup sugar
2 cups flour
1 teaspoon cinnamon
1 cup buttermilk
1 teaspoon soda

½ teaspoon salt
1 cup cooking oil
1 teaspoon cloves
1 teaspoon nutmeg
1 cup fig preserves

Mix eggs, oil and sugar. Sift dry ingredients. Alternately add egg mixture and buttermilk to dry ingredients. When thoroughly mixed, stir in fig preserves. Cook in greased tube pan for 1 hour at 300 degrees.

FIG CAKE ICING:

1 cup sugar
¼ teaspoon soda
2 teaspoons vanilla

½ cup buttermilk
½ stick margarine

Combine all ingredients in saucepan and boil 1 minute. Pour over hot cake.
Miss Julia Hickson

WHITE SEA-FOAM ICING

2 egg whites
1½ cups sugar
¼ teaspoon cream of tartar
¼ teaspoon salt

⅓ cup cold water
2 teaspoons light corn
     syrup
1 teaspoon vanilla

Put all ingredients except vanilla in a double boiler. Cook over boiling water 7 minutes, beating with electric beater. Remove from heat. Add vanilla and beat one minute. Makes enough to ice a two layer cake with plenty in the middle layer.
Mrs. Thomas Hawkins (Harriet)
Similar recipe submitted by *Mrs. George Neel (Jenny).*

GERMAN CHOCOLATE FROSTING

1 cup evaporated milk
1 cup sugar
3 egg yolks
½ cup margarine or
     butter

1 teaspoon vanilla
1½ cups coconut
1 cup nuts, chopped

Place all ingredients except coconut and nuts in a medium-size boiler and cook over medium heat, stirring until thickened (about 12 minutes). Remove from heat and add coconut and nuts. Beat until thick enough to spread.
Mrs. Oscar Mims (Candy)

Pies

KEY LIME PIE WITH
CHOCOLATE COOKIE CRUST

1 envelope unflavored
   gelatin
¼ cup cold water
½ cup sugar
½ cup fresh lime juice
¼ teaspoon salt
4 egg yolks, beaten

1 teaspoon lime rind, grated
4 egg whites, beaten with
   ½ cup sugar added
1 drop green food coloring
20 chocolate wafers, crushed
¼ cup butter, melted
½ pint whipping cream

Soak gelatin in water. Cook the following in double boiler until consistency of custard, stirring constantly: sugar, lime juice, salt, and beaten egg yolks. Remove custard from heat and add soaked gelatin. Chill. Add 1 drop green food coloring. Beat egg whites until stiff. Add ½ cup sugar and beat one minute longer. When custard begins to congeal, whip with wire whisk until fluffy. Fold in egg whites carefully. Make a pie shell by combining wafers and ¼ cup melted butter. Press into a 9-inch pie pan. Pour in filling and chill. When ready to serve, spread thin layer of whipped cream over top of pie or each individual serving. Shave chocolate over whipped cream.

From *Mrs. Haney's Phi Mu Cookbook*   *Athens, Georgia*

LEMON MERINGUE PIE

4 eggs
1 cup sugar
½ stick butter, melted
Juice of 2 large lemons

Rind of one lemon, grated
More sugar for meringue
1 9-inch pastry, shell,
   unbaked

Separate 3 of the eggs, set aside the 3 whites for meringue. Beat the 1 whole egg with the 3 egg yolks and with the sugar. Add the melted butter, lemon juice and rind. Bake in pastry shell for 30 minutes at 350 degrees. To make meringue, add 2 tablespoons of sugar for each egg white. Beat very stiff. Put meringue roughly over the cooked pie and brown slightly from the top element with the oven door partly open. It takes only a few minutes.

Mrs. Charles Watt (Julie)

HEAVENLY PIE

1 cup sugar
¼ teaspoon cream of tartar
4 eggs, separated
½ cup sugar
3 tablespoons lemon juice

1 teaspoon lemon rind,
  grated
⅛ teaspoon salt
1 pint whipping cream

Sift together 1 cup sugar and cream of tartar. Beat stiffly 4 egg whites and stir sugar mixture into egg whites gradually. Continue to beat until stiff. Line bottom of a greased 9-inch pie plate with mixture. Slightly hollow out center. Be careful not to spread meringue too close to rim of plate. Bake in a 275 degree oven for 1 hour. (Individual meringue shells may be made rather than putting mixture in the 9-inch pie plate). To make the filling, beat slightly in top of double boiler 4 egg yolks. Stir in ½ cup sugar, lemon juice and rind, and salt. Cook until very thick and smooth, stirring constantly. Remove from heat and cool. Fold into lemon mixture 1 cup whipped cream. Fill pie plate or shells with lemon mixture and refrigerate. Just before serving, pour 1 cup whipped cream over meringue and lemon mixture and sprinkle with chocolate shavings or chocolate chips.
Mrs. Richard S. Vann (Ann)

LEMON CHESS PIE
From the New Perry Motel

½ cup butter
2 cups sugar
1 tablespoon cornstarch
Juice of 2 lemons

Rind of 1 lemon, grated
4 eggs
1 pie shell, unbaked

Cream butter. Blend together cornstarch and sugar and add to the butter. Add whole eggs, one at a time, and beat well after each addition. Blend in lemon juice and rind. Pour into unbaked pie shell. Bake at 350 degrees until set, about 35 minutes.
Mrs. Bolling Jones, III (Connie)

ANNIE'S CHESS PIE

3 whole eggs,
  slightly beaten
1 cup sugar
1 tablespoon flour
1 tablespoon cold water

1½ teaspoons vinegar
¾ stick butter
1 teaspoon vanilla
1 pie shell, unbaked

Mix all ingredients. Pour into unbaked pie crust. Bake 10 minutes at 450 degrees then lower heat to 350 degrees and bake for 25 minutes.
Mrs. Ken Beverly (Mary Jo)

PUMPKIN CHIFFON PIE

1 envelope unflavored
   gelatin
¼ cup cold water
1¼ cups canned pumpkin
½ cup milk
½ teaspoon nutmeg
½ teaspoon ginger

½ teaspoon cinnamon
½ teaspoon salt
1 cup sugar
3 eggs, separated
1 9-inch pie shell, baked
   and cooled

To slightly beaten egg yolks add ½ cup sugar, pumpkin, milk, salt and spices. Cook in double boiler until thickened. Soften gelatin in cold water. Add to hot pumpkin mixture; mix thoroughly and cool. When it begins to thicken, fold in stiffly beaten egg whites to which the other ½ cup sugar has been added. Pour into baked pie shell. Chill in refrigerator or cool place. Pie may be garnished with whipped cream just before serving. Delicious served in gingersnap crust. Follow recipe for graham cracker crust, using a little less sugar. Chill gingersnap crust thoroughly and pour in pumpkin mixture.
Mrs. Leroy Edwards (Sarah Martha)

PUMPKIN PRALINE PIE

Pie crust for 10-inch pie
3 tablespoons margarine or
   butter, softened
⅓ cup dark brown sugar
⅓ cup pecans, chopped
1 cup evaporated milk
½ cup water
3 eggs

1½ cups canned pumpkin
½ cup sugar
½ cup brown sugar
1 teaspoon cinnamon
¼ teaspoon ground cloves
¼ teaspoon nutmeg
1 teaspoon salt
½ pint whipping cream

Prepare crust and put in 10-inch pie pan. Cream butter with dark brown sugar; stir in pecans and press over pie crust. This forms the praline layer. Bake at 450 degrees for 10 minutes. Cool. Scald milk with water in small pan. Beat eggs in large bowl; stir in pumpkin, sugars, spices and salt. Beat in scalded mixture. Pour over praline layer. Bake at 350 degrees for 50 minutes until set but still soft. Cool and top with whipped cream.
Mrs. Mervin Wine (Hettie Love)

SWEET POTATO PIE

2 cups sweet potatoes,
    cooked and mashed
2 eggs, beaten
1 cup milk
1½ cups light brown sugar

1 stick butter
1 teaspoon cinnamon
1 teaspoon allspice
½ teaspoon cloves
1 pie crust, unbaked

Mix all ingredients well. Pour into unbaked pie crust and bake at 350 degrees about an hour.
Mrs. Henry M. Moore (Reta)

Similar recipes submitted by *Mrs. Leon Neel (Julie) and Mrs. John H. Chastain (Cecilia).*

EGG CUSTARD PIE

4 eggs
2 cups milk
½ cup plus 2
    tablespoons sugar

1 teaspoon vanilla
Dash nutmeg
Pinch of salt
1 pie shell, unbaked

Scald milk. Beat eggs slightly. Add eggs and all other ingredients to milk. Pour into unbaked pie shell. Bake 10 minutes at 400 degrees, then about 30 minutes at 350 degrees.
Mrs. Joe E. Beverly (Mary)

BUTTERSCOTCH PIE

1 cup light brown sugar
6 tablespoons flour
1 cup milk
2 egg yolks
4 tablespoons butter

½ teaspoon vanilla
1 8-inch pie crust, baked
2 egg whites
2 tablespoons sugar

Put brown sugar and flour in top of double boiler over slowly boiling water. Add milk slowly, stirring constantly. Add slightly beaten egg yolks. Cook until thick, stirring constantly. Remove from heat. Add butter. Cool. Add vanilla. Pour into pie shell. Make meringue with 2 egg whites and 2 tablespoons of sugar. Arrange over pie and brown a few minutes in a 425 degree oven.
Mrs. R. C. Balfour, III (Virginia)

FRENCH SILK CHOCOLATE PIE

1 stick butter
¾ cup sugar
2 squares unsweetened
    chocolate, melted
1 teaspoon vanilla

2 eggs, chilled
1 pie shell, baked and
    cooled
Whipped cream
Almonds, slivered

Cream butter and sugar until light and fluffy. Blend in chocolate and vanilla. Add the chilled eggs, one at a time, beating two minutes after adding each. Pour into baked pie shell. Chill at least 3 hours before serving. Top with whipped cream and toasted slivered almonds.

Mrs. Maurice Tanner (Peggy)
Mrs. Hugh Hodges (Sally)
Mrs. Frank DeLamar (Peggy)

CHOCOLATE CHIP PIE

1 6-ounce package
    chocolate chips
2 tablespoons sugar
2 tablespoons milk
1 teaspoon vanilla or
    rum flavoring

4 eggs, separated
1 9-inch pie shell,
    baked and cooled
½ pint whipping cream

Combine chocolate chips, sugar and milk in top of double boiler and heat over boiling water to melt chocolate. Add flavoring and cool to lukewarm. Beat egg yolks, one at a time, into chocolate mixture. Beat egg whites separately and gently fold into mixture. Pour into baked pie shell and refrigerate. Garnish with whipped cream and chocolate shavings.

Mrs. Fred Allen (Winnie)

GRANDMOTHER'S CHOCOLATE PIE

2 squares unsweetened
    chocolate
2¾ cups milk, warmed
½ cup plain flour
1 teaspoon vanilla
1⅓ cups sugar

4 eggs, separated
¼ teaspoon salt
2 tablespoons butter
1 10-inch graham cracker
    crust
⅓ cup sugar

Melt chocolate in double boiler. Add sugar and flour. Add warmed milk slowly and cook until thickened. Remove from heat and add slightly beaten egg yolks. Cook until mixture thickens even more. Add butter and vanilla. Pour into 10-inch graham cracker crust pie shell. Beat egg whites with ⅓ cup sugar. Pile on top of pie. Bake at 350 degrees until golden brown.

Mrs. Tom Lear (Ann)

CHOCOLATE PIE

1 stick margarine
1 square dark baking
   chocolate
½ cup flour
1 cup sugar

1 teaspoon vanilla
2 eggs
½ cup nuts, chopped
   (optional)

Melt margarine and chocolate together over low heat. Stir together flour, sugar and eggs. Add chocolate mixture and vanilla. Add nuts. Pour into greased pie pan. Bake at 350 degrees for 25 minutes. Do not overcook. The pie should be soft in the middle.
Mrs. J. T. Higgins (Virginia)

FUDGE SUNDAE PIE

1 pie crust shell, baked
1 cup evaporated milk
6-ounce package semi-
   sweet chocolate pieces
¼ teaspoon salt

1 cup miniature
   marshmallows
1 quart vanilla ice cream
Pecans, as desired

Put evaporated milk, chocolate pieces and salt in 1-quart saucepan. Stir over low heat until chocolate melts completely and mixture thickens. Remove from heat. Stir in marshmallows until melted and mixture is smooth. Cool to room temperature. Spoon half of ice cream into shell. Cover with half of chocolate mixture. Repeat with rest of ice cream and chocolate. Top with pecans (Nuts may be added between layers also.) Freeze until firm, about 5 hours.
Mrs. Marx Gaines (Claire)

HERSHEY BAR PIE

1 pastry shell,
   baked and cooled
1 8-ounce Hershey Bar with
   Almonds

22 large marshmallows
½ cup milk
1 pint whipping cream,
   whipped

Melt chocolate, marshmallows and milk together in a double boiler. When cool, fold in 1 pint of whipped cream. Pour into browned pie shell and refrigerate.
Mrs. Richard Vann (Ann)

BLACK BOTTOM PIE

1 pie shell, baked
4 eggs, divided
½ cup dark brown sugar
1½ tablespoons corn starch
¼ teaspoon salt
1½ cups milk, scalded
5 tablespoons brandy or rum
1 2-inch square unsweetened
    chocolate, melted

¾ teaspoon vanilla
1 envelope unflavored gelatin
2 tablespoons water
1 tablespoon brandy
¼ teaspoon cream of tartar
Whipped cream and slivered
    chocolate for top

Beat 4 egg yolks in top of double boiler. Gradually add a generous ½ cup of dark brown sugar sifted with corn starch and salt. Stir in scalded milk and cook over hot water until thick. Add 5 tablespoons brandy or rum and remove from hot water. Take out 1 cup of the custard and add to it the melted chocolate and vanilla. Cool and pour into baked pie shell. To the rest of the hot custard add the gelatin, softened in 2 tablespoons cold water and 1 table-spoon brandy. Cool but do not let set. Beat 4 egg whites stiffly with cream of tartar. Fold into the custard and pour over the chocolate filling. Chill at least 3 hours. Spread with whipped cream and slivered chocolate before serving.
Mrs. James Burch (Wilma)

GRASSHOPPER PIE
Crème de Menthe Pie

20 chocolate wafers, crushed
¼ cup butter or margarine,
    melted
25 marshmallows
¾ cup milk
3 egg whites

⅓ cup sugar
3 tablespoons crème de
    menthe
3 tablespoons crème
    de cacao

Combine wafers and butter. Press into a 9-inch pie pan. Reserve a tablespoon of crumbs for garnish. Chill the crust. Melt marshmallows with milk over low heat. Cool. Beat egg whites with sugar until stiff. Add crèmes to marshmallow mixture. Fold in egg whites. Pile into crust. Garnish with reserved crumbs. Chill.
Mrs. R. C. Balfour, III (Virginia)

Similar recipe by *Mrs. Randolph Jones (Nancy).*

GRAHAM CRACKER PIE
Macaroon Pie

3 egg whites	1 teaspoon baking powder
1 cup sugar	¼ teaspon cream of tartar
1 cup graham cracker	½ cup coconut
crumbs	½ cup dates, chopped
1 cup pecans, chopped	Whipped cream

Beat egg whites with cream of tartar and baking powder. Gradually add sugar and beat until stiff, but not dry. Fold in cracker crumbs, nuts, coconut and dates. Pour into buttered pie plate and bake at 350 degrees for ½ hour. Serve with whipped cream.
Mrs. Jack Herring (Rosalyn)

ANGEL PIE

4 egg whites	1½ teaspoons vanilla
⅔ cup granulated sugar	1 cup whipping cream
½ cup confectioners' sugar	¼ square Baker's chocolate

Beat egg whites until stiff. Add granulated sugar gradually; then add confectioners' sugar the same way. Add vanilla. Butter and flour pie pan. Bake meringue 45 minutes at 325 degrees. Let cool. Cover with whipped cream and grated chocolate. Chill 4 or 5 hours.
Mrs. James Evans (Margaret)

JAPANESE FRUIT PIE

1 stick margarine	½ cup nuts, chopped
1 cup sugar	1 teaspoon vanilla
2 eggs	1 teaspoon vinegar
½ cup coconut	1 pie shell, unbaked
½ cup raisins	

Melt margarine with sugar over low heat, stirring constantly. Remove from stove and add well-beaten eggs. Then add coconut, raisins, and nuts. Stir in the vanilla and vinegar. Pour into unbaked pie shell and bake 30 minutes at 300 degrees.
Mrs. J. C. Payne (Leola)

Variation: Add ½ cup chopped dates instead of raisins and juice and rind of one lemon instead of the vinegar.
Mrs. J. Furman Stewart (Clo)

Similar recipes submitted by *Mrs. Lloyd Eckberg (Maxine), Mrs. Paul L. Sampson (Katherine), and Mrs. Robert G. Lauder (Annelle).*

PECAN PIE

3 eggs, beaten
1½ cups brown sugar
½ cup butter, melted
4 teaspoons lemon juice

1 teaspoon vanilla
1 cup pecans
Pastry for 9-inch pie

Combine eggs, sugar, lemon juice, butter and vanilla. Stir in pecans. Pour into pie shell. Bake at 350 degrees for about 40 minutes or until firm.
Mrs. Stephen Eckels (Beth)

WILLIAMSBURG PECAN PIE

4 eggs
¾ cup sugar
½ teaspoon salt
1½ cups light corn
    syrup

1 tablespoon butter, melted
1 teaspoon vanilla
1 cup pecan halves
1 9-inch pie shell,
    unbaked

Preheat oven to 400 degrees. Beat eggs lightly and add sugar, salt, corn syrup, cooled butter, and vanilla. Stir until mixed well. Spread pecan halves on bottom of crust and cover with the filling. Place in oven and immediately reduce heat to 350 degrees. Bake 40 to 50 minutes or until mixture is firm in center. Cool before serving.
Mrs. Maurice Tanner (Peggy)

NO CRUST COCONUT PIE
Makes two pies. Enjoy one, share one!

4 eggs, well-beaten
1¾ cups sugar
½ cup self-rising flour
½ stick butter or
    margarine, melted

1 teaspoon vanilla
2 cups milk
7 ounces coconut (fresh or
    Angel Flake)

Mix sugar and flour. Add beaten eggs, then remaining ingredients. Pour into two greased, 9-inch aluminum foil pie tins. Bake at 350 degrees until brown on tops about 35 minutes. No crust is needed.
Mrs. Thomas W. Efford
Mrs. Robert G. Lauder (Annelle)
Mrs. James McCollum (Wyche)
Mrs. Truman Chastain (Hazel)

CRUSTY COCONUT PIE

⅓ cup milk
1½ cups coconut
¼ cup butter
1 cup sugar

3 eggs
1 teaspoon vanilla
1 pie shell, unbaked

Pour milk over coconut and set aside. Cream butter and sugar. Add eggs. Beat. Add coconut mixture and flavoring. Pour into pie shell. Bake at 350 degrees for 35 minutes or until pie is golden brown and firm.
Mrs. Ralph Neel, Jr. (Katherine)

COCONUT CREAM PIE

5 eggs, separated
1½ cups sugar
5 tablespoons flour
3 cups milk
½ stick margarine
1 teaspoon vanilla

1 cup flaked coconut
2 9-inch pie shells,
    baked
10 tablespoons sugar for
    meringue

Mix beaten egg yolks, sugar, flour, milk and margarine in top of double boiler. Cook until thick. Add vanilla and coconut and cool. Pour into baked pie shells. Cover with meringue made from 5 stiffly beaten egg whites and 10 tablespoons sugar. Beat egg whites until stiff, then gradually add sugar a tablespoon at a time while continuing to beat. Brown meringue at 350 degrees. (Be sure pie is cool before adding meringue.) Makes 2 pies.
Mrs. Tom Vann, Jr. (Ann)

GEORGIA PEACH COBBLER

8 ripe peaches
¼ teaspoon cinnamon
½ cup flour

½ cup sugar
¼ teaspoon salt
¼ cup butter

Grease a 1-quart casserole. Peel and slice peaches and place in casserole. Mix the flour, sugar, cinnamon and salt. Cut in the butter. Spoon mixture over the peaches. Make four small holes in the crust with knife. Bake at 450 degrees for 20 to 25 minutes.
Mrs. C. B. Hitchcock (Anita)

Similar recipe by *Mrs. Harris Pope (Esther)*.

PEACH CHEESE PIE

1 pie shell, baked
1 can sweetened condensed
   milk
¼ cup lemon juice
1 3-ounce package cream
   cheese

2 eggs
1 cup fresh peaches, sliced
¼ teaspoon cream of tartar
2 tablespoons sugar

Arrange peach slices in the baked pie shell. Mix lemon juice with the condensed milk. Add the cream cheese. Separate eggs. Add one egg yolk at a time to the milk mixture. Pour over the peaches. Beat the egg whites with the cream of tartar and the sugar. Pour over pie. Bake in 325 degree oven for 15 minutes.
Mrs. Bill Gilliam (Barbara)

OLD ENGLISH APPLE PIE

2 eggs
1½ cups sugar
1 cup flour, sifted
2 teaspoons baking powder
½ teaspoon salt

¾ cup black walnuts,
   chopped
2 cups raw apples,
   finely chopped

Beat eggs. Add sugar, flour, baking powder and salt. Add walnuts and apples. Pour into well-greased 9 x 9-inch baking dish. Bake at 350 degrees for 30 minutes.
Mrs. Hartley Falbaum (Gayle)

EASY APPLE PIE

3 or 4 Rome Beauty apples
1 cup sugar
1 teaspoon cinnamon
1 cup flour

1 cup Cheddar cheese, grated
3 tablespoons butter,
   melted
Pinch of salt

Cut apples into wedges. (Not necessary to peel.) Place apples in baking dish. Sprinkle with ½ cup sugar and cinnamon. Mix flour, ½ cup sugar, cheese, melted butter and salt. Press this mixture over apples to make a crust. Bake at 350 degrees for 45 minutes. Serves 4-6.
Mrs. Scott Rich (Peggy)

CANDIED APPLE PIE

4 tart apples
1½ cups brown sugar
1 cup self-rising flour

½ cup butter
½-1 cup ground nut meats
Whipped cream

Pare apples and slice thinly. Arrange in baking dish. Sprinkle with ½ cup brown sugar. Add another layer of apples. Cream together butter, remainder of sugar, flour, and nuts. Pour this mixture over apples. Bake in 350 degree oven about 45 minutes. Serve with whipped cream.
Mrs. J. L. Turner, Jr. (Lucille)

RASPBERRY BAKED ALASKA PIE

18 ladyfingers
⅓ cup orange-flavored liqueur
1 10-ounce package
    raspberries, slightly thawed
2 pints vanilla ice cream,
    slightly softened

4 egg whites
¼ teaspoon salt
⅛ teaspoon cream of tartar
⅔ cup sugar

Line bottom and sides of 9-inch pie plate with two-thirds of ladyfingers, allowing rounded ends to extend slightly over pie-plate rim. Sprinkle with half of liqueur. In medium bowl, with potato masher, crush raspberries well to make a paste consistency. In large bowl, stir softened ice cream slightly. Drop spoonfuls of raspberries onto ice cream; with knife cut through to create a swirl effect. Spoon half of ice cream mixture into pie plate. Layer remaining ladyfingers on top of ice cream; sprinkle with remaining liqueur. Spoon remaining ice-cream mixture onto ladyfingers. Freeze until firm, about 4 hours. Preheat oven to 500 degrees when almost ready to serve. In small bowl, beat egg whites, salt and cream of tartar until soft peaks form. Beating at high speed, gradually beat in sugar, 2 tablespoons at a time; beat until sugar is completely dissolved. (Whites should stand in stiff, glossy peaks.) Quickly spread meringue over top of pie, sealing to edge. Bake 3 to 4 minutes until meringue is lightly browned. Serve immediately. Keep any leftover pie frozen. Serves 8.
Mrs. A. B. Wight, Jr. (Carolyn)

PINEAPPLE SURPRISE PIE

2 graham cracker crusts
1 cup sweetened condensed
    milk
1 tablespoon lemon juice

1 No. 2 can crushed
    pineapple, drained
1 cup pecan pieces
1 large carton Cool Whip

Mix all ingredients and pour into the pie shells. Chill for at least 2 hours. Really easy and good!
Mrs. Langdon Flowers, Jr. (Mandy)

STRAWBERRY PIE

1 frozen pie crust,
    baked and cooled
1 pint fresh strawberries,
    washed and drained
1 cup sugar

1 cup hot water
3 tablespoons corn starch
3 tablespoons wild
    strawberry gelatin
Whipped cream

Mix sugar, hot water, corn starch and gelatin. Cook until thick. Cool. Pour over strawberries in pie crust. Place in refrigerator until set and ready to serve. Top with whipped cream.

Mrs. William B. Turner (Sue Marie)   *Columbus, Georgia*

Similar recipe submitted by *Mrs. W. M. Kennington (Robbie)*.

PHILADELPHIA PIE CRUST

1 cup flour
1 3-ounce package cream
    cheese

¼ teaspoon salt
1 stick margarine
2 tablespoons ice water

Mix salt with flour in mixing bowl. Mix cream cheese and margarine with two knives or pastry blender until mixture is crumbly and well blended. Use as little ice water as possible because too much will make crust tough. Sprinkle over flour and stir together to make a ball. Wrap and chill in wax paper. When ready to bake, bake at 325 degrees until slightly browned. Excellent with delicate fruit filling.
Mrs. T. R. Sample (Nell)

Desserts

APRICOT SOUFFLÉ
This is elegant but easy.

1 tablespoon butter
Granulated sugar
5 egg whites
Dash salt

1 16-ounce jar apricot
  preserves
¼ cup slivered almonds
Confectioners' sugar

Preheat oven to 400 degrees. Lightly butter inside of a 2-quart soufflé dish. Sprinkle evenly with sugar. In medium bowl, at high speed, beat egg whites with salt until foamy. Add 1 tablespoon granulated sugar, beating until stiff peaks form. Gently fold preserves into egg whites until just combined. Turn into soufflé dish. Sprinkle with almonds. Bake 20 minutes until golden. Sift confectioners' sugar on top.
Mrs. Edward Davis (Rozzi)

RASPBERRY CREAM SOUFFLÉ

2 envelopes (2 tablespoons)
  unflavored gelatin
½ cup cold water
1¾ cups water, boiling
1 8-ounce package cream
  cheese, softened
⅔ cup sugar

1 10-ounce package frozen
  raspberries, thawed
1 tablespoon lemon juice,
  freshly squeezed
1 cup whipping cream,
  whipped

Wrap a collar of greased aluminum foil around top of a lightly greased 1½-quart soufflé dish. Soften gelatin in cold water; add boiling water and stir until gelatin dissolves. Combine cream cheese and sugar; mix until well blended. Drain raspberries and reserve juice. Gradually add gelatin, lemon juice, and raspberry juice to cream cheese mixture. Chill until slightly thickened. Fold in raspberries and whipped cream. Pour mixture into soufflé dish. Chill until firm. Remove foil collar before serving and garnish with additional whipped cream, if desired. Serves 8-10.
Mrs. A. B. Wight, Jr. (Carolyn)

SOUFFLÉ ROTHSCHILD

2 tablespoons butter,
    softened
3 tablespoons sugar
5 egg yolks
¼ cup sugar
¼ cup Grand Marnier or
    Benedictine

1 tablespoon orange rind,
    grated
2 tablespoons glacéed fruits
7 egg whites
¼ teaspoon cream of tartar

Preheat oven to 425 degrees. Grease and sugar 1-quart soufflé dish. Soak fruit in the liqueur. In double boiler, beat egg yolks; add sugar. Continue to beat as yolks heat. When thickened, add liqueured fruit rind. Pour into bowl to cool. In a mixing bowl, beat egg whites with cream of tartar until they peak. Fold into egg mixture. Pour into soufflé dish. Bake 5 minutes. Reduce heat to 400 degrees. Cook another 30 minutes. Serve at once. Serves 4 to 6.
The Editors

LEMON SOUFFLÉ

6 eggs
1½ cups sugar
½ cup water

2 envelopes unflavored
    gelatin
⅔ cup lemon juice
2 cups heavy cream

Beat eggs in copper bowl with sugar until light and fluffy, about 10 minutes. Using a copper bowl makes the eggs lighter and fluffier than beating in an ordinary bowl. Using double boiler, heat water and add gelatin. Dissolve. Stir lemon juice into gelatin mixture. Add gelatin mixture to egg and sugar still in copper bowl; blend well. At this stage it will begin to set. Whip cream until stiff. Fold into egg mixture. Pour into soufflé dish and chill. Top with whipped cream. This may be made the day before it is to be served. Serves 10.
Mrs. John L. Turner, III (Ann)

SATSUMA CHARLOTTE

2 packages gelatin
½ cup satsuma juice
½ cup water, boiling
¾ cup sugar

2 tablespoons lemon juice
2 cups satsuma juice
3 egg whites
½ pint whipping cream

Mix gelatin with ½ cup satsuma juice and when thick, add boiling water. Blend in sugar, lemon juice and 2 cups satsuma juice. Allow this mixture to thicken in refrigerator for several hours. Beat well with electric mixer. Fold in cream which has been whipped. Then fold in stiffly beaten egg whites. Chill until set and serve in bowls or sherbets. Serves 12.
Mrs. Alvin B. Wight (Anne)

CRÈME BRULÉE

1 quart heavy cream
8 egg yolks
8 tablespoons sugar

Dash vanilla
½ cup brown sugar, sifted

Heat cream in top of double boiler over hot water until it reaches the boiling point. Beat eggs lightly; add sugar and beat it with the eggs. Flavor with touch of vanilla. Slowly add the hot cream to egg mixture, beating with wooden spoon constantly. Return the cream and eggs to top of double boiler and cook, stirring constantly, until the mixture coats spoon with a thin film. Do not overcook or the eggs will curdle. Pour into heat-proof serving dish or ramekins and cool for 6-8 hours. When ready to serve, sprinkle top of crème with brown sugar, sifted, and place under broiler for just a minute to glaze the sugar. Cool before serving. Serves 8 in small ramekins.
Mrs. Charles Watt, III (Jan)

FROSTY FUDGE MOUSSE

1 cup milk
2 1-ounce squares of
    unsweetened chocolate
Dash of salt
½ pound (about 32) marshmallows
    or 4 cups tiny marshmallows

1 egg yolk, slightly beaten
1 teaspoon vanilla
1 cup heavy cream,
    whipped

CEREAL CRUNCH CRUST:

1 egg white
1 cup wheat flakes, crushed

½ cup nuts, finely chopped
¼ cup brown sugar

To make crust, beat egg white until stiff peaks form. Fold in brown sugar, nuts, and wheat flakes and press into bottom of 10 x 6 x 1½-inch baking dish. Bake in a slow oven (300 degrees) about 10 minutes. Cool. Meanwhile, heat milk, chocolate, salt and marshmallows over low heat, stirring constantly, until chocolate and marshmallows melt. Stir small amount of hot mixture into egg yolk and add egg to hot mixture. Cook and stir over low heat 1 minute. Add vanilla. Chill until partially set, stirring occasionally. Fold in whipped cream. Pour into crust. Freeze until firm. Cut into 8 or 10 squares.
Mrs. Pratt Secrest (Sara)

BLENDER CHOCOLATE MOUSSE

6-ounce package semi-sweet
   chocolate chips
2 whole eggs
3 tablespoons very strong
   coffee

1-2 tablespoons rum
¾ cup heavy cream

Blend ingredients at high speed in blender for 1-2 minutes. Pour into a small pretty bowl or 4 individual dessert cups. Chill. To serve, top with a dab of sweetened whipped cream, flavored with a tiny bit of almond extract and with sprigs of fresh mint. Serves 4.
Miss Maury Flowers

OLD-FASHIONED CHOCOLATE MOUSSE

6 ounces semi-sweet
   chocolate
1 tablespoon powdered coffee
3 tablespoons butter

6 eggs, separated
5 tablespoons sugar
½ pint heavy cream

Melt chocolate with coffee in upper part of double boiler over hot (not boiling) water. Add the butter and stir until melted. Beat the egg yolks until very light; add a little of the chocolate mixture and blend with wire whisk. Then add rest of chocolate and beat over hot water for few minutes until smooth. Cool. Whip cream and add sugar. Then beat the egg whites until very stiff. Fold the whipped cream and egg whites into the chocolate mixture. Chill. Serves 4-6. Note: This mousse is not quite as heavy as one with a liqueur added.
Mrs. Charles Watt, III (Jan)

CHOCOLATE ALMOND DESSERT

2 bars German's Sweet
   Chocolate
½ cup almonds, finely
   slivered
8 eggs, separated
¼ teaspoon salt

½ pint whipping cream
⅛ teaspoon almond
   extract
1 tablespoon shaved,
   unsweetened chocolate
   (for garnish)

Melt chocolate over warm water. Add almonds. Beat egg whites with salt until thick. Add chocolate and nuts to yolks. Mix well. Fold into egg whites. Pour into shallow serving dish and chill overnight. Top with whipped cream, slightly sweetened and seasoned with almond extract. Garnish with shaved chocolate.
Mrs. Frank Neel (Frances)

LEMON MOUSSE

This is a light frozen dessert which can be made several days ahead.

1 large can evaporated
  milk
1 cup sugar

½ cup lemon juice
3 eggs
Graham cracker crumbs

Pour can of milk into bowl and place in freezer. When it begins to form ice crystals around the edge, then use electric mixer and whip until very thick. Beat up egg yolks in small boiler and add lemon juice and sugar. Heat, stirring constantly, until mixture comes to boil. Place in refrigerator and cool. When cool, add to whipped evaporated milk, then fold in well-beaten egg whites. Line 2 9-inch pans or one large pan with crushed graham crackers. Pour in mixture and sprinkle lightly with more crumbs on top. Place in freezer for several hours before serving.
Mrs. Richard Ramsey (Elsie)

COFFEE MOUSSE

2 cups hot strong
  coffee
2 pounds marshmallows

4 tablespoons instant
  coffee
1 pint heavy whipping
  cream

Place marshmallows in top of double boiler. Add hot coffee and stir until melted. Add instant coffee. Chill mixture until almost set. Whip cream and fold into mixture. Pour into 12-cup mold. To serve, cover with shaved toasted almonds and grated German chocolate. Pass bowl of whipped cream and Cognac to serve over mousse. Serves 16-18.
Mrs. Thomas Williams (Marguerite)

COFFEE JELLY

1 cup sugar
3 envelopes unflavored
  gelatin

3 cups strong coffee
1½ cups water, boiling
Whipping cream

In pan stir sugar and gelatin together. Add coffee and boiling water. Stir until sugar and gelatin dissolve. Pour into molds or glasses and chill. Serve with whipped cream or custard sauce.
Mrs. C. B. Hitchcock (Anita)

MOM'S ICE BOX PUDDING

2 cups milk	½ cup water
4 eggs, separated	1 dozen almond macaroons
1 cup sugar	1 3-ounce jar
1 envelope unflavored	maraschino cherries
gelatin	Whipped cream

Beat egg yolks. Combine milk, egg yolks, and sugar. Boil to a medium-thick custard. Dissolve 1 envelope gelatin in ½ cup water. Mix with custard and cool. Line a 10 x 5 x 3-inch pyrex bread pan with macaroons and maraschino cherries. Beat egg whites until they stand in peaks and fold gently into cooled custard. Pour custard into macaroon and cherry-lined pan. Refrigerate at least 4 hours. Cut into slices and serve with whipped cream.
Mrs. Howard Carnes (Henrietta)

DATE NUT PUDDING

1 8-ounce box pitted	1 cup sugar
dates, chopped	1 rounded tablespoon butter
1 teaspoon soda	1 cup flour
1 cup hot water	1 cup nuts, chopped
1 egg	

Put dates in a bowl and add soda and water. Let stand while preparing the other mixture. Combine egg, sugar, butter, flour and nuts. Mix with the dates. Bake in a greased loaf pan at 350 degrees for 45 minutes.
Mrs. Marshall Woodson (Betty)

OLD FASHIONED BREAD PUDDING

2 eggs, slightly beaten	⅔ cup sugar
3 cups (½-inch) dry bread	⅔ cup seedless raisins
cubes, approximately 5 slices	2 teaspoons vanilla
1 14½-ounce can	¼ teaspoon salt
evaporated milk	¼ teaspoon nutmeg
1 cup water	

In a large bowl, combine ingredients; mix well. Pour into greased 1½-quart baking dish. Place in pan containing 1 inch hot water. Bake at 350 degrees for 45 minutes. Serve warm or cool with whipped cream, if desired. 6 servings.
Mrs. Raymond D. Hill (Virginia)

BAKED FUDGE PUDDING
A great favorite with young people!

1 cup flour
2 teaspoons baking powder
½ teaspoon salt
⅔ cup sugar
3 tablespoons cocoa

½ cup nuts, chopped
2 tablespoons shortening
½ cup milk
1 teaspoon vanilla

TOPPING:

3 tablespoons cocoa
¾ cup sugar

1¾ cups hot water

Sift flour; sift again with baking powder, salt, sugar and cocoa. Add nuts to dry ingredients. Melt shortening; cool. Add shortening to milk with vanilla. Stir the liquid ingredients into dry ingredients and mix very well. Spread batter into greased 8 x 8 x 2-inch pan. To make topping, mix cocoa and sugar. Stir in the hot water and gently pour over the batter. Bake for 1 hour at 350 degrees. After baking, the cake will be on top and the sauce on bottom. Serve warm.
Mrs. Travis Smith (Dorothy)

CARAMEL CUSTARD

½ cup sugar for syrup
5 eggs
½ cup sugar

¼ teaspoon salt
1 teaspoon vanilla
3½ cups milk

Preheat oven to 325 degrees. Sprinkle ½ cup of sugar evenly over bottom of a small heavy skillet. Cook slowly over very low heat, stirring occasionally just until sugar melts to a golden syrup. (If heat is too high or the syrup is cooked too long it will be too dark and will taste burned). Pour immediately into a 5-cup ring mold and quickly tilt mold to coat bottom and sides while syrup is still liquid. Let cool. Beat eggs with sugar, salt, and vanilla and mix well. Gradually add milk and mix thoroughly. Set prepared ring mold into a shallow pan and pour mixture into mold. Place baking pan on middle rack in oven and pour hot water into pan and into center of mold until water is 1 inch deep around mold. Bake 1 hour, but test with a knife at 50 minutes. Do not overbake. Remove from hot water to cool completely, then refrigerate at least 1 hour. Recipe may be made a day ahead. To unmold, loosen edge with knife and turn a plate upside down on mold. Quickly reverse the two and shake gently. Caramel will run down the sides. Delicious as is or served with fresh or well-drained canned fruit in center of mold. Spoon the caramel sauce over the top. Custard may also be served with whipped cream.
Mrs. Martin Cooper (Peggy)

BOILED CUSTARD

1 quart milk	6 eggs
1 cup sugar	1 teaspoon vanilla

Cook milk in double boiler until it comes to a boil. Add eggs, beaten well with sugar. Cook, stirring constantly, until it thickens. If custard curdles, beat with egg beater. Strain. Cool. Add vanilla. Delicious over sliced bananas or over vanilla ice cream.
Mrs. Richard Hackney (Mary)

Similar recipe submitted by *Mrs. Donald H. Price (Judy)*.

HUGUENOT TORTE

4 eggs	2 cups tart cooking apples,
3 cups sugar	chopped
8 tablespoons flour	2 cups pecans or walnuts,
5 teaspoons baking	chopped
powder	2 teaspoons vanilla
½ teaspoon salt	½ pint whipping cream

Beat whole eggs in electric mixer until very frothy and lemon-colored. Add other ingredients in above order, except cream. Pour into two well-buttered baking pans about 8 by 12 inches. Bake in 325 degree oven about 45 minutes or until crusty and brown. To serve, scoop up with spatula, keeping crust on top. Stack on large plate and cover with whipped cream (the real thing, please!) and a sprinkling of chopped nuts. Serves 16.
Mrs. Chip Coffin (Sheila)

FRUIT DESSERT

½ stick butter	1 teaspoon vanilla
½ cup flour	½ cup milk
½ cup sugar	½ cup blueberries or fruit
½ teaspoon baking powder	of your choice, sweetened
½ teaspoon cinnamon	

Melt butter in a quart-size casserole and spread around the sides. Mix a batter of flour, sugar, milk, baking powder, cinnamon and vanilla. Pour batter in the center of butter in the casserole. Pour fruit in center of mixture. Bake in 325 degree oven for 30 minutes.
Mrs. Marx Gaines (Claire)

LEMON CUPS

1 cup sugar
2 tablespoons butter
1½ cups milk
Rind of 1 lemon

3 eggs
Pinch of salt
5 tablespoons lemon juice
4 tablespoons flour

Cream butter; add sugar, salt, lemon juice and rind. Separate eggs; mix egg yolks with milk. Pour this into creamed mixture and stir well. Fold in stiffly beaten egg whites. Pour into custard cups, set cups in pan of water, and bake at 350 degrees for 40 minutes. When baked, each cup will contain custard with sponge cake on top.
Mrs. Al Stringer (Regina)

PINEAPPLE DESSERT

1 stick butter
1 cup confectioners' sugar
1 cup crushed pineapple,
    drained
1 cup pecans, chopped

1 egg yolk, beaten
1 egg white, stiffly
    beaten
Graham crackers
Whipped cream

Make filling by creaming butter, sugar and egg yolk. Add crushed pineapple and nuts and mix well. Fold in beaten egg white. Place a layer of graham crackers (do not crush) in bottom of 5 x 8-inch pan. Spread ⅓ of filling evenly over crackers. Make 3 layers of filling and 4 layers of crackers, ending with crackers on top. Top with whipped topping or whipped cream. Chill overnight. Cut in squares. They will look like petit-fours.
Mrs. Woody Faircloth (Millie)

RUTH'S APPLE DESSERT

3 medium apples,
    thinly sliced
¾ cup quick-cooking
    oatmeal

¾ cup brown sugar
Sprinkle of cinnamon
½ cup plain flour
½ cup butter

Arrange apples in casserole dish. Combine oatmeal, sugar, cinnamon, and flour. Cut in butter. Sprinkle this mixture over apples. Bake in 350 degree oven for 35-40 minutes. Serve warm with cream.
Mrs. Chris CoCroft (Katie)

APPLE CRISP

1 quart (8) apples, sliced
⅔ cup sugar
¼ teaspoon salt
2-4 tablespoons butter

¼ teaspoon nutmeg
1 cup flour, sifted
½ cup brown sugar
½ cup butter

Mix sugar, salt and nutmeg and combine with apples in a deep pie pan. Dot pieces of butter (2-4 tablespoons) over all. Blend the flour with the brown sugar. Cut ½ cup butter into flour mixture with a pastry blender. Sprinkle this mixture over the apples and bake at 400 degrees for 30-40 minutes. Cut in wedges and serve with whipped cream or topping.
Mrs. James Mason (Trudy)

LOVE PUFFS

1 stick butter or margarine
1 cup water, boiling
¼ teaspoon salt

1 cup flour, sifted
4 eggs

Preheat oven to 400 degrees. In small saucepan, heat butter with boiling water, stirring until butter has melted. Reduce heat to low and add flour and salt, stirring vigorously until mixture leaves the sides of pan in a smooth ball. Remove from heat and quickly add eggs, one at a time, beating well after each addition until mixture is shiny and smooth. Drop mixture by tablespoons onto a greased cookie sheet, forming light mounds that peak at center. Bake 45-50 minutes until puffed and golden brown. Do not open oven to check until end of baking period. Remove from sheet and cool on wire racks. This makes 8 large puffs. Cool. Split puffs and fill with pudding, strawberries, custard, or ice cream. Place top back on puff and ice with your favorite icing or sauce.
Mrs. Robert Sullivan (Sally)

PEACHES BLAZED WITH BOURBON

6 fresh peach halves,
    peeled
1 teaspoon orange rind,
    grated
3 tablespoons butter

3 teaspoons sugar
Juice of ½ lemon
2 tablespoons orange
    marmalade
3 ounces bourbon

Blend grated orange rind with butter and heat in a chafing dish. Sauté peaches in butter. Sprinkle on sugar. Add lemon juice and continue to baste. When peaches are brown, fill with marmalade. Sprinkle bourbon over fruit and ignite.
Mrs. W. W. Gravely (Tan)

HOT FUDGE SAUCE

2 cups sugar	2 cups milk
¾ cup cocoa	4 tablespoons butter
¼ cup flour	1 teaspoon vanilla
¼ teaspoon salt	

Combine sugar, cocoa, flour and salt in saucepan. Add milk and butter. Cook to boiling; lower heat and cook 8 minutes, stirring constantly. Cool. Add vanilla. Serve as topping for ice cream or desserts.
Mrs. William Z. Bridges (Mary)

Similar recipe submitted by *Mrs. Forrest Caldwell (Emily)*.

FROZEN ORANGE DESSERT

⅓ cup water	1 pint fresh orange juice
1 cup sugar	Juice of 1 large lemon
1 tablespoon gelatin, softened	½ pint cream
in ¼ cup of water	

Make syrup of water and sugar. Dissolve gelatin in hot syrup. Add the juices. Place in refrigerator tray and put in freezer. When partially frozen, cover with one cup of cream which has been whipped, sweetened and flavored to taste. Return to freezer to finish freezing.
Mrs. William M. Searcy, Jr. (Emily)

COCONUT MACAROON ICE CREAM

1 package coconut	½ gallon coffee ice
macaroon cookies	cream
½ cup sherry	

Crush macaroons. Set aside enough crumbs to use as topping. Soak remaining crumbs in sherry overnight. To soak, put crumbs in a quart jar, add sherry, and put lid on jar. Partially thaw ice cream and mix in macaroons that have soaked in sherry. Return to freezer. When ready to serve, top with dry macaroons.
Mrs. E. P. McCollum (Louise)

BUTTER PECAN ICE CREAM

4 eggs	½ teaspoon salt
2 cups sugar	4½ teaspoons vanilla
4 cups heavy cream	2 cups pecans, chopped
5 cups milk	3 tablespoons butter

Beat eggs. Gradually add sugar until stiff. Add cream, milk, salt, and vanilla. Refrigerate until cold. Churn in an ice cream freezer for 20 minutes. Meanwhile, sauté pecans in butter and cool. Add to mixture in the ice cream freezer and continue freezing.
Mrs. Fred Cooper (Helen)

HOMEMADE CUSTARD-STYLE ICE CREAM

3 quarts milk	2¾ cups sugar
1 dozen eggs,	3 tablespoons cornstarch
beaten slightly	3 teaspoons vanilla

Make paste mixture by adding a little cold milk to cornstarch. Then mix remaining ingredients. Cook over low heat until thickened. Cool. Add fruit (peaches, strawberries, pineapple, etc.) if desired. Place in 6-quart ice cream freezer. Add enough milk or cream to make churn ⅔ full, if it is not. Freeze according to freezer directions.
Mrs. Franklin I. Smith (Doris)

PEACH ICE CREAM

1 quart boiled custard	Juice of 1 lemon
½ pint whipped cream	Sugar to taste
1 quart peaches, mashed	

Combine all ingredients. Freeze in ice cream freezer.
The Editors.

PEPPERMINT ICE CREAM

16 large marshmallows
½ pound peppermint candy
1 cup boiling water

1 pint milk
½ pint whipping cream

Put marshmallows, candy and boiling water in the top of double boiler over hot water and stir until the candy is dissolved. Cool. Add milk to the candy mixture. Whip the cream and pour peppermint mix into cream. Freeze in ice cream freezer. Makes 2 quarts.
Mrs. Henry M. Moore (Reta)

CHOCOLATE ICE CREAM

6 cups half and half
   cream
4½ teaspoons vanilla
1½ cups sugar
4 eggs, beaten

3 cups milk
6-ounce package semi-sweet
   chocolate chips
2 ounces unsweetened
   chocolate
⅓ cup strong coffee

Mix cream, sugar and eggs. Cook, but not to boiling. Add vanilla and milk after cooking. Melt chocolate in the strong coffee. Stir into custard and chill. Freeze in ice cream freezer.
Mrs. Fred Cooper (Helen)

DIANA TORTE

28 macaroons
1 quart chocolate ice cream
1 quart coffee ice cream

Chocolate sauce
3 or 4 Heath bars

Oil an 8-inch spring-form pan, Bundt pan or angel food mold. Crush 14 macaroons and sprinkle on bottom. Spread slightly softened chocolate ice cream on top of macaroons. Dribble 2 tablespoons chocolate sauce on ice cream. Add remainder of crushed macaroons; then add the slightly softened coffee ice cream and 2 more tablespoons of chocolate sauce. Crush the Heath bars and sprinkle on top. Freeze for several hours.
Mrs. Lonnie Ferguson (Georgia)

Cookies
and
Candy

BUTTERFLY COOKIES

2 egg whites
⅔ cup sugar
1 teaspoon vanilla

1 cup nuts, chopped
1 6-ounce package chocolate
  or caramel chips

Beat egg whites as stiffly as possible. Add sugar slowly. Add remaining ingredients. Drop on wax paper on cookie sheet. Place in preheated 450 degree oven. Turn off oven and let stand overnight or 4 or 5 hours.
Mrs. J. A. Stewart (Melba)
Mrs. William King (Anne)

UNBEATABLES

2 cups confectioners' sugar
½ cup flour
⅛ teaspoon baking powder

½ cup (3 to 4) egg whites
2 cups nuts, chopped
½ cup dried apricots,
  chopped

Combine sugar, flour, baking powder and egg whites. Add nuts and apricots. Mix well. Drop by teaspoonfuls onto well-greased cookie sheets. Bake at 325 degrees for 15 to 18 minutes. Makes 3 dozen cookies.
Mrs. Forrest Caldwell (Emily)

ORANGE OATMEAL COOKIES

½ cup margarine
½ cup brown sugar
½ cup white sugar
1 egg, well beaten
1 cup flour
2½ teaspoons baking
  powder
½ teaspoon baking soda

½ teaspoon salt
1½ teaspoons orange peel,
  grated
1 teaspoon vanilla
1 cup cornflakes
1 cup oatmeal
¾ cup raisins

Cream butter and sugars. Add egg. Sift flour, baking powder, soda and salt. Mix in. Add orange peel and vanilla and blend well. Fold in cornflakes, oatmeal and raisins by hand. Drop by teaspoonful on greased cookie sheet. Bake 10 minutes at 350 degrees. Makes about 3 dozen.
Mrs. Thomas Hawkins (Harriet)

VARIETY OATMEAL COOKIES
Good and chewy!

1 cup butter
1 cup brown sugar
(dark or light)
1 cup white sugar
2 eggs
1 teaspoon vanilla

2 cups flour
1 teaspoon soda
1 teaspoon baking powder
¼ teaspoon salt
2 cups oatmeal

ADD ANY OF THESE FOR VARIETY:

1 cup walnuts or pecans,
chopped
½ cup raisins
1 cup gum drops, chopped

1 cup flaked coconut
½ cup wheat germ
1 ounce chocolate or 1 cup
chocolate chips, melted

Cream butter with sugars. Add eggs and vanilla and beat well. Sift flour, soda, baking powder, and salt; add to the mixture. Add the oatmeal. Add nuts and raisins or other of the optional ingredients. Drop by teaspoonfuls onto ungreased baking sheet 2 inches apart. Bake in 375 degree oven for 10 minutes.
Mrs. Robert Maxwell (Ruth Ann)

PEPPERMINT SNOWBALLS

Confectioners' sugar
2¼ cups all-purpose flour
1 cup butter or margarine,
softened
1 teaspoon vanilla
½ cup hard peppermint candy,
crushed

2 tablespoons cream cheese,
softened
1 teaspoon milk
1 drop red food coloring

In large bowl measure ½ cup confectioners' sugar, flour, butter, and vanilla. With mixer at medium speed, beat until well mixed. Occasionally scrape bowl with rubber spatula. In small bowl, toss together peppermint candy and ¼ cup confectioners' sugar. In another small bowl prepare filling. With spoon, blend cream cheese with milk until smooth. Gradually stir in ½ cup confectioners' sugar, coloring, and 3 tablespoons of reserved candy mixture. With hands, shape dough into ¾-inch balls. With handle of wooden spoon make a deep hole in center of each ball. Fill each hole with ¼ teaspoon of filling. Cover with bit of dough to seal. Bake 12 minutes at 350 degrees or until set, but not brown. Remove while cookies are hot and roll in remaining candy mixture. Refrigerate until served. Makes about 3 dozen cookies.
Mrs. T. R. Sample (Nell)

JELLY-FILLED BUTTER COOKIES

¾ pound butter (3 sticks)
1 cup sugar
4 cups plain flour, sifted

2 egg yolks
1 teaspoon vanilla
Apple jelly

Cream butter and sugar. Add the flour and egg yolks; then add the vanilla. This will make a heavy dough. Roll into 1-inch balls, press a hole into center (not all the way through), and fill with about ¼ teaspoon jelly. Bake 15 minutes at 325 degrees on a greased cookie sheet.
Mrs. Cleone Jackson

NEW ENGLAND LACE COOKIES

1 stick butter
1 egg
1 cup sugar

1 teaspoon vanilla
1 cup quick-cooking
   oatmeal

Melt butter, add egg, sugar, vanilla and oatmeal. Mix well. Drop by teaspoon-fuls onto heavy-duty foil-lined cookie sheet very far apart. (Cook only six cookies on a cookie sheet that usually holds a dozen.) Bake at 350 degrees for 8 minutes. Cool on foil.
Mrs. C. B. Hitchcock (Anita)

HI-PROTEIN CHOCOLATE CHIP COOKIES
One cookie equals approximately 1.5 grams usable protein.

2¼ cups whole-wheat flour
1 teaspoon baking soda
1 teaspoon salt
½ cup butter, softened
1½ cups brown sugar
3 eggs, beaten
1 teaspoon vanilla

6 tablespoons instant dry
   milk powder
1 tablespoon water
12 ounces semi-sweet
   chocolate chips
¾ cup peanuts, chopped
1 cup sunflower seeds

Stir flour, soda and salt together and set aside. In large bowl, cream the butter with the sugar. Add eggs, vanilla, milk powder and water. Beat until fluffy. Add the flour mixture and blend well. Stir in chocolate chips, nuts and seeds. Drop by tablespoonfuls onto greased cookie sheet. Bake at 375 degrees for 10 to 15 minutes or until browned. The peanuts and sunflower seeds compliment each other and increase the protein content.
Mrs. Maureen Otis Adams

HERSHEY KISS COOKIES

1¾ cups flour
1 teaspoon soda
½ teaspoon salt
½ cup Crisco
½ cup peanut butter

½ cup sugar
½ cup brown sugar
1 egg
1 teaspoon vanilla
48 Hershey's Chocolate Kisses

Cream Crisco and peanut butter. Add dry ingredients, sugars, egg and vanilla. Mix until dough forms. Shape into balls. Roll in sugar. Bake 10 minutes at 375 degrees on ungreased cookie sheet. When taken from oven, immediately press a chocolate Kiss into cookie. (Press smooth side into cookie). Makes 48 cookies.
Mrs. Ames Watkins Kindred

ICE BOX COOKIES

2 cups light brown sugar
1½ sticks butter (not
    margarine)
2 eggs

1 teaspoon soda
3½ cups self-rising flour
1 teaspoon vanilla
2 cups pecans, chopped

Cream together sugar and butter until light and fluffy. Add beaten eggs. Sift together dry ingredients. Add to mixture and mix well. Then add vanilla and pecans. This amount will make about 4 rolls the size of a half dollar and as long as wax paper is wide. Roll up each roll in waxed paper and store in refrigerator overnight or up to two weeks. When ready to bake, slice thinly with a sharp knife. Place on a greased baking sheet and bake 10 to 12 minutes in a 350 degree oven. Remove from sheet while hot.

Variations: May use plain flour instead of self-rising. May add 1 teaspoon rum flavoring with 1 teaspoon vanilla.
Mrs. E. C. Cochran (Virginia)

Similar recipes submitted by *Mrs. Homer T. Smith (Nora) and Mrs. Terrell Singletary (Nan)*.

CINNAMON COOKIES

1¼ cups flour, sifted
1 teaspoon baking powder
¼ teaspoon salt
½ cup butter or margarine
1 cup granulated sugar

1 egg, beaten
1 teaspoon vanilla
½ cup nut meats,
    finely chopped
2 teaspoons cinnamon

Sift together flour, baking powder and salt. Mix margarine, sugar, egg and vanilla until creamy. Combine with flour mixture. Chill one hour until firm. Roll level tablespoonful of dough into ball. Roll in combined nuts and cinnamon. Arrange two inches apart on greased cookie sheets. Bake at 375 degrees about 15 minutes.
Mrs. Vance Watt (Mercer)

CREAM CHEESE COOKIES

½ cup butter
½ cup shortening
4-ounces cream cheese
1 cup sugar

1 teaspoon vanilla
2½ cups flour, sifted
¼ teaspoon salt
Cinnamon and sugar

Cream butter, shortening and cream cheese. Add sugar slowly. Add vanilla. Stir in flour and salt. Divide into 2 rolls. Refrigerate until firm. Slice very thin and sprinkle with cinnamon and sugar. Bake at 325 degrees for 10 to 12 minutes.

Variation: Increase sugar to 1½ cups. Add 1 tablespoon grated lemon rind and finely chopped pecans.
Mrs. Pat Fenlon (Renie)

TEA CAKES

1 stick butter or
    margarine
1 cup sugar
1 egg

½ teaspoon vanilla
2 tablespoons milk
1¾ cups self-rising flour

Cream butter, egg, sugar, milk and vanilla together. Add flour and mix well. Put in refrigerator and let chill well for several hours. Using ⅓ to ½ of dough at a time, roll and cut in desired shapes. Bake about 8 minutes in 375 degree oven.
Mrs. Joe Whittemore (Pat)

Similar recipe submitted by *Mrs. Terrell Singletary (Nan)*.

SUGAR COOKIES

½ cup confectioners' sugar
½ cup white sugar
1 stick butter
½ cup cooking oil
1 egg, beaten

2 cups flour
½ teaspoon soda
½ teaspoon cream of tartar
1 teaspoon vanilla

Cream sugar, butter and cooking oil well. Add the beaten egg. In separate container sift together the flour, soda, and cream of tartar. Add to creamed mixture, and lastly, add vanilla. Chill in refrigerator slightly. Remove and make small balls; place on cookie sheet. Flatten balls with bottom of juice glass dipped in sugar each time (this sugar is not included in the above mentioned measurements). Bake in 375 degree oven 8 to 10 minutes.
Mrs. Ames Watkins Kindred

CRISS-CROSS BUTTER COOKIES

1 cup butter
⅔ cup sugar
2 egg yolks

1 teaspoon lemon extract
2⅔ cups flour, sifted

Cream butter. Slowly stir in sugar. Beat well. Beat in egg yolks, one at a time. Blend in lemon extract and flour with a wooden spoon to make a smooth, stiff dough. Shape into ½-inch balls. Place two inches apart on ungreased cookie sheet. Flatten each cookie to desired thickness by pressing crosswise with lightly floured fork. Bake 10 minutes or until pale brown at 375 degrees. Remove from sheet and cool on wire rack. Makes 2 dozen cookies.
Mrs. Ralph Neel, Jr. (Katherine)

BUTTER COOKIES

1 cup butter
1 cup sugar
2 eggs
1 teaspoon cream of tartar

2¼ cups flour, sifted
½ teaspoon soda
½ teaspoon vanilla
½ teaspoon lemon extract

Cream butter; Add sugar and beat well. Add beaten eggs and sifted dry ingredients. Add flavorings. Blend. Chill dough for at least two hours. Roll thin on lightly floured board. (Use only ⅓ of dough; keep the rest chilled.) Cut with cookie cutters and sprinkle with sugar, or decorate with bits of candied cherries. Bake on greased cookie sheet 8 to 10 minutes in 375 degree oven. Keep in covered tins.
Mrs. Leroy Edwards (Sarah Martha)

CHOCOLATE COVERED CHERRY COOKIES

½ cup butter or margarine,
  softened
1 cup sugar
1 egg
1½ teaspoons vanilla
1½ cups flour

½ cup cocoa
¼ teaspoon salt
¼ teaspoon baking powder
¼ teaspoon soda
Maraschino cherries

FROSTING:

6 ounces semi-sweet
  chocolate bits
½ cup sweetened condensed milk

¼ teaspoon salt
1 tablespoon cherry juice

Mix in large bowl butter, sugar, egg and vanilla until fluffy. Add remaining ingredients, except cherries. Blend until mixed. Batter will be very stiff. Shape and drop with teaspoon. Place 2 inches apart on ungreased cookie sheet. Push a well-drained maraschino cherry into each ball of dough. Then frost over each cherry by spreading ½ teaspoon frosting over each cherry. To make frosting, combine 6 ounces semi-sweet chocolate bits and ½ cup sweetened condensed milk in a heavy saucepan and melt over low heat. Stir until blended. Add ¼ teaspoon salt and 1 tablespoon cherry juice. Stir well. Bake cookies at 350 degrees for 10 minutes until puffed up.
Mrs. George Clark (Gladys)

CHRISTMAS COOKIES

1 cup shortening
2 cups light brown sugar
2 eggs
½ cup sour milk
3½ cups flour
½ teaspoon soda
1 teaspoon salt

1 teaspoon vanilla
1 teaspoon almond flavoring
2 cups pecans, chopped
1 package dates, chopped
1 package candied cherries,
  chopped

Cream shortening and sugar. Add eggs. Stir in milk. Sift the flour, soda and salt and blend into shortening mixture. Add vanilla and almond flavoring. Stir in the pecans, dates and cherries by hand. Chill overnight. Drop about 2 inches apart on lightly greased baking sheet. Bake at 350 degrees for 10 to 12 minutes.
Mrs. J. M. Hancock (Leafy)

MINCEMEAT COOKIES

1 cup Crisco or butter,
  softened
1 9-ounce package mincemeat
2 cups sugar
4 eggs
4 cups flour
½ teaspoon cinnamon

¼ teaspoon allspice
1 teaspoon cloves
Pinch of salt
1 teaspoon soda
2 tablespoons water,
  boiling

Cream shortening, mincemeat, sugar and eggs. Sift together flour, cinnamon, allspice, cloves and salt and combine with the first mixture. Mix well and add soda, dissolved in the boiling water. Blend. Drop by teaspoonfuls on greased cookie sheet. Bake at 375 degrees for approximately 10 minutes.
Mrs. William King (Anne)

BUTTER PECAN TURTLE COOKIES

CRUST:

2 cups flour
1 cup brown sugar

½ cup butter, softened

CARAMEL LAYER:

⅔ cup butter

½ cup brown sugar

OTHER INGREDIENTS:

1 cup whole pecan halves

2 6-ounce packages milk
  chocolate chips

Combine flour, brown sugar and butter for the crust. Mix well. Pat firmly into an ungreased 13 x 9 x 2-inch pan. Sprinkle pecans evenly over unbaked crust. Prepare caramel layer by combining brown sugar and butter in a heavy sauce pan. Cook over medium heat, stirring constantly, until entire surface of mixture begins to boil. Boil ½ to 1 minute, stirring constantly. Pour evenly over pecans and crust. Bake at 350 degrees for 18-22 minutes or until crust is light, golden brown. Remove from oven. Immediately sprinkle with chips. Allow chips to melt slightly (2 to 3 minutes), then swirl. Cut into 3-4 dozen bars.
Mrs. Russell Fryar (Carol)

MAPLE NUT BARS

1 stick butter or margarine
1½ cups dark brown sugar
2 eggs
1½ cups flour
2 teaspoons baking powder

½ teaspoon salt
1 teaspoon maple flavoring
½ teaspoon vanilla flavoring
1 cup chopped nuts

Melt margarine and stir in sugar. Cool. Add eggs. Add flour, baking powder and salt. Add flavorings and nuts. Pour into a greased 9 x 13-inch pan. Bake at 350 degrees for 20 to 25 minutes.
Mrs. Alvin B. Wight (Anne)

MYSTERY BARS
Good for a coffee or for Christmas goodies.

2 eggs
1 box dark brown sugar
1½ cups flour, sifted
2 teaspoons baking powder

Dash of salt
1 teaspoon vanilla
1 cup butter, melted
1 cup pecans, chopped

Beat the eggs. Add the brown sugar. Sift the flour with the baking powder and salt. Add to mixture. Add the melted butter and vanilla. Mix well. Stir in the chopped pecans. Bake in a greased pan (8 x 12-inch or 9 x 13-inch) for 45 minutes in a 325 degree oven. Cool before cutting into bars. Roll the bars in powdered sugar.
Mrs. A. D. Caley (Helen)

CONGO BARS

2 sticks butter, melted
1 box light brown sugar
3 eggs
2¼ cups plain flour
2½ teaspoons baking powder

½ teaspoon salt
1 teaspoon vanilla
1 12-ounce package
        chocolate chips
1 cup nuts, chopped

Combine butter and sugar. Add eggs, one at a time. Add dry ingredients, vanilla, nuts, and chocolate chips. Bake in a greased 9 x 14-inch pan for 25 to 30 minutes in a 350 degree oven. Let cool and cut into squares.
Mrs. J. D. Hall (Willene)

Similar recipes submitted by *Mrs. Harry Brown (Etta)*.

DATE BARS

1 cup sugar (white or good
    with brown, too)
3 eggs
1 cup flour
1 teaspoon baking powder

Pinch of salt
1 cup dates, pitted and chopped
1 cup nuts, chopped
1 teaspoon vanilla
Confectioners' sugar

Cream eggs and sugar. Sift dry ingredients over fruit and stir into the eggs and sugar. Add vanilla. Bake in a greased pan 15 or 20 minutes at 300 degrees. Cut in squares and roll in confectioners' sugar while hot.
Mrs. Archie Pittman (Hattie)

Similar recipe submitted by *Mrs. J. Howard Arnold (Margaret).*

DATE CHEWS

1 stick butter
1 cup dark brown sugar
1 small box dates, chopped
2 cups Rice Crispies
1 cup pecans, chopped

1 cup coconut
1 teaspoon vanilla
Dash of salt
Confectioners' sugar

Mix the butter, brown sugar, and dates in heavy saucepan. Cook on low heat until the mixture bubbles, stirring often. (It will burn easily.) After it bubbles, cook 4 or 5 more minutes. Remove from stove and add remaining ingredients. Shape into balls and dip in confectioners' sugar.
Mrs. E. C. Oliver (Clancy)

PECAN FINGERS

1 cup butter
¼ cup confectioners' sugar
1 teaspoon vanilla
1 tablespoon water

2 cups cake flour
¼ teaspoon salt
2 cups pecans, chopped

Cream butter, add sugar, vanilla and water. Mix well. Add flour, salt and nuts. Chill 1 hour. Form into fingers. Bake at 250 degrees for 1 hour. Roll in powdered sugar.
Mrs. William Z. Bridges (Mary)

Similar recipe submitted by *Mrs. Dan Bain (Sally).*

HERSHEY'S SYRUP BROWNIES

½ cup margarine
1 cup sugar
4 eggs
1 16-ounce can Hershey's
   Chocolate Syrup

1 cup plus 1 tablespoon
   flour
½ teaspoon vanilla
½ cup nuts, chopped

FROSTING:

6 tablespoons margarine
6 tablespoons milk

1½ cups sugar
¾ cup chocolate chips

Cream margarine and sugar. Add eggs; beat until light. Add chocolate syrup and flour alternately. Add vanilla and nuts. Bake in 11 x 15-inch jelly roll pan at 350 degrees for 20-25 minutes. To make frosting, mix margarine, milk and sugar and boil for 30-45 seconds. Add chocolate chips. Remove from heat and stir until it becomes a spreading consistency. Frost brownies.
Mrs. Elliott McCollum (Lorna)

DELICIOUS BROWNIES

2 sticks margarine
4 squares unsweetened
   chocolate
4 eggs

2 cups sugar
1½ cups flour
1 cup nuts, chopped
1 teaspoon vanilla

FROSTING:

½ cup Hershey's Chocolate
   Syrup

½ box confectioners' sugar

Melt margarine and chocolate. Cream eggs with sugar. Add flour, nuts, and vanilla. Pour into 9 x 13-inch greased pan. Bake 15-20 minutes in 325 degree oven. Ice while warm with mixture of chocolate syrup and confectioners' sugar. Cut into squares when cool. This recipe freezes well.
Mrs. Billie Schneebeli
Similar recipes by *Mrs. Paul Bryan (Barbara) and Mrs. J. H. Faulk (Agnes).*

BUTTERSCOTCH BROWNIES

Recipe may be halved for a 9 x 13-inch pan.

1 stick margarine
1 stick butter
4 cups dark brown sugar
4 eggs
3 cups flour

1 teaspoon salt
4 teaspoons baking powder
2 teaspoons vanilla
1½ cups pecans, chopped

Melt the margarine and butter in a large saucepan. Remove from heat and add remaining ingredients. Spread in greased 17 x 11½-inch pan and bake 30 minutes in 350 degree oven. Cut in squares while warm with very sharp knife. Dust with powdered sugar if desired. Whole recipe makes 64 squares.
Mrs. Randy Malone (Mary)
Similar recipe submitted by *Mrs. William Young (Ruth) and Mrs. Jim Horner (Zee).*

Variation: Use light brown sugar instead of dark.
Mrs. Randolph Jones (Nancy)

LUSCIOUS APRICOT BARS

⅔ cup dried apricots
½ cup butter or margarine, softened
¼ cup granulated sugar
1⅓ cups all-purpose flour, sifted
½ teaspoon double-acting baking powder

¼ teaspoon salt
1 cup brown sugar, packed
2 eggs, well beaten
½ teaspoon vanilla
½ cup pecans, chopped
Confectioners' sugar

Rinse apricots and cover with water. Boil 10 minutes. Drain, cool, and chop. Grease an 8 x 8 x 2-inch pan. Mix butter, granulated sugar, and 1 cup flour until crumbly. Pack into pan. Bake 25 minutes at 350 degrees. Sift ⅓ cup flour, baking powder, and salt. In large bowl, with mixer at low speed, gradually beat brown sugar into eggs. Mix in flour mixture and then vanilla. Stir in nuts and apricots. Spread over baked layer. Bake 30 minutes. Cool in pan and cut into 32 bars. Roll bars in confectioners' sugar.
Mrs. T. R. Sample (Nell)

LEMON SQUARES

2 cups flour
1 cup butter
½ cup confectioners' sugar
4 eggs
2 cups sugar
5 tablespoons lemon juice

Rind of one lemon, grated
1 teaspoon baking powder
Pinch of salt
Confectioners' sugar to sprinkle
    on top

Blend well the flour, butter and ½ cup confectioners' sugar with pastry knife or hands. Press this mixture into bottom of 9 x 13-inch greased pan. Bake at 350 degrees for 15 minutes. While this cooks, beat the eggs. Then add the sugar, lemon juice and rind, baking powder and salt. Pour over first mixture and bake at 325 degrees another 20 minutes. While still hot, sift confectioners' sugar over top. Let cool well before cutting into small squares.
Mrs. Roy C. Johnson (Mary Belle)   *Americus, Georgia*

FRUIT BARS

1 stick butter or margarine
1½ cups brown sugar
3 eggs
1 cup self-rising flour

1 teaspoon vanilla
3 slices candied pineapple
½ pound candied cherries
2 cups nuts, finely chopped

Cream butter and sugar. Add eggs. Add flour and vanilla. Grease a 9 x 13 x 2-inch pan. Sprinkle nuts on the bottom. Drop dough, a little at a time, over nuts. Slice fruit on top. Cook at 300 degrees for one hour. Cut immediately.
Mrs. Leroy Edwards (Sarah Martha)

SPICY NUTS

2½ cups nut halves
1 cup granulated sugar
½ cup water

1 teaspoon cinnamon
½ teaspoon salt
1½ teaspoons vanilla

Heat nut halves in oven at 375 degrees for 5 minutes, stirring once. Butter sides of heavy 2-quart saucepan. In it combine sugar, water, cinnamon, and salt. Cook and stir until sugar dissolves and mixture boils. Cook, without stirring, to soft-ball stage (236 degrees). Remove from heat. Beat by hand 1 minutes or until mixture just begins to get creamy. Add vanilla and warm nuts; stir gently until nuts are well-coated and mixture is creamy. Turn out on buttered platter or cookie sheet. Separate at once, using two forks. Makes about a pound.
Mrs. Paul McCollum (Nancy)

CREAM PRALINES

1 box (1 pound) light brown
    sugar
¾ cup evaporated milk
2 cups pecans, halves or
    broken bits

⅛ teaspoon salt
1 tablespoon butter

Mix sugar, salt, milk and butter. Cook and stir over low heat until sugar dissolves. Add pecans and cook over medium heat to soft-ball stage, stirring constantly. Remove from heat; cool 5 minutes. Stir rapidly until mixture thickens and coats pecans. Drop rapidly from spoon onto foil or wax paper, forming patties. If candy gets too thick, add a few drops of hot water. Let patties stand until set and cool. If you like brown sugar flavor without other flavoring, make according to above. If you prefer additional flavoring, add 1 to 1½ teaspoons vanilla or rum flavoring. Makes 3½ dozen.
Mrs. W. J. Vaughan (Virginia)

DIPPED CHOCOLATE CANDIES

1 cup graham cracker crumbs
1 cup nuts, chopped
1 box confectioners' sugar
2 sticks butter or margarine
1 cup coconut

½ cup peanut butter
1 6-ounce package chocolate
    chips
½ block paraffin

Mix all ingredients except butter, chocolate chips and paraffin. Pour melted butter over mixture. Mix well. Shape into logs or balls. Melt chocolate and paraffin mixture in top of double boiler over hot water. Dip balls into chocolate-paraffin mixture and place on greased cookie sheet or wax paper. Makes 3 dozen.
Mrs. D. P. Suber (Winnie)

Similar recipe submitted by *Miss Eunice Singletary*

BOURBON BALLS

1 pound confectioners'
    sugar, sifted
½ stick butter, softened
¼ cup bourbon
Dash vanilla flavoring

Dash salt
½ cup pecans, minced
¾ bar of paraffin
4 squares bitter chocolate

Cream sugar and butter. Add vanilla, bourbon and salt. Stir in pecans. Chill thoroughly. Roll into bite-size balls. Place on cookie sheet. Chill again. Melt paraffin and chocolate in double boiler. Dip chilled candy, one piece at a time, into chocolate mixture. Dip twice if necessary. Store in refrigerator.
Mrs. Fred Cooper (Helen)

NO-COOK MINT PATTIES

4 tablespoons butter or
    margarine, softened
⅓ cup light corn syrup
1 teaspoon peppermint extract
½ teaspoon salt

4¾ cups (about 1 pound)
    confectioners' sugar, sifted
1 drop each red and green
    food coloring

Thoroughly blend butter or margarine, corn syrup, extract and salt in large mixing bowl. Add sugar, mix with spoon and hands until blended and smooth. Divide into thirds; knead red food coloring into one portion of the mixture, green into the other, and leave one portion white. Shape into small round balls; flatten with fork on wax paper-lined baking sheets. Let dry several hours. Makes six dozen.
Mrs. Rudolph Fletcher (Barbara)

SALLY'S FAVORITE FUDGE

2 cups sugar
4 tablespoons cocoa
¾ cup milk
½ teaspoon salt

2 tablespoons light corn syrup
¼ stick butter
1 teaspoon vanilla
1 cup pecans, chopped

Combine sugar, cocoa, milk, salt and syrup in large saucepan and bring to rolling boil. Lower heat and continue to cook rapidly for 12 minutes or until soft-ball stage. Add butter. Cook until butter melts. Remove from heat and beat until partly cool. Add nuts and vanilla. Continue beating until thick. Pour into buttered platter. Cut into squares. Do not stir while cooking.
Mrs. Frank Neel (Frances)

Similar recipes submitted by *Mrs. Charles D. Reichert (Eddie) and Mrs. Gene Walker (Hilda).*

Men's
Recipes

ROLLED MAYONNAISE BISCUITS

2 cups self-rising flour
1 cup milk

4 tablespoons mayonnaise

Combine all ingredients and mix with fork. Knead gently. Roll on floured foil. Cut and place on ungreased baking sheet. Bake at 450 degrees for 10 minutes. Yield: 12 crisp biscuits.
Rocky Ivey

CHEF'S OPEN-FACED SANDWICH

1 French-style roll, 3 x 7
    inches, baked
1 tablespoon white dry wine
Garlic

1 slice each: Swiss cheese,
    American cheese, ham and
    salami

Split roll in half. Rub crusty edge of roll with cut side of garlic bud. Sprinkle wine on soft sides of bread. Cut cheeses and meats in half. Alternate layers of cheese and meat in roll. Bake in oven at 350 degrees until cheese is melted.
Howard Carnes

HOT ASPARAGUS-DRIED BEEF SANDWICH

White toast
1 jar dried beef
1 small can asparagus spears

Mustard
White sauce with cheese

Spread toast with mustard. Place layer of dried beef on toast. Top with asparagus; then layer more beef and top with cheese white sauce. Put under broiler until sauce bubbles and begins to brown.
Joe Griffin

FRESH MUSHROOM SALAD DRESSING

2 egg yolks
1 teaspoon leaf oregano
1/4 teaspoon powdered mustard
1/2 teaspoon Italian seasoning
Olive oil or vegetable oil

Juice of 1 lemon
Salt and freshly ground
    pepper to taste
1 pound fresh mushrooms

Combine all ingredients except oil and lemon juice and beat well. While beating mixture with wire whisk, gradually add oil, pouring in steady stream until mixture thickens. Add lemon juice and taste to correct seasoning. Let dressing stand for one hour before tossing with 1 pound of thinly sliced mushrooms. (To insure freshness, make sure mushrooms are almost white and have closed caps.)
Al Wight

RARE ROAST BEEF SALAD
Hearty salad to please a man's appetite!

½ pound or more rare roast
  beef or leftover steak,
  thinly sliced
⅔ cup salad oil
1 teaspoon lemon peel, grated
⅓ cup lemon juice
1 teaspoon Worcestershire sauce
1 teaspoon prepared mustard

½ teaspoon salt
4 ounces natural Swiss cheese,
  cut in strips (1 cup)
¼ cup green pepper, diced
2 tablespoons green onion,
  sliced
6 cups romaine or lettuce,
  torn into pieces

Combine oil, lemon peel and juice, Worcestershire, mustard, and salt. Cover and shake vigorously to blend. Pour over beef and let marinate while preparing salad or for several hours in the refrigerator. In salad bowl toss together the dressing, beef, lettuce, Swiss cheese and onion with salt and pepper to taste. Serves 3-4.
Al Wight

GOURMET FROG LEGS

Frog legs
2 cups vegetable oil
1 cup white vinegar
3 tablespoons poultry
  seasoning

2 eggs
1 teaspoon salt

Combine all ingredients except frog legs and blend for 10 minutes with electric beater. Pour over frog legs and allow to marinate at least 3 hours and preferably 12 hours. When ready to cook, place legs over low coals for approximately 30-45 minutes or until fork tender, basting frequently with marinade. Note: Marinade is good on chicken for which recipe was originally intended.
Mike Goldie

PAELLA ALFRESCO
Cooked outdoors on charcoal grill!

Basic components (no substitutions):

3 cups white, unprocessed rice
½ cup olive oil
½ cup white, round onions, diced
1 large tomato, finely chopped
and drained
1 teaspoon garlic, finely chopped
¼ teaspoon saffron, ground or
1/16-ounce strand, pulverized
2 teaspons salt (approximately)

½ teaspoon black pepper,
coarsely ground
1 teaspoon paprika
6 cups hot water
3 chorizo (This is a chili-
spiced pork sausage. One may
substitute ½ pound pork sausage
plus 1 tablespoon chili powder.)
2 lemons

Variable components (should contain some meat and some seafood):

*12-16 pieces chicken (fryer)
or rabbit
*12-24 large shrimp, depending
on size
*4 lobster tails
*1 8-ounce can clams,
whole or minced
*8 live clams, in shell

*1 8-ounce can oysters
(not smoked)
8 live mussels, in shells
*½ cup English peas, fresh
or frozen
½ cup green beans
*1 ounce pimento, cooked,
preserved

*Denotes recommendations for the first try at this dish.

This dish requires a very hot, long burning fire for proper cooking. Start a charcoal bed 3 inches thick using at least 5 pounds of charcoal. Arrange to be able to add more later if necessary. The cooking pan should be not more than 3 inches from the coals. The coals will require 30 to 45 minutes to be ready.

Meanwhile, wash but don't peel the shrimp. Scrub the clam shells and dry and lightly salt the chicken. Open the canned oysters and clams, drain, and save the liquid. This liquid will count as part of the 6 cups of water. (For the rice, of course.) Have some Sangria if you can complete the above just before the fire is ready. Wait to chop the onion and garlic until just before putting them in, or they will lose some flavor.

Set up a work table near the grill. Have everything you need at hand. Place a 12 to 15-inch heavy skillet or paella pan on the grill and pour in ¼ cup olive oil. Heat until it appears slightly hazy. Put in the chicken pieces, skin side down. Sprinkle on the pepper and paprika. Turn chicken regularly until browned evenly and the meat becomes uniformly opaque (15 to 25 minutes, depending on fire.) Remove chicken to a pan lined with paper toweling.

Cut the lobster tails into 1-inch thick sections on a cutting board and place them and the shrimp into the pan. Cook until the shells have become bright red and the meat opaque. This takes about 5-10 minutes. Remove and drain like the chicken.

Chop the chorizo (or the pork sausage and chili powder) with a knife and fry it likewise. When well browned, remove with a draining spoon (the ones with the holes in it). Remove the pan carefully and drain it of the fat into a receptacle. (A large empty coffee can works well.)

Now, to make the sofrito, place the pan back on the fire and add another ¼ cup olive oil. When hazy add the tomato. Chop the onion and garlic and add them to the tomato and stir. Have some more Sangria at this point as this is your last chance for a while.

When the sofrito has thickened enough to nearly hold its shape in the center of the pan, add the entire 3 cups of rice and stir continuously but slowly to keep it from burning. Add the fried chorizo at this point. When the rice becomes translucent, add the saffron and continue stirring for a minute or so. Check the fire and add some charcoal at this point if needed.

Add enough very hot tap water to bring the volume of the clam and oyster liquid up to 6 cups. Add this to the rice and sofrito. Stir thoroughly and carefully as the pan will be fairly full at this point. Taste the liquid and correct the flavor with salt as desired. Stir again and distribute the rice evenly. Now, with a flair, arrange the chicken, shrimp, lobster, oysters, clams, etc., into the liquid which should now be coming to a boil. Do this with respect to symmetry, balance, and color composition. Push them down gently into the liquid as you go and don't leave anything out. It will all fit in, but you won't believe it until it's done. Sprinkle the peas on top. Now leave it alone and make sure it is boiling around the edges. If not, add more charcoal.

Soon the paella will start to rise out of the pan; when the liquid has all cooked away, it is done (18-25 minutes depending on the fire). Remove from the fire, garnish with lemon wedges and pimento strips in an artistic design and serve with pride. You have earned it! Serves 8.
Hartley Falbaum

SHRIMP NORMANDE

2 pounds fresh shrimp
¼ pound butter
1 clove garlic, minced
1 teaspoon dried tarragon
1 teaspoon parsley, chopped
½ cup bread crumbs

Salt and pepper to taste
Dry vermouth
1 cup heavy cream
Slice of lime
Bay leaf

Shell and devein shrimp and cook for four minutes in enough boiling water to cover, with bay leaf, lime slice and 1 teaspoon salt. Blend butter with garlic, tarragon, parsley, seasonings, and bread crumbs. Roll shrimp in butter and crumb mixture and then place them in greased baking dish. Pour in enough wine to cover. Top with cream and bake about 5 or 10 minutes at 475 degrees. Serves 4.
Al Wight

CHAR-BROILED KING MACKEREL

Fish, about 4 pounds or less
½ cup Worcestershire sauce
½ cup cooking sherry

½ stick butter
Juice of 1 lemon

Make a stretcher of foil on which to cook fish. Lay cleaned fish, skin side down, on foil. Place fish on grill. Make sauce by mixing ingredients together on stove until butter melts. Spoon this mixture over fish and baste as it cooks. Close grill cover for smoked flavor. When fish is done (meat will be flaky), sprinkle with Parmesan cheese and then paprika. Serve on stretcher (sauce will carmelize around fish) on platter.
Joe Griffin

JERRY WADDELL'S BASS

Bass
Salt
Milk

Bread crumbs
Butter

Skin, filet and heavily salt bass. Cover with whole milk and allow to marinate ½ hour. Butter casserole dish and add unrinsed fish filets which have been rolled in bread crumbs. Dot with butter. Bake at 350 degrees 15 minutes per inch of thickness. Broil to brown. Pour marinade to side (not over) fish in casserole.
Thomas Hawkins

VENISON STEAK EXOTIC

2 large venison steaks
½ cup vinegar

1 tablespoon salt

SAUCE:

1 tablespoon parsley, chopped
1 tablespoon Worcestershire
    sauce
2 ounces Roquefort cheese
1 medium onion, chopped

¼ teaspoon Tabasco
1 tablespoon lemon juice
Salt and pepper
⅛ pound butter

Marinate steaks in mixture of vinegar, salt, and enough water to barely cover meat for 12 hours in the refrigerator. To prepare sauce, blend ingredients thoroughly with a wooden spoon until a firm paste results. Rub steaks with butter and broil rapidly under hot flame. When almost done, remove and coat one side of each steak with paste. Return to broiler, 2 inches from flame, for ½ minute. Serve immediately!
Thomas Hawkins

DOVES IN FOIL

In middle of each dove (divided) put chopped onion, diced potato, salt, pepper and one pat of butter. Wrap each dove with slice of bacon; then wrap each in heavy aluminum foil. Bake in hot oven, 375-400 degrees, for 1 hour.
Al Lookabaugh

HEAVENLY DOVE

6 doves, cleaned and dressed
Flour
2 tablespoons butter or
    margarine
⅛ teaspoon thyme
⅛ teaspoon rosemary
1 teaspoon parsley, finely
    chopped

1 medium onion, finely
    chopped
1 4-ounce can mushrooms,
    undrained
1 cup Sauterne
1 teaspoon salt

Cut doves along backbone; butterfly by removing the large bones of the lower back and legs. Press flat and roll in flour. Brown lightly in butter. Sprinkle with herbs and parsley. Cover and cook slowly for 15 minutes. Add onions, mushrooms with liquid and Sauterne. Cover and simmer for 1 hour or until tender. Add salt 5 minutes before removing from heat. Serve with wild rice or hot buttered rice. Note: Quail or squab may be substituted for doves. Yield: 2 servings.
Mickey Cooper

WILD DUCK IN CROCK POT

1 wild duck
½ cup catsup
2 tablespoons mustard

10 tablespoons A.1. Sauce
1 cup red wine
½ cup water

Mix all ingredients except duck in bowl. Place duck in bottom of crock pot. Pour sauce over duck. Cook on low temperature 8-12 hours.
Hartley Falbaum

CHICKEN SANTA ROSA

Each serving is prepared in an individual packet of heavy duty aluminum foil approximately 20 x 20-inches square. Ingredients for each serving:

2 generous pats butter
½ stalk celery, sliced
    lengthwise in quarters
4-5 strips of green
    bell pepper
1-2 tablespoons onion, chopped
½ clove garlic, minced
    (if you like garlic)
1 small carrot, scraped and
    sliced in thin strips
4 chunks of ripe fresh tomato
    (each the size of a walnut)
Celery Salt

2 tablespoons white wine (not
    too important what kind so
    long as it is fairly dry
    —Sauterne, Rhine, Chablis)
3 small or 2 medium pieces
    of chicken (thighs work best)
Black pepper, coarsely ground
Accent or monosodium glutamate
Marjoram leaves
Paprika or turmeric
    (Add paprika if you want it
    reddish, or turmeric if you
    want it yellowish. Neither will
    add nor detract much from flavor
    Put some of both if you'd like
    it on the orange side.)

Place butter on square of heavy duty aluminum foil. Arrange a bed of the vegetables on top of butter. Place chicken pieces, which have been seasoned with Accent, celery salt, and coarsely ground pepper, on top of vegetables. Sprinkle marjoram leaves on top of chicken pieces and then, if you wish, color with your choice of paprika, turmeric or both. Add wine, pouring beneath, not over, chicken pieces. (Be sure sides of foil are turned up.) Fold foil over chicken and press carefully to seal. Place in shallow pan just in case you have a minor puncture in your foil. Bake in 350 degree oven (preheated) for exactly one hour. Serve with rice (see Simple Rice Recipe) pouring juices from packets over all. Easier than it sounds, and best of all, quick to prepare and will stay on "hold", if necessary, for a long time. Extra packets freeze well for those "single" meals that are, regrettably, sometimes necessary.

Variation: Sprinkle a very little curry powder on chicken before cooking. Be
    careful! A little curry goes a long way.
John L. Turner, III

CHICKEN BREASTS PONTALBA

½ cup butter
½ cup white onion,
   thinly sliced
¼ cup shallots or green
   onions, chopped
1 tablespoon garlic, minced
1 cup mushrooms, chopped

½ cup ham, chopped
½ cup white wine
1 tablespoon parsley, chopped
2 whole chicken breasts,
   halved and boned
1½ cups Béarnaise Sauce
   (See Sauces)

Melt butter and sauté onion, shallots and garlic until tender. Add mushrooms and ham and continue cooking about 5 more minutes. Add wine and parsley; heat through. Remove sauce from heat and keep warm, covered. Lightly flour the chicken breasts and fry in butter until golden brown. To serve, arrange chicken pieces on bed of above sauce and cover chicken with Béarnaise Sauce. Serves 4 for lunch or 2 for dinner.
Al Wight

RAIN CHICKEN*

Fresh chicken breasts with wings

SAUCE:

1 lemon, squeezed, per
   breast
1 tablespoon corn oil or
   butter per breast
1 tablespoon Worcestershire per
   breast

1 tablespoon water per breast
1 teaspoon sugar per breast
Salt to taste

Start chicken on low charcoal fire and cook at least 45 minutes. Baste continuously with sauce during last 10 minutes as chicken browns. *Recipe is so named because it rains each time chicken is prepared.
Thomas Hawkins

EASY BACHELOR'S PIE

1½ cups beef, cooked and
   cut into bite-size pieces
2 cups milk
⅓ cup onions, chopped
1 teaspoon salt
¼ teaspoon pepper

4 tablespoons flour
¾ cup carrots, cooked and
   diced
½ cup celery, cut up
½ cup green pepper, chopped
Mashed potatoes

Combine onion, celery, beef, and pepper in big frying pan with a little cooking oil in it. Brown slowly and stir constantly. When browned, add the rest of ingredients, stir until hot again, and pour into a greased baking dish. Spread mashed potatoes on top. Bake at 350 degrees until brown.
Jimmy Vaughn

FLANK STEAK BOURGUIGNON

2½ pounds flank steak or
London broil
5 tablespoons butter
½ cup Burgundy (or other
red wine)
½ tablespoon paprika

Salt
Black pepper, freshly ground
6 slices crustless bread,
fried in butter

To prepare flank steak for cooking, make shallow, diagonal incisions on membrane side of steak. Then sprinkle steak with salt and ground pepper on both sides and rub into meat. Broil steak close to broiler until very rare. While steak is broiling, make sauce. Brown the butter, slowly, in a skillet. Add wine and paprika; allow mixture to bubble slowly until sauce is a little reduced. Slice flank steak on a very steep diagonal, arrange on toast pieces, and spoon sauce over all. Serves 4.
Al Wight

AL'S PEPPER STEAK

1½-2 pounds round or
sirloin steak
1 large head celery, sliced
crosswise
4-5 green peppers, cut in
strips
1 large onion, sliced
1 head Chinese cabbage, cut
crosswise (optional but good!)

1 can beef consommé or
bouillon
1 can bean sprouts, drained
¼ cup soy sauce
1 tablespoon cornstarch
Salt to taste

Cut meat into strips approximately ½ or ¼ inch by 2 or 3 inches long. Brown in vegetable oil. Add bouillon. Bring to boil. Add vegetables to meat. Simmer 20 minutes, covered. Mix soy sauce, cornstarch and salt. Add to meat mixture and simmer until it thickens. Serve over rice or noodles.
Al Lookabaugh
Theo Titus

POTTER VALLEY LEG OF LAMB

1 leg of lamb
1 bottle Cross and Blackwell
Mint Sauce

1 bottle Escoffier sauce

Have butcher butterfly a leg of lamb. Marinate the leg for 24 hours in a combination of Escoffier sauce and mint sauce. Barbecue over fairly slow coals using the marinade to baste the leg.
C. Martin Wood, III

CHINESE BEEF WITH PEPPERS AND TOMATOES

1 pound round steak, cut
    about ½ inch thick
2 tablespoons soy sauce
Salad oil
1 tablespoon cooking sherry
4 teaspoons cornstarch
½ teaspoon sugar
¼ teaspoon ginger

2 medium peppers, cut into
    lengthwise strips
2 small onions, quartered
1 teaspoon salt
2 small tomatoes, cut
    into wedges
3 cups hot, cooked rice

Cut steak lengthwise in half; slice halves diagonally into thin slices. In large bowl, combine steak, soy sauce, 1 tablespoon salad oil, cornstarch, sugar and ginger; set aside. In large skillet over medium-high heat, in 2 tablespoons hot salad oil, cook green peppers, onions and salt, stirring quickly and frequently until vegetables are tender-crisp; remove to another large bowl and set aside. In same skillet over medium-high heat, heat 3 tablespoons salad oil. Add meat and cook until well browned. Stir in vegetables and tomatoes; cook until tomatoes are heated through. Serve with rice. Serves 4.

Paul McCollum

CHRIS' BAKED BEANS

1 pound bacon
2 pounds baked beans
1 bell pepper, chopped
6 ounces maple syrup

Salt to taste
1 ounce Worcestershire sauce
2 medium onions, chopped

Fry bacon and pour off most of drippings. Add beans and chopped onions to pan and cook on slow simmer. When beans are hot and a skim forms on top, add syrup and salt. When mixture starts to thicken, add Worcestershire. Stir and continue to cook slowly until thickened. About 10 minutes before serving add diced bell pepper. At serving time stir in crumbled bacon.

Chris CoCroft

RUDY'S SPECIAL VEGETABLE BAKE
Let's eat outdoors!

Individual packages of:
1 ear corn, shucked and
    silked
1 medium tomato, firm
1 onion, peeled

1 yellow squash may be added
    or used as a substitute for
    the corn
Salt and pepper

Rinse and arrange vegetables on a sheet of heavy-duty foil. Salt and pepper to taste. Bring foil up and twist ends together to seal. Cook on a charcoal grill with vented hood or a gas grill over low heat. Place 8-10 inches above coals for about 1 hour. The blend of flavors is delicious. Great for a winter night cookout. Serve with grilled steak and buttered bread.

Rudolph Davis

SIMPLE RICE RECIPE

Haven't you always wondered how the simple, rather primitive people over so much of the eastern world could have depended on rice as the mainstay of their diet if it were as difficult to cook as most of our western cooks tell us it is? Well . . . Throw away your double boilers, your steamers, and whatever else you have, and try this *just once*. The secret: They cook rice just the same as Italians cook spaghetti — lots of water! It boils out all the sticky part. Get a big boiler — much too big. Put in too much water — much too much. Bring to boil, having added either salt or bouillon cubes (not necessary if you're going to put something salty on rice after cooked). If you're moderate eaters, put in 2 tablespoons of regular raw rice for each person (three, if you're really rice lovers). Stand by, stirring, while rice cooks. This is crucial. You can't leave it to cook alone. There's no time set on this, so what you do is taste occasionally, until the grain "bites" right (not hard in center — not really soft; depends on your stove how long this takes). When it suits you, pour out into colander. Drain; with fork, fluff up until amost dry. Remove to a bowl. Fluff again with fork; then cover with aluminum foil. Can be done ahead of time. Can even be refrigerated and re-heated several days later. It's good rice.
John L. Turner, III

ONION RINGS

2 cups buttermilk	Large white onions
2 eggs	1-2 cups cracker meal
¼ teaspoon yellow food coloring	Salt and pepper

Peel onion and cut into round slices ½ inch thick. Separate slices into rings. Mix buttermilk, eggs and food coloring in a deep bowl. In a shallow pan mix 1 to 2 cups of cracker meal with salt and pepper to taste. Dip onion slices in buttermilk mixture; then cover with cracker meal. Repeat for extra thick batter. Deep fat fry at 350 to 375 degrees until golden brown. Drain on paper towels.
Fred Cooper

AL LOOKABAUGH'S KOSHER DILL PICKLES

20-25 4-inch cucumbers,
    whole or cut in strips
1 cup salt

3 quarts water
1 quart cider vinegar
Grape leaves

PER QUART:

⅛ teaspoon powdered alum
1 clove garlic
1 hot red pepper

2 heads fresh dill or
    1 teaspoon dill seed

Wash cucumbers. Refrigerate or let stand in cold water overnight. Pack in hot sterilized jars. To each quart add above amount of alum, garlic, dill and pepper. Combine salt, water and vinegar and heat to boiling. Pour over cucumbers in jars. Put a grape leaf in each jar. Seal. Makes 6-8 quarts. Note: Same recipe may be used for pickled okra.
Al Lookabaugh

MY BLACKBERRY PUDDIN'

2 cups blackberries
2 cups flour, sifted
⅓ cup margarine or butter
2 cups boiling water

2 cups sugar
2 teaspoons baking powder
1 cup milk
¼ teaspoon vanilla

Cream butter and 1 cup sugar together. Add flour, baking powder, salt, milk, vanilla and mix well. Pour blackberries on top; then pour 1 cup sugar and the 2 cups boiling water over berries. Bake in 350 degree preheated oven for 50-60 minutes or until top is golden brown and crisp.
Jimmy Vaughn

BOB'S CARAMELS

2 cups white sugar
¼ pound butter
1 cup white corn syrup

1 teaspoon vanilla
1 14-ounce can sweetened
    condensed milk

In saucepan mix sugar, butter, corn syrup and condensed milk. Cook over low heat until mixture reaches soft-ball stage (240 degrees), stirring constantly. Remove from heat and stir in vanilla. Pour into a thickly buttered pan. When cold, cut into small squares using heavy, buttered knife or scissors. Wrap in wax paper.
Robert Maxwell

EQUIVALENTS

Beans, green	1 pound	3 cups, cut (uncooked)
Beans, dried	1 cup	½ pound
Bread	2 slices	1 cup crumbs
Butter	½ cup (8 tablespoons)	1 stick
Butter, packed solid	2 cups	1 pound
Carrots	7-9 carrots (2 cups, cooked)	1 pound
Chocolate	1 square	1 ounce
Chocolate	1 square	3-4 tablespoons, grated
Cocoa	4 cups	1 pound
Coffee, ground	5 cups	40-50 servings, 1 pound
Cheese	4-4½ cups	1 pound
Cheese, grated	1 cup	¼ pound
Cheese, cream	3-ounce package	6 tablespoons
Cream, heavy	½ pint	2 cups, whipped
Cucumbers	2 6-inch cucumbers	1 pound
Dates, pitted	2 cups	1 pound
Eggs	1	¼ cup
Eggs, white	1	1½ tablespoons
Egg, yolk	1	1 tablespoon
Egg, whites	4-6	½ cup
Egg, yolks	6-7	½ cup
Flour, all-purpose, sifted	4 cups	1 pound
Flour, cake flour	4½-5 cups	1 pound
Graham cracker crumbs	11 crackers	1 cup, rolled fine
Lemon	1 juiced	2-3 tablespoons
Macaroni	1 cup	2 cups, cooked
Meat, cooked & diced	2 cups	1 pound
Meat, crab	2 cups	1 pound
Marshmallows	16	¼ pound
Milk, condensed	1¼ cups	14-ounce can
Milk, evaporated	⅔ cup	6-ounce can
Milk, evaporated	1⅔ cup	14½-ounce can
Noodles	1 cup raw	1½ cups, cooked
Nuts, shelled	2 cups, coarsely chopped	½ pound
Orange	1 juiced	½ cup or 6-8 tablespoons
Peas, in pod	1 pound	1-1½ cups, shelled, or 1 cup, cooked
Potatoes, white	1 pound	2-5 medium or 2-3 cups cooked, mashed
Prunes	1 pound	4 cups, cooked
Punch	4 quarts	About 40 3-ounce punch cups
Raisins, seedless	3 cups	1 pound
Rice, raw	2¼ cups	1 pound
Rice	1 cup	About 3 cups, cooked
Saccharin	¼ grain	1 teaspoon sugar
Spinach	1 pound	2-2½ quarts raw or 1½ cups, cooked
Sucaryl	1 tablet	1 teaspoon sugar
Sugar, granulated	2 cups	1 pound
Sugar, brown (firmly packed)	2¼ cups	1 pound (1 box)
Sugar, confectioners'	3-3½ cups	1 pound (1 box)
Tea, loose	1 pound	5 cups, about 155 teacup servings

"HEART HEALTHY" RECIPE SUBSTITUTIONS

ORIGINAL INGREDIENT	ALTERNATIVE
1 pound ground beef	• 1 pound ground turkey (breast)
1 ounce cheddar, Swiss, or American cheese	• 1 ounce lowfat cheese • 1 ounce part-skim cheese (Mozzarella)
1 egg	• 2 egg whites • ¼ cup low cholesterol egg substitute
1 cup whole milk	• 1 cup skim milk
1 cup cream	• 1 cup evaporated skim milk
1 cup sour cream	• 1 cup nonfat sour cream • 1 cup plain nonfat yogurt • 1 cup lowfat cottage cheese plus 1 to 2 teaspoons lemon juice, blended smooth
1 ounce cream cheese	• 1 ounce nonfat cream cheese • 1 ounce Neufchâtel cheese
1 cup butter	• 1 cup margarine • 1 cup vegetable oil
1 cup shortening	• 7 ounces vegetable oil
1 ounce baking chocolate	• 3 tablespoons cocoa powder plus 1 tablespoon vegetable oil
roux: 1 part fat, 1 part starch	• ½ part fat to 1 part starch
1 can condensed cream soup	• Mix together: ½ cup nonfat dry milk 2 tablespoons cornstarch 2 teaspoons low-sodium chicken bouillon ¼ teaspoon onion powder ⅛ teaspoon garlic powder ¼ teaspoon basil ¼ teaspoon thyme ¼ teaspoon white pepper 9 ounces cold water Add the following if desired: ¼ cup chopped celery or ½ cup sliced mushrooms Heat to a boil; stir frequently. Per "can": 215 calories, 1 g fat, 8 mg cholesterol, 200 mg sodium
Broth, Chicken or Beef (1 cup)	• 1 bouillon cube or 1 teaspoon granules mixed with 1 cup boiling water

Pebble Hill Plantation
Menu Additions

PINES AND PLANTATIONS
1815 East Clay Street
Thomasville, Georgia 31792

Please send me _____ copies of PINES AND PLANTATIONS. Please enclose the direct shipping cost of $23.95 per book, which includes postage and handling fees. Thank you for supporting the children of Vashti Center.

Enclosed is my check or money order for $ _____

Name _____

Address _____

City _____ State _____ Zip _____

- -

PINES AND PLANTATIONS
1815 East Clay Street
Thomasville, Georgia 31792

Please send me _____ copies of PINES AND PLANTATIONS. Please enclose the direct shipping cost of $23.95 per book, which includes postage and handling fees. Thank you for supporting the children of Vashti Center.

Enclosed is my check or money order for $ _____

Name _____

Address _____

City _____ State _____ Zip _____

- -

PINES AND PLANTATIONS
1815 East Clay Street
Thomasville, Georgia 31792

Please send me _____ copies of PINES AND PLANTATIONS. Please enclose the direct shipping cost of $23.95 per book, which includes postage and handling fees. Thank you for supporting the children of Vashti Center.

Enclosed is my check or money order for $ _____

Name _____

Address _____

City _____ State _____ Zip _____

Please check our webpage www.vashti.org for additional order forms and complete pricing information.